BOLSHEVIKS AND THE BOTTLE

Drink and Worker Culture in St. Petersburg,

1900-1929

L A U R A   L .   P H I L L I P S

Northern

Illinois

University

Press

DeKalb

2000

© 2000 by Northern Illinois University Press

Published by the Northern Illinois University Press,

DeKalb, Illinois 60115

Manufactured in the United States using acid-free paper

All Rights Reserved

Design by Julia Fauci

Library of Congress Cataloging-in-Publication Data

Phillips, Laura L., 1959–

    Bolsheviks and the bottle : drink and worker culture in St. Petersburg, 1900–1929 /

Laura L. Phillips.

      p. cm.

Includes bibliographical references and index.

ISBN 0-87580-264-8 (alk. paper)

    1. Drinking of alcoholic beverages—Russia (Federation)—Saint

Petersburg—History—20th century. 2. Working class—Russia (Federation)

—Saint Petersburg—History—20th century. I. Title.

HV5515.15 .P48 2000

394.1′3′094721—dc21   99-087014

CONTENTS

ACKNOWLEDGMENTS

■ I am happy to thank publicly the many individuals and institutions that have assisted me with this project. Major grants from the International Research and Exchanges Board, the Kennan Institute for Advanced Russian Studies, and the Northwest Institute for Advanced Study financed the research and writing of this manuscript. Helen Sullivan and the staff of the Slavic Reference Service at the University of Illinois provided invaluable help on numerous occasions; the International Labor Organization kindly assisted with the cover illustration. An earlier version of Chapter 6 was published in *The Russian Review* (1997), and portions of Chapter 5 previously appeared in *The Journal of Women's History* (1999). Permission to use this material was granted by the *Review* and the Indiana University Press.

During my graduate career and beyond, colleagues from the University of Illinois have offered advice and perspective of all kinds. I especially thank Jim Barrett, Heather Coleman, and Tom Trice for their many suggestions. Andrew Verner's intellectual enthusiasm and boundless energy contributed more to this project than he realizes. Current and past colleagues at Eastern Washington University were highly supportive of the project and most tolerant of the absences required to complete it. Ann LeBar contributed gracious and helpful advice, and Greg Smits shared his enthusiasm for intellectual inquiry, his practical expertise with computers, his distrust of "magic," and his steady friendship. Christine Worobec and Choi Chatterjee offered insightful comments on major portions of this manuscript. W. Arthur McKee has been a most generous intellectual colleague. In addition to allowing me to read his then unpublished dissertation, he offered detailed comments on the study as a whole. His own mastery of the sources and subject matter provided me with great insight. Even though Alex and Laurie Martin regularly contributed to merriment entirely inappropriate to a Soviet metro, they allowed my ex-husband and me to maintain our sanity and weight during our major stint in Leningrad. May we never be in such dire need of a 7-Eleven again.

Two other people have lived with this work as long as I have. My main academic advisor, Diane Koenker, generously managed to find promise in early graduate papers. Her ability to see beyond the problems of a manuscript and to envision where it *can* go have been invaluable to me. I have been fortunate to benefit from her careful advice for many years now, and I thank her for putting up with me during some of my more stubborn phases.

Even under normal circumstances, it would be difficult to find the right words to thank someone who spent hours shopping during the height of a Russian food crisis, thus allowing me to remain happily ensconced in a library and still have my morning coffee *"s molokom."* That same person listened to countless stories about the antics of drunken Russians and made intellectual contributions to this work that are now quite inseparable from my own. Properly acknowledging such support becomes yet more difficult when the two of you are not celebrating a book's release in the way you had once planned. I hope that Loyal Cowles nonetheless understands my deep appreciation for his many efforts and companionship.

And now, I ask that you please excuse me, for I owe these fine people a drink.

BOLSHEVIKS AND THE BOTTLE

INTRODUCTION

■ Decades of scholarship have been devoted to understanding the Russian revolution of 1917. Thanks to the work of many dedicated scholars, we now know a good deal about the course of revolution, its underlying causes, and the goals of its participants. Yet even before the tired edifice of the Bolshevik state came tumbling down in 1991, some scholars began to think that the dynamics of revolution might be better understood if more attention were committed to exploring the importance of 1917 as a cultural divide. In the effort to understand the dramatic change wrought by revolution, perhaps vital elements of continuity had been missed.

An increasing number of scholarly studies are thus bypassing traditional periodizations in an effort to explore Russian and Soviet history in new ways. Among them, Katerina Clark's investigation of culture in early twentieth-century St. Petersburg is truly exceptional.[1] Clark shows that many important artistic ideas traversed the revolutionary divide: the attempt to collapse time and create idealized space; the promotion of "Perceptual Millenarianism" and "Romantic Anticapitalism"; alternate efforts to harness Russian society's centripetal and centrifugal forces. According to Clark, only in the late 1920s did the avant garde's iconoclastic, centrifugal tendency finally give way to its monumentalist, hierarchical one. This "second revolution," she asserts, produced "a more fundamental re-structuring of the country" than had the one in 1917.[2]

And yet, Soviet Russia's "second revolution" reinforced a great many "pre-revolutionary" values. This "restructuring" mimicked the formation of conglomerate rock: throughout the 1920s, bits and pieces of pre-revolutionary culture that would not wash away intermixed with Soviet clay. By decade's end, the ongoing dialogue between state and society clearly foreshadowed certain elements of Nicholas S. Timasheff's famous "Great Retreat," that is, a meeting of revolutionary goals and Russian national culture.[3] As the revolutionary state learned to accept the population's maintenance of certain behaviors antitheti-cal to revolutionary precepts, citizens learned how to negotiate a new political order.

More than Clark's work, this study explores the impact of the Octo-ber Revolution by self-consciously placing 1917 in its chronological and conceptual middle. Although the question of continuity and change is at least implicit in virtually any historical investigation of late tsarist and early Soviet Russia, scholars' customary proclivity for choosing 1917 (or 1914) as a terminal point for study means that they have generally relied on secondary works or indistinct impressions to understand the other side of revolution. Examination of roughly equal periods on either side of 1917 facilitates a more systematic reassess-ment of this commonly observed chronological divide.

Interest in 1917 and its legacy also makes the October Revolution an important conceptual center of historical investigation: focus here is on the ways in which this "workers' revolution" affected the everyday life of its main constituency. Although the workers who were allegedly destined to build the world's first socialist state have already attracted a great deal of scholarly attention, preoccupation with the overtly po-litical aspects of laborers' lives has generally led historians into the or-ganizations, workshops, and minds of worker activists, as well as to moments of political crisis. In the search for the Soviet regime's social basis of support, the working masses, the more unsavory elements of working-class culture, and workers' "ordinary" lives have tended to be consigned to the margins of history. Recent investigations that discuss misogyny, anti-Semitism, reactionary politics, and "hooliganism" show that this has begun to change,[4] but focusing on drink—one of the more notorious, pervasive features of daily life in the working commu-nity—solidly roots us in the world of the working mass.

To the extent that this investigation concentrates on workers who spent their evenings drinking instead of attending night classes, it does so deliberately. It is of course true that many labor activists viewed the heavy use of alcohol among Russia's workers with considerable consternation. Activists' attitudes about drink do help provide valuable insight into many issues critical in the history of the Russian working class, including the nature of intraclass conflict and the effect that cultural life had on the legitimacy of tsarist and Soviet regimes alike. Laborers who intently sought self-improvement through education and the "sensible" use of leisure have, nonetheless, attracted a great deal of attention in historical inquiry on the Russian working class. Concentration on the less well understood working mass begins to redress this imbalance; it does not ignore the laborers who adhered to a different cultural code.

Given alcohol's prominent place in worker's lives cross-culturally, it is surprising that the drinking customs of Russian workers have not previously inspired deliberate historical analysis. Certainly scholars of the working class in other Western countries appreciate how strikingly questions about alcohol reflect larger political and cultural concerns. Not only have workers historically viewed alcohol—along with cigarettes, watches, and respectable Sunday clothes—as among the few luxuries they could afford, at least on occasion, but also as symbolically reflecting inclusion or exclusion from particular communities. Important political and social constituencies have thus been exemplified in workers' drinking practices. Drinking customs of working communities express their interdependence and exclusivity, their hopes and dreams, their compromises and disappointments.

One student of nineteenth-century British politics, for example, has argued that the temperance movement in Britain "helped to prevent English society from splitting apart," since the aspiration on the part of many workers to attain a "respectable" lifestyle united middle- and working-class reformers in a common cause. Another scholar alternatively suggested that various forms of entertainment—including the time laborers spent in English pubs—exhibited their declining interest in politics, their acceptance of the class system as a fact of life, and their willingness to settle for amusement over substantive changes in their economic situation. The defensive functions of drink have also been noted elsewhere: in French cafés, where workers enjoyed a comfortable camaraderie with coworkers and neighbors while sheltering themselves from economic, social, and political upheaval; in early modern Augsburg, where local officials promoted social order by holding tavern keepers responsible for activities occurring within their establishments—rather than attempting to monitor what happened in private homes. At the same time, the tavern's prominence in the political mobilization of working-class movements has also been well established, particularly in reference to German Social Democracy. Finally, Lynn Abrams has argued that a masculine workers' culture centered around alcohol and the tavern gave way in late-nineteenth- and early twentieth-century Germany to a more inclusive, commercialized mass culture: cinema, theater, sport, and mass media attracted women and middle-class elements as well as workingmen.[5]

In Russia, too, workers' drinking practices are a brilliant prism reflecting the deeper political and cultural attitudes of early twentieth-century laborers. It would be astonishing if they were not. After all, customs surrounding drink permeated every facet of working-class life, including leisure, shop-floor culture, politics, and family life. A Russian worker might bypass the theater, the club, movies, lectures, or books without great difficulty, but an omnipresent culture of drink inevitably confronted all who moved within the working community. Drinking in Russia—and elsewhere—was a predominantly male activity, and the tavern a predominantly male world. Nonetheless, drinking husbands affected family life and the family economy; any study into worker drinking is therefore necessarily propelled into the realms of gender and family. Russia's working-class women (i.e., women employed in manufacturing and domestic service as well as wives and daughters of male laborers) had their own approach to drink, though they seldom categorically opposed "masculine" consumption of alcohol, as anti-alcohol activists consistently hoped they would do.

Great resilience in workers' drinking customs confirms a tenacious persistence in cultural life, even in the face of the severe social and political dislocation characteristic of early twentieth-century Russia. Alcohol's significance as a symbolic indicator of working-class masculinity, sociability, and festivity emerged from the revolutionary maelstrom unscathed. So, too, did tavern culture as a masculine habitat, women's preoccupation with alcohol's economic implications, and prominent drunkenness in the workplace. If workers' cultural lives were not transformed by revolution, however, certain elements of pre-revolutionary worker culture were severely deflated, depleted, and under siege by the late 1920s—among them the former integration of work and leisure, the previously rich diversity of tavern life, and commonly accepted markers of masculinity. Through it all, laborers and the state disputed the working-class's proper role in Russian society by contesting the meanings of drink.

Some readers will undoubtedly wonder how the "disease" of "alcoholism" has affected Russian workers. The disease concept of alcoholism is relatively new, having gained widespread currency in the West only in the second half of the nineteenth century. Furthermore, in the last decade, the understanding of alcoholism as a disease with a distinct set of physical symptoms has been seriously challenged in anthropological and historical literature on alcohol. "Alcoholism," writes Jean-Charles Sournia, "does not obey the laws of a system that distinguishes between the normal and the pathological." Since the presence of alcoholism can only be determined by thorough consideration of psychological, social, and cultural factors, he concludes, it does not fulfill many of the criteria for "disease." Patricia Prestwich similarly maintains that alcoholism is "an almost infinitely variable set of syndromes" and that it is "a social construct that varies with the society, the period, the users, and the observers." Assumptions that "heavy" drinking is coterminous with "problem" drinking have also been convincingly challenged. Anthropologists, who led the way in investigating the social functions of alcohol, conclude that alcohol-related problems are "rare, even in many societies where drinking is customary and drunkenness is commonplace."[6]

For most people, alcohol is a normal component of social interaction. The social functions of alcohol in Russia have been treated sensitively, albeit briefly, by David Christian and N. S. Polishchuk, but historians of Russia—unlike specialists in the social history of alcohol in the West—still tend to focus on the consumption of alcohol in Russia as a social problem.[7] Of course, in the late nineteenth and early twentieth centuries, drunkenness in urban Russia *was* a significant social problem—from the perspective of temperance activists. But the very same behaviors that concerned reformers were considered entirely normal in working-class communities. Although workers did have an understanding of problem drinking, the clinical effects of drink on physical and mental health were virtually irrelevant to their considerations. Alcohol's contribution to specific physical ailments is not a matter of dispute; as a "problem" within Russia's working community, though, drink stood out much more for its economic and political implications than for its perceived contribution to ill health. For the vast majority of Russia's male laborers, drink was more commonly viewed as an essential element of sociability, and the tavern was a locus of working-class life.

Producing a study sensitive to the meaning of drink among workers requires sifting through a wide variety of sources: temperance and medical literature; trade union materials; government records on the drink trade; budget studies; memoirs; and daily and factory newspapers. The investigation therefore focuses on a single city. St. Petersburg was the logical choice: for much of the period under consideration, the most active temperance efforts in Russia were centered in the capital, and memoirs of St. Petersburg's workers are more abundant than are memoirs of workers in other Russian cities.[8] Geographic concentration allows for a more in-depth study of drinking customs than would otherwise be possible. At the same time, generalizations for a broader spectrum of the Russian working class can be made, since much of the anti-alcohol literature consulted was not directed at St. Petersburg alone, and secondary literature on workers' drinking habits in other industrializing countries facilitates cross-cultural comparisons.

St. Petersburg serves as the focus of this investigation for another important reason. As Andrey Biely, the great literary chronicler of the early twentieth-century city observed, an "impetuous surge of words" spewed from this "black dot" on the map. So, too, did the impetuous surge of revolution. In its splendor and its squalor, St. Petersburg frequently assumes mythical significance for Russian and westerner alike. From the beauty of Smol'nyi Cathedral to the polluted water of sluggish canals, there is plenty in St. Petersburg to charm, intrigue, and repulse even the city's most casual visitor. In Biely's vision, St. Petersburg was a place where revolutionaries donned fearsome masks to the delight of children, where social classes were separated by islands and flimsy carriages, where gray bureaucrats scurried about like frightened mice (or frightful rats), where sons unwillingly plotted to kill fathers. It was a place where everyone sensed impending explosion but did little to prepare for or avoid it. In any case, the actions Biely's characters took never had the intended effect. Time, sound, and space were all deceptive. But St. Petersburg is not merely deceptive myth: this "black dot" was the eye of revolution. If the workers' revolution was to influence the life of cobblers in Moscow, miners in Iuzovka, and spinners in Ivanovo—in short, if it could be expected to have affected the lives of Russians anywhere—it would have to change them here. And so, with Biely, we ask: "What'll happen to Petersburg?"[9]

CHAPTER 1

ALCOHOL AND THE STATE

■ Russia greeted the twentieth century deeply embroiled in a series of overlapping crises. Just as the earlier industrial revolution in western Europe had led to the emergence of new social groups and to their demands for a political voice, by 1900 Russian industrialization was creating social actors who had no clear place in the old order. Most noticeably, *sosloviia*—the hereditary legal categories that had long divided the population of the empire into groups with specific rights and obligations—did not take account of the mass of workers now inhabiting Russia's urban areas. In terms of their juridical position, most laborers remained "peasants" who were formally subject to the authority of village communes. Yet Russia's competitiveness in the modern world increasingly depended upon the state's ability to successfully integrate urban labor into Russia's economic, political, and social life.

The discrepancy between *sosloviia* and the actual configuration of the population was not the only anomaly emerging between Russian society and the institutions intended to bring order to it. Traditionally, the behavior of peasant youth and women was to be monitored by elders and by male heads of households, but industrialization blurred these lines of authority as well. Men who sought work in urban industries often left their wives and children behind, at least temporarily, in Russia's villages; even married lower-class women who worked in Russia's major urban centers typically did not live with their husbands.[1] Furthermore, lower-class women and adolescent men who migrated to industrial cities were able to secure independent incomes. Though the authority of age and gender were far from obliterated by industrialization's social and economic effects, in the urban setting the comportment of lower-class women and youth was not always monitored in traditional ways. This subtle erosion of disciplinary boundaries contributed to liberal perceptions that society in turn-of-the-century Russia was suffering from cultural and moral crisis. Lower-class women working as registered prostitutes provided legitimate services in pre-revolutionary Russia, but after 1905 liberal reformers were increasingly inclined to see the sale of sex as a sign of pathological disorder. Indeed, as Laura Engelstein has shown, the urban boulevard seemed to foster an atmosphere of sexual licentiousness and vice, an indiscriminate mixing of bodies and social classes. In the streets of the capital city, even the empire's most "respectable" citizens could be unexpectedly pestered by rowdy, unsupervised youths or accosted by women wise to the ways of the world.[2]

Tsar Nicholas II, the titular head of this dynamic society, appeared less concerned with its creative cultivation than with passing the Russian crown, autocratic power fully intact, to his biological heir. Such limited political vision was anachronistic in early twentieth-century Europe, but Nicholas faithfully pursued what he believed to be his God-given duty. Although a general strike in 1905 forced the unwilling tsar to grant constitutional reform, the liberal and working-class hope for meaningful inclusion in the political process remained frustrated as Nicholas and his advisors soon ensured that conservative voices came to dominate the new Duma. Such conservatism unfortunately did not serve the needs of the Russian state well: a poor showing in the Russo-Japanese war was perhaps the clearest sign that autocracy had witnessed brighter days. Partly because of the autocracy's conspicuous inability to ensure the country's basic security, liberal professionals argued that their specialized training and expertise qualified them to help bolster Russia's competitiveness. But Russia's autocrat remained wary of the benefits to be had from granting greater initiative to civil society.

In the early decades of the twentieth century, disputes over alcohol and its use were an integral part of these questions concerning the future of the Russian state. After all, vodka had long been considered an essential part of Russian life. The legend that the tenth-century prince

Vladimir refused to adopt Islam because the religion forbade drink has been widely cited. More directly here, early twentieth-century observers noted that Russians learned to drink "with mother's milk," had more opportunities for "hospitable" drinking than other peoples, and brought "grief" to the Russian land through their enthusiastic drinking bouts.[3] Alcohol played a central role in discussions of the "worker question" in particular. In Russia as well as in other industrializing countries, alcoholic beverages were an integral feature of working-class sociability. Furthermore, proceeds from a state monopoly on the sale of spirits, introduced in 1895 and gradually expanded throughout the empire, provided the imperial government with one-quarter to one-third of its annual income.[4] Along with alcohol's ubiquitous presence in workers' lives, the Russian state's heavy dependence on alcohol income made it impossible to extricate questions about alcohol from broader discussions about the fate of the autocracy and the future of the working class.

To judge from the remarks of contemporaries, the problem of drunkenness in prewar Russia was becoming steadily worse. From the turn of the century until the outbreak of world war, temperance literature and newspapers repeatedly warned that drunkenness was growing "with unusual rapidity," that never before had there been such a "broad wave of drunkenness" as in recent years.[5] It might seem reasonable to anticipate that particularly energetic anti-alcohol efforts would coincide with these types of observations; heightened concern about the role that alcohol played in Russian society could logically be rooted in increasing public consumption of alcoholic beverages. But whether in Russia or elsewhere, the history of alcohol shows no simple correlation between high levels of consumption and heightened public debate over the "problem" of alcohol.[6] Statistical data for late imperial Russia suggest no precipitous rise in the population's use of alcoholic beverages. In St. Petersburg, the annual per capita consumption of vodka, Russia's favorite alcoholic beverage, fluctuated between 1900 and 1913, but no menacing upward trend in consumption patterns can be discerned (see table 1).[7] The widespread concern with drink in late imperial Russia was not rooted in a sudden elevation in use; instead, social activists argued about drunkenness because it seemed to embody the many ills plaguing a society in turmoil. As Prestwich has observed of France, anti-alcohol movements attract public support when alcohol becomes "a symbol of some deeper crisis."[8]

. . .

The best place to begin a discussion of state politics and drink is with the First All-Russian Congress for the Struggle against Drunkenness (the Congress against Drunkenness), for this signal meeting in Russian temperance history made the broader implications of alcohol use abundantly clear. A national congress to discuss the problem of drunkenness had been proposed as early as 1900 by leading temperance activist and psychiatrist M. N. Nizhegorodtsev, but the idea did not come to fruition until Prime Minister Petr A. Stolypin agreed to convene a series of meetings—including a congress of people's universities, a women's congress, and a congress of factory doctors—in the aftermath of the 1905 revolution.[9] The Congress against Drunkenness was one of those meetings. Although most of the approximately 450 conferees in attendance at this anti-alcohol meeting were physicians, temperance activists, and educational leaders, a group of some 35 to 40 Social Democrats was able to propel its revolutionary message into the heart of the event, making the Congress against Drunkenness more combative than previous congresses on other public issues had been. This study of working-class drinking necessarily focuses on the political maneuvering of these labor activists.[10] The strident political position assumed by the Social Democrats brought repeated censure by congress organizers and the state—but the isolation of workers' delegates was mirrored by the parallel isolation of the regime. As workers and more moderate political actors united in their condemnation of the government's alcohol policy, the state's estranged relationship with Russian society was put on full public display.

The first of two highly divisive debates arising at the Congress centered on a draft resolution endorsing temperance education, a matter that raised fundamental questions about state secularism and control of education. During discussion of the matter, a member of the workers' group proposed that a phrase advocating temperance education based in "strong religious-moral foundations" be dropped from the declaration, because of the public's diverse views on religious matters.[11] When the Congress subsequently adopted the measure as amended, the ruffled Orthodox clergy exited the hall in protest. Workers reportedly met accusations that they alone favored the proposed omission with "laughter and ironic applause"; other participants noted the impossibility of resolving such questions "when a workers' group participates."[12]

A second major dispute at the Congress erupted during deliberations on the government's liquor monopoly. The monopoly made the regime highly vulnerable to charges that it profited from the people's

Table 1—Per Capita Consumption of Vodka in Saint Petersburg, 1900–1913 (In buckets)[*]

1900	2.12	1905	1.84	1910	1.57
1901	2.03	1906	1.85	1911	1.72
1902	1.95	1907	1.80	1912	1.75
1903	1.85	1908	1.70	1913	1.84
1904	1.83	1909	1.57		

Source: Didrikhson, *Alkogolizm,* 10.
[*] A bucket [*vedro*] is 12.3 liters.

misery, and the tsarist administration was well aware of this problem. Official nervousness had in fact prompted the St. Petersburg city governor [*gradonachal'nik*] to ban the reading of reports that addressed the system of alcohol sale in Russia. Discussion of the monopoly system ultimately went ahead after the Ministry of Internal Affairs reversed the governor's decision, but the debate that transpired at the Congress undoubtedly caused the security agency to regret its permissiveness.[13]

Perhaps it came as little surprise that workers' representatives, typically forthright in their criticisms, accused the government of trying to raise as much revenue as possible by "spreading drunkenness."[14] But severe censure of the state's alcohol monopoly came from more moderate quarters as well. During a particularly caustic exchange of remarks, liberal physician Dmitrii N. Borodin accused the government of condoning the illegal sale of liquor, former minister of finance Sergei Iu. Witte was branded a "state criminal" for his role in pioneering the alcohol monopoly, an unidentified delegate called the state sale of drink "a crime," and the Ministry of Finance representative quit the Congress.[15] A jittery presidium informed delegates that "similar incidents" would result in the closure of the Congress. In an attempt to ensure that the Congress's final declarations would be palatable to the government, the presidium subsequently edited the meeting's resolution on the liquor monopoly, insisting that it possessed authority to "soften sharp content." The presidium's heavy hand nonetheless provoked widespread dissatisfaction among conferees. A report from the Ministry of Internal Affairs reveals that news of the revisions gave rise to an "unimaginable commotion" lasting "about ten minutes." Led by the workers' group, "almost all of the audience and a significant part of the doctors" left the meeting in protest.[16] The most important public discussion about drunkenness in pre-revolutionary Russia thus ended in scandal.

These two debates underscore the political isolation of workers and government alike. Although the workers' position on temperance education prevailed in a vote on the matter, many delegates present at the Congress were not convinced that the resolution's secular emphasis was the most sensible alternative. Significantly, when clerics left the Congress, the conference blamed the workers. Dr. Nikolai I. Grigor'ev, the chair of that contentious meeting, specifically asked for the record to reflect that "the customary decision"—that is, a resolution in *favor* of religious education—had not passed because "the meeting [was] small and . . . representatives of workers' organizations predominated."[17] Delegates were disturbed by the departure of the clerics, and tearful presidium members urged Russia's religious leaders to return to the meeting.[18] In contrast, many conferees considered the workers' voice dispensable. The liberal majority worried that workers' representatives threatened the peaceful conduct of the Congress, and they wearied of the vituperative speeches that the workers continually directed at the government and moderate reformers alike.

To be sure, the Social Democrats had arrived at the Congress disinclined to cooperate with Russian liberals. An article published shortly before the Congress announced that the workers' delegation intended to "disassociate" itself from "bourgeois" reformers.[19] According to worker activists, the bourgeoisie wrongly believed that poverty resulted from drink. Precisely the opposite was true, they maintained: poverty and the capitalist system of labor exploitation produced alcoholism. Questionnaires that worker delegates had compiled in advance of the Congress showed as much. Laborers who drank heavily were poorly paid and malnourished; they worked long hours and lived in desperate conditions. The delegates asserted that working-class drunkenness could be successfully addressed only if labor organizations were allowed to agitate for improved conditions. Any hope that alcoholism could be destroyed within the current system—whether though devoted prayer or through moderate reform—was a "laughable, naive utopia."[20] In short, eliminating the factors that propelled working-class drinking required a revolution in Russia's economic and political life. Clerics and liberal reformers failed to understand this critical point, and worker activists were unwilling to work toward lesser goals. Any attempt at cooperation with the bourgeoisie, Bolshevik Semen I. Kanatchikov concluded, was of no use. The interests of workers, he said, were "in contradiction" to the interests of other social groups.[21]

The superior organization of workers' delegates allowed them to move their agenda to the forefront of public discussion. Drawing important lessons from their unorganized, uncoordinated participation in similar public gatherings in the past, worker activists preparing for the anti-alcohol gathering were determined to see that "unanimity and discipline" allowed them to prevail at this meeting. They therefore resolved to prepare all proposals in advance and to collectively sponsor all resolutions "in the name of the workers' delegation."[22]

The success of their tactics produced alarm among other delegates. On advice that a resolution of the workers' group had passed "again," the exasperated Dr. Ivan V. Sazhin implored: "*What* are we to do? *They* are organized!"[23] Chairmen at the Congress against Drunkenness frequently manipulated the agenda to prevent voting on resolutions brought forth by worker delegates, stripped labor activists of the right to speak, and reproached workers for disrupting the meeting.[24] Though labor activists presented plausible arguments, liberal participants, including Borodin, had little patience for the delegation. "The workers' movement doesn't have any bearing on drunkenness," the long-time temperance advocate protested.[25]

The participation of working-class delegates caused similar concern for the tsarist regime. A number of worker activists originally slated to attend the meeting had been prevented from doing so through their timely incarceration; in addition, the Ministry of Internal Affairs informed the St. Petersburg metalworkers' union that it would not be permitted representation at the Congress. The metalworkers subverted the ministry's prohibition by reclassifying their delegates as representatives of workers' clubs and temperance societies, but official Russia's misgivings about the workers' attendance were unmistakable.[26] The postscript to the Congress could not have come as a surprise to anyone: when certain members of the workers' group were arrested, the Duma refused to protest their detention.[27] Only workers themselves defended their right to deliver such disturbing messages in such disturbing ways.

Yet isolation was not a fate suffered by workers alone. On the sensitive issue of the alcohol monopoly, the regime failed to bridge the gap between itself and the rest of society. As the sole legal source for liquor, the state was implicated in crime, prostitution, venereal disease, and tuberculosis, all ailments that temperance activists commonly attributed to drink. By 1909, the sensitivity of the government's position vis-à-vis the drink trade was compounded by assurances that Witte had made when the alcohol monopoly was introduced in the 1890s. Government control of the drink trade, Witte had affirmed, would moderate consumption patterns—but things only seemed to be getting worse.[28] Government-sponsored temperance efforts inaugurated with the monopoly had been limited and largely ineffective. In the view of temperance activists, the state had proved singularly incapable of solving the alcohol problem on its own.

By 1909, the regime found itself in an unenviable position. Even if it agreed with the criticisms that temperance activists leveled against drink, liquor sales produced substantial revenue for the state. Eliminating the government monopoly on spirits had the potential to cripple government operations. It might seem curious, then, that the Congress against Drunkenness was permitted to meet at all, particularly during this infamous "period of reaction." In 1907, Stolypin had christened his conservative premiership with a "coup d'état" revising Russian electoral law. Though these actions ensured more malleable representation in the state Duma, the prime minister frequently bypassed the legislature altogether. He also had more than one thousand people executed during his crackdown on the revolutionary movement. The temperance congress met in the middle of this reactionary period, which reached its denouement in 1911 with the assassination of the prime minister himself. It does not seem that the state would have thought this a propitious moment for a frank public discussion of matters related to drink.

In assessing the government's motivations for consenting to a congress on temperance, a Menshevik journal hypothesized that the state hoped to emerge as the "victor" from a "more or less open clash of opinion."[29] If this was indeed the government's aim, it badly misjudged its ability to manage the situation. In debate on the alcohol monopoly, the rift between state and society was made manifest, the state's isolation all the more obvious in light of the repeated sparring between the workers' group and moderate delegates in the conference's previous meetings. In the view of liberals, the liquor monopoly contributed to numerous social and physical problems that could be ameliorated if physicians, psychiatrists, teachers, and local government officials were permitted to bring their expertise to bear on the situation. The final moments of the Congress against Drunkenness saw significant elements of the liberal faction join the workers in a mass exodus that underlined a common opposition to the monopoly system. When it came to the liquor monopoly, censure coming from liberal constituencies was no less threatening to the government than the critique of the workers' group. The Ministry of Finance stood uncomfortably alone in defense of the government's alcohol policy.[30]

The criticism to which the regime was subjected at the anti-alcohol congress might have produced salutary long-term benefits if it had prompted the state to reach an accommodation with its more moderate critics. Instead, the government cut off the possibilities for reconciliation by eliminating any chance for further similar rebukes. Though clerics were allowed to convene a far more benign temperance congress in 1912, that same year the Ministry of Internal Affairs denied a petition submitted by one of the 1909 Congress's original organizers: Nizhegorodtsev had hoped to establish a permanent committee on anti-alcohol congresses. The ministry's refusal to grant the physician's request was partially due to the experience of the 1909 Congress. Many of the 1909 conferees, the St. Petersburg city governor advised, had been observed in the company of "criminal" or "revolutionary" elements; in addition, some of the reports given at that gathering had borne a "revolutionary slant." The ruinous lesson the state culled from the First All-Russian Congress against Drunkenness was to never again allow the likes of Borodin the opportunity to end a report on the liquor monopoly with the ambiguous words, "Down with the whole system."[31] Lessons like this doomed the autocracy.

· · ·

It was not until the outbreak of world war in 1914 that there was a dramatic change in state alcohol policy and in the population's overall consumption patterns. In 1904, military mobilization for the Russo-Japanese War had been accompanied by drunken disorder as troops took leave of their families. Primarily because military leaders wanted to ensure that mobilization for the impending European conflict would be accomplished in a more organized manner, the tsar banned vodka sales throughout the empire in July 1914. With national survival at stake, Nicholas forfeited a critical source of state revenue. By August, the tsar had decreed that the temporary ban on the sale of strong drink be maintained until the conclusion of war.[32] Local constraints on alcohol sale were often more severe. In December, St. Petersburg's city governor extended the ban on vodka to beer and wine.[33] Restrictive laws on alcohol use, confirmed by both the Provisional and early Soviet governments, were destined to outlive the tsar who had inaugurated them.

The prohibition initially resulted in a dramatic decline in the Russian population's use of intoxicating beverages. No consumption statistics exist that would lend support to this assertion, but there are many other indications of a sharp decline in consumption following the tsar's July 1914 decision. According to numerous observers, "drunkards" were "not seen" and "not met" on the streets of Petrograd during prohibition. The Briton Ernst Gordon attributed a change in the appearance of Russia's working people to the dry laws: workers were suddenly well clothed and well fed, he reported, and they were now at work on Mondays. A resident of St. Petersburg's Vasil'evskii Island wrote her relatives that the "drunkards" in this working-class district had become "people."[34] Even if such enthusiastic accounts exaggerate prohibition's effects, a range of statistical data similarly suggest that the consumption of alcoholic beverages dropped dramatically in the second half of 1914. For example, both the number of people arrested for public drunkenness and the number seeking treatment for alcoholism at major relief facilities in Petrograd plummeted.[35] The new restrictions on drink produced a few scattered disturbances in urban areas, but temperance activists generally applauded the population's seeming acceptance of prohibition and the ease with which the transition to a sober society had apparently been accomplished.

It was not long, though, before a more somber side to prohibition emerged. Dry laws have proved difficult to enforce in many countries, and Russia was no exception. More telling than accounts enthusiastically singing the praises of prohibition is one Dr. Mikhailov's observation that in 1914 drunkenness "truly" declined—"but only at first."[36] The most desperate and dangerous response to legal prohibitions against alcohol sales was the use of lethal surrogates. Methylated spirits, perfumes, and varnishes ranked high among the urban population's substitutes for vodka. In St. Petersburg, the sale of methylated spirits, the most popular of the three alternatives, jumped from 103,400 buckets in 1913 to 170,200 buckets in 1915, an indication that not all of the product sold was destined for its intended industrial uses.[37] Devotees of drink adopted a variety of techniques designed to make surrogates more palatable and less dangerous. Methylated spirits went down easier when diluted with fruit juice, water, or wine; adding salt to varnish reportedly caused the most harmful resinous material to fall to the bottom of the container, and the purer liquid near the top could itself be filtered through cotton or black bread.[38] The consumption of substances capable of causing blindness and death is a sign of the extreme measures that some individuals were prepared to take to achieve intoxication, but severe poisoning does not seem to have been a particularly widespread occurrence.[39]

Of far greater significance for urban workers was moonshine, although its implications and effects were less sensational. The production and consumption of home brew did not become widespread immediately with the inauguration of prohibition in 1914. Rather, the urban population's use of illegal spirits developed gradually and expanded over time. The relative novelty of replacing state alcohol with moonshine in prohibition's early months is indicated by a 1915 report appearing in *Nashe delo*. People had "begun" to find new ways to get alcohol, and substitutes bearing "new names"—*khanzha, vodka samosidka*, and *samogon*—had recently appeared. David Christian maintains that the production of moonshine probably originated in Siberia, spreading inexorably and becoming more prevalent throughout the empire as the population mastered the manufacturing process.[40] The end of Russia's participation in World War I and the new alcohol policies of the revolutionary governments do not seem to have significantly affected this trend. In the wake of the February revolution, the Provisional government did relax the restrictions on alcohol by permitting the sale of wines with a potency of up to 12 percent, but prohibitions on the sale and use of strong drink were maintained.[41] The early Soviet regime adopted draconian legal penalties for selling or using spirits; the deterrent effect of this legislation is doubtful, though, since the laws reportedly were not enforced.[42] With the huge secession of territory demanded by Brest-Litovsk, Allied troops intervening in Russia's civil war, non-Communist White troops advancing against the state center, and peasant revolt in the south, the infant regime necessarily devoted its attention to challenges more pressing than the illegal distillation of liquor and public intoxication. Especially in major urban areas like Petrograd, overall alcohol consumption nonetheless appears to have remained quite low during World War I and the early years of revolution, if only because persistent shortages of grain limited the population's ability to produce affordable home brew. A man named Lobanov, for example, reported that he did not drink in the early Soviet period because he had "no money" and there was "no vodka." Raids of liquor supplies in the Winter Palace and elsewhere in Petrograd following the Bolshevik seizure of power also indicate that the supply of alcohol in the capital was not meeting the demand.[43]

The illegal manufacture of inexpensive moonshine received a clear boost in 1921 with the government's adoption of the New Economic Policy (NEP). When their obligations to the state had been met, agricultural producers were now free to dispose of their surpluses; and using excess grain to make bootleg liquor proved much more profitable than selling the raw agricultural products. According to the journal of the Ministry of Internal Affairs, the previously limited production of home brew reached "huge dimensions" during NEP.[44] At the same time, the perception that the production of moonshine diverted grain

from the food supply prompted the revolutionary government to liber-
alize the alcohol policy. In August 1921, the sale of 14 percent wine was
legalized; in February 1922, beer became available. The maximum al-
lowable alcoholic content of beverages was then steadily increased until October 1925, when the Soviet government reintroduced the sale of
full-strength (40%) vodka.[45]

Accurately determining the levels of alcohol consumption in Russia
during the 1920s is exceedingly difficult. It is clear, though, that the use
of intoxicating beverages in Petrograd and other urban areas increased
markedly after the legalization of beer in 1922. One individual who
had quit drinking in the 1890s affirmed that in 1922 he began to drink
again because "wherever" he went he "saw beer."[46] The rise in alcohol
consumption characteristic of early NEP seems to have leveled off in
the second half the 1920s. According to official statistics, the per capita
consumption of beer and vodka remained fairly steady after the state
reintroduced the sale of full-strength vodka in 1925 (see table 2).[47]
Though the figures in table 2 do not take moonshine into account, in
urban areas like Leningrad the use of bootleg liquor fell as affordable
beverages with comparable alcoholic content were legalized. Sources
certainly mention the consumption of home brew much more frequently in the first half of the 1920s than later in the decade. According
to a major study of the Russian population's alcohol use, by late 1926
administrative bodies no longer unearthed bootleg liquor in
Leningrad. At an anti-alcohol congress in 1929, economist Iurii Larin
asserted that high grain prices in the Leningrad region discouraged the
production of illegal alcoholic beverages; resolutions from that congress referred to Leningrad as a "non-moonshine region."[48] Even if
limited use of moonshine is assumed, alcohol consumption in the city
was probably somewhat lower in the late 1920s than it had been in
1913. In this respect, patterns in the capital corresponded to what was
happening in Russia's urban areas more generally: whereas in
1927–1928 the consumption of vodka and moonshine in the countryside had mushroomed to 150 percent of prewar levels, the state economic planning agency (Gosplan) and the Central Statistical Administration estimated that during that same period the use of spirits in
cities had declined to 75 percent of prewar levels.[49]

In sum, the state's policy toward drink had a significant impact on
the urban population's alcohol consumption patterns. The consumption of alcohol in St. Petersburg, fairly stable in the prewar era, declined sharply in the second half of 1914, when restrictive laws on the
sale of alcoholic beverages were adopted. It did not rise significantly

Table 2—Per Capita Use of Vodka and Beer in Leningrad, 1924–29 (In buckets)

	1924–25	1925–26	1926–27	1927–28	1928–29
Vodka	—	—	1.1	1.1	1.2
Beer	4.15	4.4	4.3	3.2	2.7

Source: *God bor'by s alkogolizmom*, 4.

until the population learned how to make home brew, the inauguration of NEP resulted in surplus grain harvests, and the state again allowed the sale of weak alcoholic beverages in the early 1920s. After full-strength vodka was again legalized in 1925, alcohol use appears to have stabilized slightly below its prewar level. Despite instances of poisoning by harmful surrogates during prohibition, most citizens of Petrograd shunned the most dangerous alternatives to vodka; in later years, some stalwart individuals even claimed never to have touched "a drop" of the more potable moonshine.[50]

This outline of consumption patterns is important not only for what it reveals about the population's overall use of intoxicating beverages but also for what it says about the motivations of anti-alcohol activists in early twentieth-century Russia. If the concern over temperance had been linked primarily to heightened levels of alcohol use, increased anti-alcohol activity should have emerged between 1922 and 1926, when the population's intake of alcohol was rising most precipitously. But the most energetic anti-alcohol activity in the early Soviet years erupted in 1928–1929, after renewed legalization of vodka sales had stabilized the urban population's intake of intoxicating beverages.[51] Furthermore, a significant shift in the terms of temperance discussions in the late 1920s signaled that deeper issues were at stake. Pre-revolutionary temperance activists had emphasized the effects of the government monopoly on public health and morality as a way to impugn the authority of the regime. The debate during the Soviet period, in contrast, stressed the implications of alcohol consumption for economic growth. In the late 1920s, disputes over alcohol-related issues became a component of the deep disagreements within the political power structure over how socialism in Russia would be built.

• • •

Although the tsarist government's dependence on income from the liquor monopoly had exposed the regime to harsh public criticism, by 1925 the revolutionary state found itself also forced to turn to alcohol for financial relief. In 1918, the Soviet government reinstituted an alcohol monopoly, in effect, through its nationalization of the liquor industry. The evident failure of prohibition may have facilitated the steady repeal of restrictive alcohol laws, but the profit harvested from the renewed alcohol sales left the fledgling socialist government vulnerable to charges that it was repeating the mistakes of its capitalist predecessor. The regime endeavored to put the best face possible on its alcohol policy, especially after full-strength vodka was reintroduced in 1925. In the public arena, drinking was consistently discouraged as wasteful, outmoded behavior ultimately targeted for complete elimination. Any citizen confused about Soviet alcohol policy could consult a whole series of pamphlets and articles intended to resolve the apparent contradictions between the Soviet state's words and deeds. The state's acceptance of alcohol sales, literature explained, had been motivated by a concern for public health and the need to preserve grain supplies: state-produced spirits did not contain the dangerous impurities characteristic of bootleg liquor; the state could produce spirits with greater economic efficiency than purveyors of moonshine; in any case, the Soviet government did not rely on alcohol income to the extent that the tsar had.[52]

Even if the government's professed concern for public health and secure grain supplies is assumed to have been sincere, contemporary historians have shown that the primary determinant of the Soviet state's alcohol policy was fiscal. The government, writes T. S. Prot'ko, introduced the liquor monopoly as a measure "necessary for the economic development of the country."[53] As Joseph Stalin explained the situation to a foreign workers' delegation in 1927, in the mid-1920s the Soviet state had been faced with two alternatives: either reach an accord with capitalists, "handing over a whole series of mills and factories to them," or institute an alcohol monopoly that would generate the capital necessary for "development of our [own socialist] industry." The lesser of two evils had been chosen, Stalin asserted, and he attempted to lend legitimacy to his choice by claiming that Lenin had himself approved the state sale of vodka, at least as a temporary measure.[54] Stalin purportedly intended alcohol proceeds to reinvigorate the country's industrial base.

The arguments made by Stalin did not go unchallenged. Those working-class activists who had attended the 1909 Congress against

Drunkenness would have paled at the thought that fifteen years hence, a victorious workers' government would profit from the state sale of drink—and the tradition of those delegates lived on among broad strata of the Communist Party and the state apparatus. As Emilian Iaroslavskii noted in 1926, the state sale of vodka caused "bewilderment and dismay" among some party members.[55] Incipient efforts to minimize the perceived social and cultural harm that alcohol brought to Soviet society emerged soon after vodka's reintroduction. Most importantly, in 1926 Sovnarkom passed legislation calling for stronger cultural measures against drink and approved compulsory treatment for "socially dangerous" alcoholics.[56] The clearer it became that influential elements within the party were prepared to use income from liquor as a source of capital accumulation, the more the debate over alcohol intensified. In 1927–1929, the discussion of alcohol thus became an important part of the party's fierce debates over industrialization, a symptom of the strong differences of opinion that party members held about the appropriate path to socialism.

Sovnarkom's adoption of legislation intended to moderate alcohol use through cultural measures shows that Stalin was not the only high-ranking official concerned about alcohol's proper role in Soviet society. Considerable intragovernmental antipathy to the nature of Stalin's fund-raising plans was again evidenced in March 1927, when Sovnarkom passed extensive legislation prohibiting liquor sales in cultural establishments and allowing local government bodies to limit sale under certain circumstances.[57] Later that same year, Sovnarkom called on local soviets to create anti-alcohol cells, the germ of the future Societies for the Struggle with Alcoholism (OBSA). Established in Moscow in February 1928, the OBSA became the organizational center of opposition to the government accumulation of capital by means of alcohol sales. Not only did *Pravda* report that the OBSA was organized with the "active sympathy of leading centers of the state,"[58] but also many of the central organization's founding members were already eminent members of Soviet society: they included leading Marxist theorist and economist Nikolai I. Bukharin; Bukharin's father-in-law, economist Iuri Larin; poet Demain Bednyi; military leaders Semen M. Budennyi and Nikolai I. Podvoiskii; and É. I. Deichman, a physician prominent in alcohol research. At the behest of Larin, a Leningrad branch of the OBSA was created a few months later, in June 1928.[59]

Although many of the individuals involved in Soviet anti-alcohol campaigns were concerned about the ethical and cultural implications of alcohol use, in the 1920s the principal struggle over state alcohol policy was fought on economic ground, with each side claiming that its proposed course would best enhance the productive capabilities of the state. In 1929, Deichman, the OBSA secretary, summed up the position of anti-alcohol activists. The sale of alcohol, he asserted, resulted in a net loss to the government: alcohol revenue brought the state 728 million rubles, but expenditures associated with alcohol-related problems cost even more—1.2 billion rubles. Sound economic policy would therefore seek the elimination of alcohol sale; state income would be enhanced through greater worker productivity and through reductions in absenteeism, crime, and health care expenditures.[60] By June 1928— only about four months after its inception—the anti-alcohol organization had presented Sovnarkom with a comprehensive plan for raising the cultural level of the population and eliminating alcohol as a source of state revenue. The proposals put forward by the OBSA included a series of prohibitions on alcohol sales: alcohol was not to be sold on nonworkdays or to minors; the sale of alcohol was to be forbidden in cultural establishments; new places of sale should not be approved. Additional suggestions were to increase the production of nonalcoholic beverages, ban alcohol advertisements, and devote more attention to improved cultural facilities. The OBSA also proposed annual reductions of at least 10 percent in the production of alcohol and recommended that Gosplan and the Commissariat of Finance should be entrusted with the task of developing a comprehensive strategy to replace the proceeds gained from alcohol with alternative sources of income.[61]

Six months later, in January 1929, Sovnarkom codified many principles of the OBSA plan into law.[62] The anti-alcohol organization's work would seem to have come to fruition. Certainly the activities undertaken by the OBSA throughout 1928–1929 demonstrate the society's own intention to expand its political authority. In late 1928, activists formed the All-Union Soviet of Anti-Alcohol Societies (VSPO), an umbrella organization designed to coordinate the work of local OBSA cells; the VSPO sponsored a national congress on the alcohol problem the following summer. In an attempt to spread its anti-alcohol message and enhance its social basis of support, the OBSA organized courses to train anti-alcohol agitators and waged extensive anti-alcohol campaigns in all levels of the press during 1928–1929.[63] The widespread publicity devoted to the OBSA efforts in the late 1920s affirms that broad sections of the party and state apparatus facilitated the organization's effort to popularize its message.

Nonetheless, in retrospect, the anti-alcohol movement's imminent demise was foreshadowed by the 1929 law's omission of key elements present in the OBSA's original proposal. Most importantly, in an indication that certain quarters continued to view alcohol revenue as an important consideration in the state budget, Sovnarkom failed to incorporate the OBSA's suggestion for a yearly 10 percent reduction in the production of alcohol. Other signs that the OBSA goals might not enjoy universal support within the Soviet apparatus emerged later that year. At the Fifth Congress of Soviets in May, Gosplan chair Gleb M. Krzhizhanovskii announced a seemingly auspicious plan to effect a 70 percent reduction in the urban population's per capita alcohol consumption by the end of the first Five Year Plan; at a VSPO congress held that very same month, though, Ia. I. Lifshits expressed surprise upon hearing conferees speak about plans to reduce alcohol production: the information available to him indicated that increased production was envisioned in Ukraine.[64] By September, the OBSA was presenting Gosplan with a letter of protest criticizing the Commissariat of Finance's plan to increase alcohol production. Krzhizhanovskii's repeated assurances that Gosplan would adhere to reductions in alcohol production as outlined at the Fifth Congress ultimately proved unwarranted. After Krzhizhanovskii lost his position at Gosplan, the Central Committee reversed the decision.[65]

Despite the flurry of activity in 1927–1929—and despite support from prominent members of the Soviet apparatus—the anti-alcohol movement ultimately fell victim to disputes then raging at the highest levels of the Communist Party. Because they were unwilling to adopt any possible means to accomplish industrialization as rapidly as possible, leading anti-alcohol activists were easily implicated in the more general attacks against the Right Opposition. Bukharin, the most prominent spokesperson for the Right, had argued that the capital required for industrialization should be accumulated gradually, through a continuation of market relations and NEP. But by 1929, Bukharin's forces were rapidly losing ground to Stalin's call for class war and an end to NEP's "temporary" compromise with the peasantry. In April 1929, the Central Committee of the party relieved Bukharin of his responsibilities as editor of *Pravda*; in November, the Old Bolshevik was expelled from the Politburo. Compared with Bukharin's hopes, what Stalin envisioned was in many ways a more optimistic scenario: industrialization, he asserted, could be accomplished much more quickly than his opponents on the Right imagined. After eliminating foreign loans and the market as appropriate mechanisms for capital accumulation, the guardian of the Left turned to alcohol revenue as an indispensable component of his plan to forge "Socialism in One Country."

The ascendent Stalin summed up his position at the Fourteenth Party Congress: it was impossible to build socialism with "white gloves."[66] Members of the Soviet apparatus who sought to accomplish industrialization without the proceeds from alcohol were allegedly attempting the impossible.

In early 1930, the anti-alcohol leadership was publicly censured. The presence of the now discredited Bukharin on the OBSA board, the long friendship between Bukharin and Larin, and Larin's Menshevik background could not have helped matters. Larin and Deichman lost their leadership positions in the OBSA, the VSPO was liquidated, and the OBSA's criticism of plans to increase the output of vodka was condemned as a "gross political mistake." The OBSA was reproached for its campaigns to close drinking establishments, and it was admonished to concentrate instead on enlightenment work.[67] According to contemporary Soviet scholars, Larin and Deichman's insistence on sharp reductions in the production of vodka was seen as "unrealistic" at a time when it was necessary "to concentrate maximum material resources on . . . the industrialization of the country."[68] By May 1930, the Central Committee had sounded the final death knell for cultural reformers' serious efforts to effect an immediate reduction in the importance of alcoholic beverages to proletarian life: among others, Larin was personally singled out for his misplaced desire to concentrate on restructuring daily life when rapid industrialization was a more pressing issue.[69] For all practical purposes, institutions concerned with the issue of drunkenness ceased active work, and discussions of alcohol largely disappeared from the press. Problem drinking, no longer presented as a phenomenon dependent on social conditions, was attributed instead to abnormal individual psychology. When the first Five Year Plan drew to a close in 1932, vodka production in the Soviet Union was higher than it had been in 1928.[70]

• • •

State control of drink made alcohol use a more volatile matter in Russia than it was in other industrializing countries. Whether before or after 1917, widespread sobriety in Russia would inevitably deprive the government of an important source of revenue. At the same time, the state's dependence on alcohol income made it vulnerable to charges that it was inept and that it was unconcerned with the physical and cultural degradation of the Russian people. Although workers' delegates at the 1909 Congress issued strong condemnations of state alcohol policy, by the end of the 1920s a revolutionary workers' government proved no less able to forgo taxes from the sale of drink and no more willing to tolerate sensitive criticism than its predecessor had been. Between 1927 and 1929, Stalin's opponents had considerable success in bringing alcohol-related issues to the press and in passing legislation targeted at discouraging drink. But despite their ability to win some important battles, the opponents of drink were defeated in the end: though OBSA activists insisted that reducing alcohol consumption was sound economic policy, by early 1930 their argument had been rejected and their organizational body had been all but disbanded.

The workers' delegation at the 1909 Congress, the anti-alcohol activists of the 1920s, and the Soviet government all claimed to have the interest of the working class at heart, but the working mass viewed drinking much differently than any of these groups. In working-class communities and on the shop floor, the politics of drink assumed entirely different dimensions.

MEANINGS OF DRINK

■ Within the more prosaic context of life, and despite extreme personal hardship in early twentieth-century Russia, there was great constancy in
many social and cultural functions that workers
assigned to alcohol. During the difficult years of
world war, revolution, and civil war, Russia's urban population struggled with physical insecurity, epidemic disease, and food shortages. Personal hardship increased as the country's
economic infrastructure, already unequal to the
demands of the military conflagration in Europe,
collapsed in the wake of the 1917 revolutions.
Major urban centers, including Petrograd, suffered extreme depopulation during the Russian
civil war; millions of urban residents simply
abandoned the cities in hopes that sustenance
would prove easier to find in the countryside.
The population of Petrograd, 2.5 million in 1917,
had plummeted to 700,000 just three years later.[1]
Individuals who did remain in the capital during
the civil war survived by gathering firewood
from deserted housing stock, foraging in rural
districts, and relying on train-traveling "bag-
men" to transport commodities between city and
country. In the midst of such hardship and
hunger, laborers' circumscribed time and resources permitted little opportunity for frivolous
pursuits: of necessity, energy was directed toward sustaining life. Even if a period of legal

prohibition had not interfered, a dramatic disruption in drinking customs might well be expected of the period 1914 to 1921.

Yet, after the dust settled and a new political authority began to emerge in place of the old regime, possibilities for rejuvenation remained. With the inauguration of the NEP in 1921, Russia's cities began to bustle again: by 1926, Leningrad was repopulated; housing was being built rather than disassembled; traders offered wares that had been unavailable in the more troubled years.[2] As scholars have previously noted, the revival of "proletarian" cities like St. Petersburg was important to the legitimacy of a state rooted in Marxist theory—but the revolutionary blueprint of course did not envision the mere duplication of pre-revolutionary urban life. Leaders of the revolutionary state hoped that the end of civil war would motivate their working-class constituency to look forward in new political and social directions and that workers' enthusiastic participation in building socialism would be evident in all spheres of worker activity, including the cultural realm. In the view of Soviet Russia's working-class activists, workers' "old" culture had been characterized by drunkenness, banality, sexual segregation, and religious superstition; their "new" cultural life was to be sober, sensible, collective, and atheistic.

For their part, workers made adjustments to the state's cultural prescription when they found it necessary or convenient, but restoring the pre-revolutionary sources of self-identity and strength in their lives often came more easily than did setting out in new directions. Indeed, a comparison of drinking practices in the years preceding World War I with those of the 1920s shows that many of the meanings of drink remained remarkably stable. Workers' discursive conventions, in particular, reflect a steady persistence in the symbolic significance that laborers attached to alcohol consumption. Whether before or after 1917, fractures within the laboring community were revealed through the use of alcohol, which visibly displayed the boundaries that workers constructed between the categories male and female, adult and child, worker and intellectual. Furthermore, alcohol remained a fundamental element in shaping worker identity: most workingmen found it virtually impossible to demonstrate shared fraternity or celebration without drink. While the Soviet regime sanctioned new holidays and alternate modes of celebration as appropriate to life in a workers' state, many laborers continued to celebrate "old" holidays, or observed "new," revolutionary holidays in now "inappropriate" ways.

. . .

In recent decades, historians have devoted considerable study to the ways in which language reflects underlying relations of power, social attitudes, and identity. Within the history of labor, William H. Sewell and Gareth Stedman Jones were among the early craftsmen of this approach. Sewell's outstanding study of workers in early nineteenth-century France demonstrated the continued importance of corporate values in workers' protests, whereas Stedman Jones pointed to workers' political apathy in late-nineteenth-century Britain. More recently, attention to language has enabled scholars such as Anna Clark to produce invigorating studies that shed new light on domesticity and gender relations among workers.[3] Historians of Russia, slower to embrace discursive strategies as a way to interrogate their sources, are relative newcomers to this intellectual discussion. Although the critical question of how and why a revolutionary working class formed in Russia has received the attention of many historians, these investigations have tended to center on the worker's migration to the city, the development of (usually) his revolutionary consciousness, and the nature of working-class political commitments.[4] Calls for increased attention to how the Russian working class was discursively constructed have surfaced only more recently.[5] An examination of the language surrounding working-class drinking helps to advance this discussion, for Russia's workers employed language in ways that reflected both significant intraclass divisions among them and a common identity separating workers from other social groups.

Within the context of alcohol and its use, evidence bearing on the linguistic conventions of the working class is most abundant in fictional short stories written to encourage laborers to stop drinking. Although there are difficulties inherent in these sources, it is not difficult to determine their intended messages: these stories are simple sketches with obvious didactic lessons aimed at an unsophisticated reading audience. If their conspicuous moral message is set aside, such vignettes remain a rich source on working-class conceptions of drink. After all, in attempting to make their lessons accessible to the intended audience, temperance stories necessarily incorporated many "unimportant" details. To paraphrase Louis Chevalier, the story is important not for what "it purports to say" but for what "it cannot help saying."[6] In addition to the repeated appearance of certain linguistic patterns— which is itself suggestive of their relevance to working-class life— much of the language used in fictional depictions of workers' drinking practices is analogous to that contained in other, "factual" accounts appearing in memoirs and newspapers.

The language of workingmen shows that their most persistent assumption about alcohol concerned its relationship to gender: they understood drinking to be conduct befitting male workers; abstinence from alcohol—and from spirits in particular—was portrayed as the appropriate behavior for women. The perception that men drank and women did not underlay Koz'ma G. Rozhkov's 1929 announcement that he was giving up vodka: he urged all other *men* to do the same. Despite the fact that his appeal was published in a journal addressed to women, the representation of the drinker in Rozhkov's mind was distinctly male. Similarly, D. Ia. Kurdachev's roommate declared, "You are a fool, Miten'ka. . . . You don't drink, you don't love women—what kind of a man [*chelovek*] are you?[7] Gendered language linking alcohol with the masculine world and abstinence with the feminine world was most starkly expressed in the remarks that laboring men directed at peers hesitant to join a drinking circle. In their good-natured attempts to encourage abstemious men to participate in drinking festivities, male workers consistently employed feminized epithets calling the sexual identity and maturity of nondrinking men into question.

Of three standard taunts intended to persuade diffident men to imbibe, *krasnaia devitsa* [red maiden] appears to have been the most widely applied.[8] Used pejoratively with reference to men, a *krasnaia devitsa* was an excessively shy, bashful person, and the adoption of the feminine form indicates that men properly distinguished themselves by behaving in more sociable ways. In the working-class milieu, men were expected to share strong drink with their peers. Workingmen were neither to abstain nor to limit their alcohol consumption to "weak, women's drinks" such as beer, wine, and liqueurs.[9] Reference to maidens—who, at least in theory, were sexually inexperienced—also clearly challenged the nondrinker's sexual maturity. Implanted in the rhetorical construction *krasnaia devitsa* was a presumption that those who abstained or who sipped only sweet drinks had not shown themselves to be men. Such bashful behavior was appropriate to women alone.

A second epithet that laboring men directed at nondrinking comrades illustrates a similar identification of temperance with femininity. A man who abstained, or who drank insufficient quantities of alcohol, could find himself dubbed a *mokraia kuritsa* [wet hen] by more enthusiastic peers.[10] The gendered construction of this common expression cannot be dismissed, for not only was the feminine *kuritsa* [hen] selected over the masculine *petukh* [rooster], but in addition, the sexual implications of the insult increase when it is considered within the broader context of Russian popular culture. Secondary understandings of *petukh*, including "bully" and "penis," are absent from *kuritsa*. Furthermore, many Russian workers would have been quite familiar with the prominent equation between women and chickens contained in the well-known Russian proverb "A chicken is not a bird, and a woman is not a person." Similarly, popular prints dating from the eighteenth century depict a male figure astride a cock while his female counterpart jaunts about on a hen.[11] No less than "red maiden," the expression "wet hen" reflected male workers' conviction that men drank; the avoidance of alcohol was a feminine trait.

An association between femininity and abstinence also figured in a third epithet of this kind: *baba* [peasant woman]. When the fictional protagonist in *Pochemu on ne pil?* resists his comrades' invitation to join their drinking party, the revelers chatter gleefully: "Hey Senia . . . [Do you know] what you are like?! A *baba* . . . Is this the way to be a man, not to drink?!" In adopting the disparaging term for peasant women to refer to nondrinking laborers, working-class men implicitly precluded belittlement via *muzhik*, the *baba*'s masculine equivalent. If laborers had considered *muzhik* an appropriate way to characterize nondrinkers, they might have chided an abstainer's social status while leaving his manhood intact.[12] Their failure to adopt this approach illustrates the striking consistency with which male workers associated abstinence with the feminine world.

Since the "way to be a man" was to drink, alcohol served as a visible behavioral mechanism for differentiating men from women. The expectation that individuals who aspired to adult male status would partake of strong alcoholic beverages made the consumption of drink a critical component in the social maturation of young male workers. By drinking, a young man publicly both affirmed that he was no longer a mere child and demonstrated his independence from the formerly intrusive feminine influence. Again, epithets that men directed at nondrinking companions make this distinction clear. In one story, for example, the main character was chided for refusing to drink with friends: "Petr, it is time for you to stop sitting by your mother's skirt! Show that you are a grown man." A youth's need to demonstrate his autonomy from maternal control through drinking was also expressed in a story by V. Mikhailovskii. When a young worker declines invitations to drink, the crowd chortles: "Come with us! If you don't know how to drink . . . we'll teach you! He still has a nanny, he has a mummy! They are [still] minding the baby. Child! He is afraid of his mother!"[13]

The male community collectively determined when it was time for a young man to enter the adult world, and the son who unduly delayed the onset of his drinking career could be a source of consternation for his father. A father named Kheiso, uneasy about his son's reluctance to imbibe, worried: "I look at you and I am embarrassed. Are you [really] my son? How long have you lived on the earth . . . and still you haven't gotten drunk once." In the elder Kheiso's view, getting drunk was a normal part of the maturation process for young men. His son's lingering sobriety was a disturbing indication that the young man's social development was retarded, a sign that Kheiso himself had failed to successfully guide his son into adulthood. Though Kanatchikov's father remained in the village, he, too, worried about a son who "drinks no vodka, smokes no tobacco, [and] doesn't play cards." His neighbors attempted to console the old man: "It's all right, Ivan Egorych, he'll turn out right when he gets older."[14]

The vital role alcohol played in distinguishing grown men from children meant that young men tended to take up drink in their maturing years. Statistical investigations of drinking habits conducted in both the pre- and post-revolutionary eras indicate that at least 90 percent of male workers drank and that young men typically began to use alcohol when they were between fifteen and nineteen years old.[15] For working-class youth, these years coincided with their initiation into the world of work (see chapter 3). Here it is important that a cluster of working-class idioms anticipated adult male workers' joining their peers in the consumption of strong alcoholic beverages. Every epithet that drinking working-class men commonly directed at abstainers—"red maiden," "wet hen," "baba," and "baby"—contested the nondrinker's manhood. Abstinence, whether seen as characteristic of women themselves or of children under female control, was ultimately attributed to the feminine domain. Furthermore, the expectations embedded in the language of laboring men were indicative of actual worker behavior. It is not mere coincidence that drinking was far more typical of laboring men than it was of working women, or that it was usually working-class fathers (not mothers) who encouraged sons (but *not* daughters) to drink. When a young boy grimaced at the taste of alcohol, his father chuckled, encouraged the tyke to "get used" to it, and praised the child who gulped down a swig.[16]

Just as workers viewed alcohol consumption as an essential element of adult male identity, they also considered drinking an important way to distinguish workers from nonworkers. "I left half of my first earnings in the tavern," recalled P. K. Ignatov, "but I was proud: now I was a 'real' worker!" Similarly, Vasia Zaitsev coaxed a friend to linger a little longer in the beer hall. "Eh, you're a wet hen," he objected. "What kind of worker are you, when you don't drink beer or spirits."[17] Of course, there were men in working communities who did not drink; outside of the restrictive period from 1914 to the mid-1920s, however, they consistently comprised a minority of 10 percent or less. As the characterization of the fictional Semen Bobrov indicates, the non-drinker was an oddity in working-class ranks. "In the eyes of [other] workers, nothing made Semen stand out more than his abstinence. He didn't drink vodka, beer, or wine. No one remembered a time when Semen had taken part in the drinking bouts and binges of his comrades."[18] It was commitment to sobriety, not drunkenness, that made a worker unusual among his peers.

For the vast majority of Russian laborers, there was nothing disgraceful about alcohol use or drunkenness. This does not mean that workers possessed no understanding of problem drinking. Solitary alcohol consumption, drinking on the street, guzzling directly from the bottle, or relying on the money of others might be signs that an individual's habits had become unhealthy—but heavy drinking alone was not considered a violation of social norms.[19] Most workers would not have called the individual who drank heartily from time to time, or whom friends occasionally led home by the arm, a "drunkard."[20] Drinking was instead seen as an external behavioral manifestation of worker self-identity.

For Russia's workers, as for any other group, the forging of a collective identity was accomplished through the twin processes of inclusion and exclusion. Observation of a stranger's drinking practices was one way that Russia's early twentieth-century workers distinguished workers from nonworkers, as their use of language shows. "Workers" consumed alcohol, and drinking was a necessary sign of inclusion in the working community. By definition, then, nondrinkers belonged to different social groups; abstinence was a means by which certain categories of people could be conceptually excluded from working-class ranks. As a young man named Krasinskii told Komsomol investigators in the late 1920s, if a laborer did not accompany fellow workers to the tavern on payday, "they look upon you as an 'intellectual,' [or] a 'baba,' not as 'one of the guys [nesvoego parnia].'"[21] Krasinskii's assertion makes it clear that "drinker" was a part of his coworkers' definition of "worker." They could not accept abstemious "intellectuals" and "babas" as "real" workers.

Krasinskii's reference to "intellectuals" was a snub directed at the intellectuals most commonly encountered by workers: that is, *worker* intellectuals, the Russian counterparts to Britain's more renowned (but sometimes allegedly more reformist) labor "aristocrats."[22] This segment of the Russian working class—more positively identified in Social Democratic lexicon as "conscious" or "advanced" workers—subscribed to a set of behavioral norms stressing rationality and self-discipline, values that were inevitably reflected in dress, language, and leisure activities. As expressed in the sharply polarized political discourse of Russia's worker activists, "backward" or "rank-and-file" workers inhabited a coarse and bawdy world—a world in which heavy drinking, brawling, womanizing, and cursing were common. "Conscious" or "advanced" workers, in contrast, valued sobriety, clean language, neat dress, sexual restraint, political involvement, and educational improvement.[23] Vasilii D. Rubtsov, an "underground worker intelligent" was one such personage: "he didn't drink, he didn't smoke, and he was always ready to talk seriously and thoughtfully."[24] But in the eyes of the working-class rank and file, people like Rubtsov had little in common with other workers.

Among other historians, Charters Wynn has observed that rank-and-file workers frequently rejected the paternalistic tutelage offered by their "conscious" brethren.[25] This examination of language suggests the magnitude of that rejection: in the eyes of most workers, the "conscious" or "advanced" workers' puritanical code of conduct transformed them into unmanly intellectuals who did not truly belong to the working community. The view of worker intellectuals as feminine may have been reinforced by the prominence of Jews in the revolutionary leadership. Sander L. Gilman, Laura Engelstein, and George L. Mosse have shown in other contexts that European Jews were broadly perceived as "feminine"—in Russia, even as *"babas."*[26] Igal Halfin's recent assertions that Marxism in Russia marked the proletariat as male and the intellectual as female can thus be extended to include rank-and-file workers' conception of the worker as masculine and the worker intellectual as feminine.[27]

The linguistic conventions employed by St. Petersburg's early twentieth-century laborers thus expose significant fractures within the Russian working class. In discriminating between the kinds of people who drank and those who did not, the working-class rank and file theoretically denied presumed "abstainers"—women, children, and worker intellectuals—full status as workers. Alcohol was ultimately symbolic of the potential power that the drinking collective held against the abstaining others. More concretely, drink was a symbol of the power that adult male workers held over women, children, and worker intellectuals. The attitudes and practices surrounding working-class drinking speak loudly about the social and political life of the Russian working class, as well as about the difficulty inherent in attempts to cultivate lasting worker solidarity.

. . .

Even as drink symbolically divided the working class's "masculine," "adult," and "backward," elements from its "feminine," "juvenile," and "advanced" components, it served as a foundation supporting sociability among workingmen. Anthropologists have shown that collective drinking practices prevail in most world populations; indeed, the solitary use of alcohol is typically considered symptomatic of problem drinking.[28] Alcohol use among Russia's male workers was no less rooted in sociability: as the journal of the food working industry put it in 1928, only the "very rare worker" drank alone. The essential accuracy of that observation is confirmed by every important statistical study of drinking in early twentieth-century St. Petersburg; both before and after 1917, Russian laborers were far more likely to drink in company than in solitude.[29]

The mutual respect expressed through shared drink—underscored by toasts to "comradeship" and "friendship"—was so fundamental to life in the working community that it was virtually impossible for laborers to affirm cordial intentions without consuming alcohol.[30] Contemporary literature repeatedly emphasized the preeminent role that drink played in initiating and reinforcing friendships between workingmen. "Eh, [you are a bit of a] fool for not drinking," an old man gently advised Boris I. Ivanov. "If you drank, you would find comrades and friends, and it is hard to live without them." The difficulty in establishing friendly relations without alcohol also surfaced in Zhizn' Kass'iana. As a nondrinking peasant made his way to St. Petersburg, he met a passerby who advised him to turn back. A temperate man, the stranger warned, would find "neither work nor comrades" in the city.[31] As might be expected in this social milieu, laborers commonly attributed their own consumption of alcohol to the influence of companions. When questioned about their reason for drinking, 73 percent of the men treated for alcoholism at certain pre-revolutionary clinics claimed that "comrades and drinking customs" compelled them to drink. Though the explanations for drinking provided to researchers at the Nevskii Machine-Building mill in 1928 were more varied, 12 percent of the respondents in that study claimed to drink primarily "for company"; a 41 percent plurality cited companionship as the reason for their first drink.[32] For most male workers, the consumption of alcoholic beverages was a decidedly social act.

The intimate connection between drink and comradeship brought with it the expectation that any solicitation to drink "for company" would be met positively. The vast majority of Russia's workers understood such invitations as friendly gestures; declining would be interpreted as a personal rejection, a sign of "'coldness' toward friends."[33] Demonstrating goodwill and friendship toward others made drinking "for company" a social imperative. "For company, Sania . . . Among us [drinking] for company is not declined," a fictitious young knife sharpener's friends urged.[34] Refusing to join a drinker for the sake of companionship was reportedly "disgraceful, shameful," even for those who normally did not partake of alcoholic beverages.[35]

Reciprocity and friendship expressed through shared drink was reinforced by the practice of sharing a common bottle and by the customs of treating one another. Dividing a common drinking stock, whether a bottle of vodka or a dozen beers, seems to have been the Russian workers' usual approach. By dividing a common drinking fund, laborers symbolically affirmed each individual's bond to the collective. Drinking from a shared source implied that all members of the group profited equally from group membership. It also established collective controls on the amount of alcohol consumed and the amount of time devoted to conversation. All members of a drinking circle were expected to tarry until the alcohol supply had been exhausted. Those who attempted to leave prematurely were likely to be reprimanded by the others: "Well, my lad, don't try that; that is not comradely. How will I drink twelve bottles [of beer] by myself? After all, I am not a horse."[36] Although treating by rounds appears to have been less typical of Russian workers, similar social mechanisms characterized that practice when it did occur. When members of a drinking circle took turns having "one comrade pay for all," the size of the group was an important factor in determining how much alcohol would be purchased and how long the group would tarry. Individuals could not conveniently depart of their own volition, for drinking vodka that someone else had purchased obliged the recipient to stay long enough to treat in return.[37] Whether laborers shared a common bottle or took turns paying for rounds, the collective controls that workers established over alcohol consumption enforced social equality and reciprocity within their ranks.

The importance of collective consumption within working-class ranks is compelling, and it suggests the need to refine the distinction that David Christian has drawn between "traditional" and "modern" drinking cultures. In his study of vodka's role in nineteenth-century Russia, Christian argues that drinking in traditional rural cultures "tended to be collective . . . while modern [urban] drinking cultures were (and are) more individualistic." Traditional drinking, says Christian, is "social and ceremonial, shaped more by convention than by individual whim." In contrast, the decision to imbibe in modern drinking cultures "reflect[s] the desires of individuals, rather than the traditions of the community." Although there may well be important distinctions between urban and rural (or worker and peasant) drinking styles, the drinking pattern of Russia's early twentieth-century laborers cannot suitably be characterized as "individualistic," nor could it be said to have been governed more by recreation than by sociability and obligation.[38] The collective voice governing the drinking practices of urban workers may have been different from that in Russian villages, but collectivity nonetheless remained a self-conscious component of workers' drinking experience. In addition, as will become even clearer from the discussion of alcohol and the workplace in chapter 3, drinking conventions among urban laborers embodied strong social requirements and collective obligations. A systematic comparison of rural and urban drinking cultures far exceeds the purpose of this investigation, but it would undoubtedly enhance historical understanding of changing social structures, conceptions of community, gender relations, and leisure among lower-class citizens in early twentieth-century Russia.

Workers' most extended opportunity for social drinking came in their leisure hours; throughout the early twentieth century, cultural activists in Russia expressed serious misgivings about the ways ordinary laborers spent their time away from work. At the dawn of the century, new laws that forbade employers to require Sunday labor heightened upper-class concerns about workers' leisure forms. The journal of the Guardianships for Public Sobriety, for example, took pains to point out that the new legislation did not *prohibit* anyone from working on Sundays. An anxious essay appearing in another temperance publication observed that the law had dramatically increased the number of "modest toilers" patrolling the city on Sunday afternoon. St. Petersburg's streets, it went on, were now populated by a "huge quantity" of "entirely new faces," a situation that made the street "dreadful" to frequent, especially during the Easter and Christmas seasons. The article concluded that workers' intellectual poverty prevented them from using their new-found leisure in constructive ways. People visiting St. Petersburg's rich museums, for example, "look[ed] at the exhibited objects with bewilderment, not understanding what significance and meaning this or another thing has. No one provides any explanation to these ignorant [*temnye*] people, and they walk among all these riches as if in a forest." Temperance activists believed that workers wasted their free days in aimless carousing; this perverted the entire purpose of holidays, which laborers should have used to restore their "spirit and body."[39]

Virtually the same sentiment was repeatedly expressed in the Soviet press. Soviet Russia's cultural activists advocated the "sensible," "healthful," and "intelligent" use of laborers' leisure time. Workers could then return to work "fresh, [and] hearty"—something they would not do if they spent their time away from work engaged in "drunken debauchery."[40] Unfortunately, workers "did not know how" to use leisure in appropriate ways.[41] In addition to traditional worries, though, the Soviet state had new concerns about the way workers spent their leisure hours. Cultural activists in the 1920s believed that workers' observance of "old," "senseless" religious holidays reinforced discarded ideologies and power structures. In principle, tsarist Russia's celebrations were incompatible with the goal of creating a new, socialist way of life.

Clearheaded revolutionaries quite logically concluded that outmoded religious holidays and old forms of celebration should be eradicated—that revolutionary goals would be fostered most successfully with the adoption of secular celebratory practices. Working-class leisure should be consistent with revolutionary precepts: it should be "rational," "organized," and "collective."[42] Notwithstanding the conspicuously collective nature of workers' traditional drinking practices, the bottle could not be squared with activists' prescriptions for the "rational" and "organized" use of workers' time. Above all, cultural activists maintained that *"the new, revolutionary holidays [must] not be clouded by the repulsive sight of drunkards."* If that happened, the significance of the Soviet state's holidays would be *"reduced to nothing."*[43] Ideology required that the revolution and its promises be celebrated by workers in full control of their faculties and cognizant of their goals. The revolutionary blueprint left no room for allegedly irrational and unproductive drunken behavior, especially on the part of workers.

Activists' attempts to replace pre-revolutionary traditions with suitable modes of celebration did not proceed easily. Alcohol was an integral part of workers' very concept of celebration. True, the exigencies of world war and civil war temporarily made the traditional use of leisure time exceedingly difficult. Although paper shortages meant that few contemporaneous publications touch on the celebration of holidays between 1914 and 1921, the circumscribed observance of holidays in those years is nonetheless clear from subsequent publications.[44] In 1925, for example, *Vestnik profsoiuzov* observed that "in the stormy years of revolution, in the years of collapse, hunger, and the struggle with the enemy advancing from all sides . . . no one thought about drunkenness or vodka." Even festivities surrounding the critical Easter holiday had been severely constrained during civil war, as a 1922 article appearing in *Petrogradskaia pravda* makes clear. It had been a long time since so many Easter cakes had been seen in St. Petersburg, the paper remarked, and bootleg liquor was still hard to get and expensive. Local conditions during civil war varied tremendously; a 1923 story appearing in *Rabotnitsa* suggested that it had been more difficult to celebrate traditional holidays in Red-controlled areas such as Petrograd. Though the geographical setting for this story is unclear, the inhabitants of the depicted area rejoiced when Whites surrounded the region shortly before the Easter holiday. This happy turn of events meant that the populace would be able to celebrate Easter "in the [Russian] Orthodox manner"; whenever Bolsheviks were in charge "a holiday [was] not a holiday."[45]

In the mid-1920s, when life in Soviet Russia began to assume some modicum of predictability and stability, citizens could once again entertain the possibility of spending leisure hours in festive ways. Despite activists' hopes that workers would abandon pre-revolutionary forms of celebration as outmoded and irrational, the impulse of many laborers was to return to traditional leisure patterns or to adjust to Soviet political culture in ways that combined customary practices with new components. In the 1920s, then, many "pre-revolutionary" drinking customs reappeared; in addition, a host of adaptations emerged that skillfully blended "old" celebratory elements with "new" revolutionary observances.

The drinking practices that proved most resilient in early twentieth-century Russia marked rites of passage and the arrival of the weekend. Both before and after 1917, drink played an integral role in the celebration of christenings, name days, weddings, and funerals. "Is it really possible to have a christening, wedding, or holiday without treating?" asked one observer. "People laugh and put [you] to shame."[46] At marriage celebrations, which frequently lasted several days, drinking "to insanity" was not uncommon.[47] Alcohol consumption was also an important element of funeral rites, and clever workers might even wrestle a pay advance from the office for such a purpose.[48] Some funeral processions stopped at each tavern along the deceased's final route.

Near the turn of the century, when one group of workers observed the passing of their friend Misha, for example, they paused at each tavern, "put down the coffin, stopped in to drink, remembered, and again took up Misha's coffin and carried it." Their drinking binge continued at the grave site, where companions saluted Misha's memory for two days. That this practice persisted into the late 1920s is clear from the nearly identical procession workers at Pechatnyi Dvor conducted in honor of foreman Arem'ev.[49] Since funeral processions often stopped at places important in the life of the deceased, the individuals whom friends remembered by visiting taverns may have been particularly prodigious drinkers.[50]

Alcohol bestowed a festive air and expressed celebratory intentions that extended beyond any abstract meaning implicit in such rituals. As one pre-revolutionary publication observed, revelers who marked name days were more preoccupied with drinking than with the health of the celebrant or the honored saint; people allegedly thought about prayer "least of all."[51] Workers' traditional observance of rites of passage in the 1920s suggests that the sober alternatives promoted by the state—"red" weddings, civil funerals, and *Oktiabriny*—failed to satisfy the desire of many workers to mark these important life events in meaningful ways. Without specific research into laborers' responses to revolutionary substitutes, it is difficult to draw firm conclusions about just what the new alternatives lacked. Nonetheless, for Russia's workers, the very absence of alcohol itself denoted a regrettable lack of festivity. As Dr. I. D. Strashun observed, many people believed that "a holiday without a drinking-bout [was] impossible."[52]

The drinking tradition most impervious to "revolutionary" encroachments was also the most mundane: the working community's celebration of the weekend's arrival. Drinking and talking with friends required time and money, and the weekend often provided both. At many establishments, workers' pay packets were distributed on Saturday, and Sunday was a day of rest. According to one worker, the normal weekend routine consisted of quitting work at 2 P.M. Saturday, heading for the baths, and then getting drunk or going shopping; on Sundays, the workingman drank; on Mondays, he skipped work and nursed his hangover.[53] The accuracy of this characterization is supported by the large number of individuals who spent time in St. Petersburg's drunk tanks on Saturday, Sunday, and Monday.[54] The practice of drinking on weekends was so entrenched in working-class life that some individuals seem to have oriented their schedules around it. When one Vasil'ev was arraigned before a public trial in the Stalin club, the court inquired whether he was inebriated when the machine he operated had been ruined. "And what day was it? Friday?" Vasil'ev asked. "No," he responded, "I don't drink on Fridays, I drink on Saturdays and Sundays."[55] Vasil'ev's statement was socially credible, even though it probably had been designed to mitigate his guilt. Together with many other laboring men, Vasil'ev may well have spent his weekends crowding into drinking establishments and competing for a place to sit. Even before the factory bell rang on Saturday afternoons, taverns' tables were reportedly taken up by "those who had to take their wife to the hospital, those who begged the foreman for a pass to break loose from the factory a little earlier, and those who regularly sit in the beer hall every payday."[56]

The onset of the weekend brought workers a sense of relief from the week's daily drudgery—a relief that was undoubtedly enhanced by widespread public participation in common celebration and the fresh acquisition of money. At most factories, payday came only once every two weeks or once a month, so workers eagerly anticipated it.[57] When, at long last, the appointed day arrived, the workers' joyful mood engulfed factory districts. St. Petersburg's working-class regions took on a "different air" as workers eagerly bolted out of the factories, filling the taverns until they overflowed "to the last degree."[58] If only briefly, workers with pay packets apparently felt well-off enough to allow themselves the luxury of a drink with friends. The relationship between a worker's perceived monetary well-being and his proclivity for robust drinking was clear and tangible: the worker was most likely to drink, asserted *Vestnik trezvosti*, when a pay packet "bulges in his pocket."[59] Individuals who happened to receive higher than normal wages saluted the occasion by drinking more than usual. As one Iakovlev recalled, "[he who] earned a lot also drank a lot; [he who] earned less also drank less."[60]

For certain individuals, it was difficult to bring this merry weekend celebration to a close in time for the return to work Monday morning. Indeed, the traditional drinking pattern in Russia worked against such punctuality. Although per capita alcohol use was actually lower in Russia than in other major European countries, nowhere else was such a "savage, uncultured" pattern of alcohol consumption said to prevail.[61] The "Russian" proclivity for punctuating long periods of abstinence with drinking binges lasting several days contrasted sharply with the regularity of "German" drinking, that is, the consumption of "a little glass of Russian vodka" at frequent intervals throughout the day.[62]

It is difficult to judge how often workers actually missed work on Mondays, though the incidence appears to have declined over the course of the first three decades of the twentieth century. Early in the century, workers were almost as likely to find themselves in the detoxification shelters on Monday as during the weekend proper, and certainly pre-revolutionary temperance literature leaves the impression that workers considered Monday little more than an opportunity to continue "Sunday debauchery."[63] In the 1920s, the press similarly complained that at some factories as many as one-fifth to one-third of all workers failed to report for work after paydays.[64] Scattered investigations of absenteeism held in archival records suggest more moderate elevations in worker truancy following paydays and weekends. At the Kalinin mill in 1927–1928, for example, 1.44 percent of workers were absent for "inadequate reason" on regular weekdays, whereas 2.15 percent missed work after paydays. An investigation of eighteen Leningrad mills conducted in February 1929 showed that on Mondays absenteeism for insufficient reason exceeded that of other weekdays by about 21 percent.[65] Yet drunkenness was not solely responsible for Monday truancy: female workers, who were far less likely to spend the weekend drinking than were laboring men, also displayed increased rates of absenteeism on Mondays. Whereas men spent Mondays with hangovers, female absenteeism was attributed to "laundry, illness of relatives, and so forth." It appears that both workingmen and workingwomen endeavored to secure extra time free from work.[66] In the 1920s, prolonged celebration of the weekend may have ebbed in comparison with the prewar years, but blue Mondays did survive. Workers' steadfast insistence on reviving their weekend drinking customs after an obligatory hiatus shows not only the remarkable strength of those traditions but also how deeply they cherished this time.

In the 1920s, workers' weekends were greeted with the same revelry and tone characteristic of prewar celebration. In addition, alcohol retained its prominent place in working-class observances of major holidays. The essential link laborers made between holidays and alcohol consumption became unmistakable when the St. Petersburg city governor inauspiciously banned alcohol sales during the three-day Easter holiday in 1914. In the workers' view, the prohibition was a patronizing nuisance. As they explained to *Gazeta kopeika*'s reporter, they were "sufficiently grown-up people and they know themselves what is harmful and what is useful for them, and they do not need administrative guardianship." Forced to endure the temporary postponement of their holiday celebration, the working population met Easter "in its own way, according to tradition" when the ban on alcohol was lifted. An estimated fifteen thousand to twenty thousand workers celebrated Easter a day late, but celebrate they did.[67] The 1914 observance of Easter foreshadowed the resourcefulness workers would display in meeting other challenges to their conception of proper holiday celebration in the 1920s.

With the consolidation of Soviet power, both the religious content and the celebratory mode of pre-revolutionary holidays were brought into official disfavor, a situation that elicited a variety of responses from the working-class rank and file. Although the manner of celebration and the extent of religious conviction cannot always be determined, into the late 1920s worker absenteeism was elevated on major religious holidays, including Christmas, Easter, and New Year's Day. At the Karl Marx mill in 1928, for example, approximately 4 percent of the workforce failed to appear on old Christmas; that was an absentee rate four times the mill's nonholiday rate. Perhaps more telling, laborers continued to miss work on a number of secondary religious holidays, including the Kazan', Il'in, Smolensk, and Pokrov holidays.[68] Continued observance of Whitmonday, which honored the spirits of dead relatives, was characteristic in St. Petersburg's Okhta region. On Whitmonday, Okhta's laborers enjoyed a mass fete at the local cemetery, where they raised toasts to deceased relatives and entertained themselves with fistfights. According to L. Zheleznov, the Whitmonday fight held in the Okhta region "from time immemorial" had once died out, but it revived, along with drinking, in the 1920s.[69] Similarly, pre-revolutionary construction workers had toasted the end of the working season in St. Petersburg with a celebration in honor of Saints Kuz'ma and Dem'ian. In the years immediately following the revolution, when there was little construction work to be had in Petrograd, builders reportedly lamented the loss of their "outstanding holiday." But in 1924, as the city and construction work revived, the industry's laborers could once again honor the saints "in the old way."[70] Neither years of hardship nor the maturation of a new generation dulled construction workers' enthusiasm for their annual celebration.

Some workers would adjust to parts of the state's holiday prescription and resist others. Responding to the state's strictures against religion and drink, workers might agree to forsake the former but not the latter. Those who disavowed the religious importance of conventional holidays could still welcome them as opportunities to celebrate with enthusiasm. Thus, Ivan Sergeevich, who reportedly did not believe in God, rejoiced on Christmas in 1926, generously entertaining guests with food and drink.[71] Other individuals displayed comparable behavior: on religious holidays, noted Zheleznov, the "inveterate atheist" frequently placed a bottle of liquor on the table; even Komsomol members saluted Christmas with drink.[72] For certain laborers, then, religious holidays like Christmas and Easter assumed secular significance, even when celebrated in "old" ways.

Still other workers appear to have renounced both drink and religion—but not the observance of the holiday. Comrade Matrosov, a fictional character, resolves to forgo church services on Easter. Being upset at the idea of missing church on such an important holiday, his wife scoffs, "Without services? And without preparing bread, decorating eggs, and treating the priests? What else have you dreamed up?" But then she cleverly remembers an anti-alcohol journal a neighbor has shown her. The couple ultimately agree that they will observe Easter not by drinking vodka or attending church, but by eating well and going to the cinema.[73] Certainly designed to send a moral message to its readers, the story nevertheless represents adjustments that some individuals were indeed making to the transformations in Soviet society. When Rozhkov gave up drinking, for example, he found new ways to celebrate Christmas and New Year's Day: on Christmas he bought a book and went to the theater; New Year's Day he celebrated with checkers and a book.[74]

Only on rare occasions did workers demonstrate "class consciousness and firmness" by agreeing to work on holidays like Easter.[75] More commonly, laborers continued their holiday celebrations though consenting to reasonable compromises with Soviet Russia's official political culture. The proximity of the "old" Easter holiday and the "new" May Day, for example, seems to have made some workers willing to sacrifice the former in favor of the latter. In the theoretical view of the state, the contrast between the class content of the two holidays could not have been more striking. Easter's emphasis on "love and forgiveness" called for "class peace," whereas May Day summoned workers to class struggle.[76] It is doubtful that the class content of these two holidays was of critical importance to many rank-and-file workers. In 1924, workers from a series of chemical factories in Leningrad agreed to substitute the celebration of Easter with the observance of 1 May. Some initiative from the trade union must have been present for so many chemical workers to decide at the same time to make this substitution. Nonetheless, for these workers, adapting to the new political atmosphere in the country meant little more than demonstrating a willingness to relinquish one set of days off for another. The quid pro quo

was made explicit in the resolutions of factories that agreed "not to celebrate the days of Easter, but to *transfer* free days to the holiday of 1
May."[77] For workers in Leningrad's chemical industry, securing the expected number of days off appears to have been at least as important
as any abstract desire to commemorate either the "religious" significance of Easter or the "class struggle" epitomized by 1 May. In this respect, their goals were not ideological but profoundly practical. The
same skillful pragmatism also surfaced in workers' response to other
efforts to transform cultural life. Internal memos of the Supreme Council of the National Economy (VSNKh) noted an unanticipated result of
the adoption of the Gregorian calendar: "a significant part" of laborers
were celebrating leading religious holidays twice—"according to tradition in the old style [calendar] and, in addition, . . . in the new style."[78]

In practice if not in principle, the adaptations made by Rozhkov
and the chemical workers were more or less acceptable to cultural activists hoping for the "rational" use of workers' leisure time—at least,
neither adaptation was as bothersome as workers' obvious penchant
for celebrating the new, "revolutionary" holidays in unseemly ways.
Because Soviet officialdom believed that working-class improprieties
gave fuel to its enemies, it was extremely self-conscious about workers' comportment on revolutionary holidays. "Our mistakes," *Iskry*
warned, are criticized in the "foreign White Guard press."[79] As the
only surviving workers' state, the Soviet regime believed it imperative
to maintain extremely high ethical and moral standards. Tiapugin explained: "Now, . . . when we are building a new state of labor, when
workers of other countries are watching us in order to learn the expe-
riences and lessons of revolutionary struggle and construction, more
than anyone else we need to remember that alcohol must not have a
place in our new life."[80] Though the Soviet regime proposed to eradicate inebriation from the "new way of life," workers continued to see
alcoholic beverages as a vital component of holiday celebration, "even
on revolutionary days."[81]

Not even May Day, perhaps the most "proletarian" of all the revolutionary holidays, was immune from drunken celebration. The May
holiday was preceded by articles in the press suggesting that the day
be spent at a concert, at the Russian Museum, for tourism or a walk—
but not for drinking.[82] But *Zorkii glaz* intimated that the recently renewed sale of alcoholic beverages had made May Day 1924 particularly eventful. The sketch portrayed a worker eagerly anticipating the
holiday. He hoped pay advances would be forthcoming; in the event
that they were not, he would need to sell something at the second-

hand shop in order to acquire the alcohol necessary for a proper celebration.[83] Although May Day did not become a state holiday until after the 1917 revolution, the practice of spending the day drinking was rooted in the pre-revolutionary past. Iakov K. Amtus recalled that in the 1890s, "very, very few [people] knew about the aims of 1 May," and many saw the holiday as an opportunity to greet spring "on the green grass with drinking."[84] Though the scene in pre-revolutionary bakers' dormitories was less idyllic, May Day there was also an opportunity to imbibe. As Boris I. Ivanov reports, bakers who went out on strike on May Day became so intoxicated that a newspaper reporter sent to investigate the strike was frightened away by "ragged people with faces swollen from alcohol and lack of sleep."[85]

It would be a mistake to suppose that Soviet May Days were corrupted by their pre-revolutionary past alone. Instead, workers appropriated this state-sanctioned holiday for their own celebratory ends. Even when no pre-revolutionary equivalent for a given holiday existed, the impulse of many laborers was to observe the "new" holidays in much the same manner that they had celebrated the "old" ones. Indeed, one Lushov seemed not to have sensed any irony in his suggestion that the October Revolution holiday be extended to three days in order to ensure its sufficient celebration. A two-day holiday, after all, made it "impossible to drink the necessary quantity of vodka . . . the third day it was necessary to drink in the mill."[86] Other workers demonstrated their revolutionary spirit with libations on International Cooperation Day, leaving a garden that had served as the site of celebration "crammed" with empty vodka bottles.[87] Even the revolution's smaller accomplishments were marked with drink. At a celebratory picnic in Petergof, Putilov workers toasted the production of the factory's thousandth tractor.[88]

. . .

Workers defended their traditional modes of sociability and celebration with determination and inventiveness. Although individual workers adapted to Soviet political culture in a variety of ways, they nonetheless exhibited a common tendency to accept elements of official culture that were advantageous to their own interests and to dispense with the rest. Thus, workers eagerly adopted new holidays—though they might not relinquish the old ones. And celebrations, whether "old" or "new," very often were not spent in the sober, "sensible" way the revolutionary regime favored but with the festive drinking that workers preferred. For workers, after all, drinking symbolized celebration itself, and holidays spent without alcohol were thereby stripped of their festivity. The arrival of the weekend, greeted with a light heart in workers' districts, constituted a shared celebration of a small but tangible working-class victory. The attainment of a bit of extra time and money was adequate cause for jubilation in a community that often enjoyed precious little of both.

Because a weekend of shared celebration and drink reinforced equality and fraternity among rank-and-file working men, it was virtually impossible for nondrinkers to reside comfortably in this world of working-class sociability. The workingman who refused to drink with his fellow laborers—seemingly indifferent or even hostile to potential companions—insulted the dignity of his peers. Drinking enthusiasts might tease and taunt the abstainer, expending some effort to persuade him to join the rest of the group, but there were other ways for celebrants to maintain personal and collective dignity in the face of refusal. The discourse of workingmen proclaims their ability to scorn any nondrinker as excessively "feminine," "childlike," or "intellectual." As a worker in one vignette bluntly put it, he and his companions had no "need" for "red maidens."[89]

MALE SOCIABILITY IN THE WORKPLACE

■ Although modifying the content of working-class leisure was critical to activists' efforts to foster a more edifying cultural life for workers, their more fundamental ambition had always been to alter the nature of working relationships. In the view of pre-revolutionary Social Democrats, labor in tsarist Russia was based on little more than capitalists' greedy expropriation of surplus value from an exploited working mass; if workers assumed power, the factory would become a more egalitarian institution. But pre-revolutionary shop-floor culture was more variegated and complicated than the Social Democrats acknowledged. Daily life in Russia's turn-of-the-century workshops was in fact marked by male laborers' careful efforts to reinforce a sense of community, equality, and justice in the workplace, and the observance of drinking rituals was an important way of ensuring the working community's symbolic cohesiveness.

Many of alcohol's symbolic meanings revived in the 1920s, but drinking traditions that had been important in the pre-revolutionary workplace were significantly weakened with the consolidation of Soviet power. Though such traditions were not obliterated, one of the greatest transformations in the drinking practices of Russia's early twentieth-century workers was precisely the deflation of rituals that had permeated the pre-revolutionary factory. Somewhat ironically, enhanced equality of opportunity among workingmen in the 1920s decreased the need for drinking rituals to reinforce reciprocity in working relationships. Despite drink's changed role in the workplace of the 1920s, however, laborers had no intention of giving up work-centered drinking entirely. Their continued insistence that alcohol served important social and physiological functions connected with work brought laborers into sharp conflict with the cultural activists who hoped to eliminate drunkenness from the Soviet workplace. In the 1920s, administrative efforts to keep alcohol out of factories increasingly forced laborers to gulp their alcohol down outside the mill itself, but the revolutionary state's cultural activists were hardly successful in eradicating drunkenness on the job.

■ ■ ■

Alcohol occupied a central place in the life of the pre-revolutionary factory, serving as a primary mechanism for ensuring a cohesive working community. Through shared drink and socially obligatory treating, workers were symbolically and pragmatically linked to each other, and paternalistic factory owners expressed their appreciation for workers' cooperative behavior. Nowhere were the integrative functions of drink more evident than in the freshly hired laborer's duty to buy drinks for his new coworkers. This practice had a variety of names, depending upon the region and industry involved, but St. Petersburg's workers typically knew this welcoming ceremony as *prival'naia*.[1]

Immediately after being hired or after receiving his first pay packet, at a nearby tavern or in the workshop itself, a new worker signaled his desire to be included in an established working community by treating his more experienced acquaintances to vodka and snacks. The provision of drinks was neither voluntary nor gratuitous; the members of a new laborer's workshop fully expected the rookie to treat them, and in meeting that expectation he implicitly obliged them to teach him skills needed in his new job. *Prival'naia* thus embodied social imperatives that benefited both treater and treated: the workshop was granted a free party; the new worker obtained promises of assistance in learning his craft. After Mikhail Nikolaev pleased new acquaintances by providing them with the requisite vodka, they promptly set out to fulfill their part of the bargain. "Well, Mishka," they proclaimed, "[get to] work. Now—you are one of us! We will show you . . . how to work. Don't gape, get used to it. . . . Here are the machines."[2] That a worker's provision of drinks compelled those who were treated to reciprocate with favors is clearly evident in a case from the Glebov mill. There a metalworker dismissed only two days after treating his coworkers "began to curse" because members of the workshop "would drink with him" but did not help him to retain his position. By taking up a collection and reimbursing the dismissed laborer for the money he had spent on *prival'naia*, the workshop demonstrated its recognition that its debt to the metalworker had not been repaid.[3]

In the pre-revolutionary era, publications written and controlled by worker activists denounced the economic hardship that *prival'naia* imposed on recent hires, particularly those workers who had been previously unemployed. A newly hired worker was likely already in debt, and every kopek counted, worker activists asserted. In the midst of this difficult financial situation, the newcomer's "worker brother" would demand: "Give [us] three rubles for *prival'naia*."[4] Though a worker might have been able to bear the economic burden of *prival'-naia* if he had himself could have decided when and how much he could afford to donate to the cause, this was seldom the case. In joining a workshop, a laborer usually needed to comply with its customary norms. It was the workshop—not the new worker—that typically set the price for admission to the working community.[5] An empty pocket did not absolve the new laborer of his responsibility to furnish his acquaintances with drink, since those who stood to benefit could invariably devise some clever method to drum up the necessary cash. "I'm not against [buying drinks]," Pavel Zinov'ev told new coworkers at the Landau print shop, "but I don't have any money." Nonplussed, the printers quickly replied, "[That's] OK, we'll get it." Soon after Zinov'ev and his new acquaintances agreed to settle accounts on payday, generous portions of snacks and vodka appeared in the print shop. As the festivities drew to a conclusion, Zinov'ev discovered how the drinking money had been obtained: the revelers handed him a receipt for his overcoat, which they had surreptitiously pawned.[6]

Initiation into a working community was not cheap. Although two to three rubles was the most common outlay required for *prival'naia*, laborers at some mills sacrificed up to eight rubles or, alternatively, purchased a certain quantity of vodka.[7] For many workers in turn-of-the-century St. Petersburg, even the commonly accepted three-ruble expenditure consumed the equivalent of several days' wages. For lower-paid unskilled workers, the financial burden imposed by *prival'naia* was greater yet: as *Gazeta kopeika* observed, three rubles constituted "a week's existence for an entire family."[8] Nevertheless, historians investigating working-class culture in other contexts have made note of workers' disinclination to plan budgets or accumulate monetary savings. The possibility thus must be raised that St. Petersburg's laborers seldom considered *prival'naia* expenditures in such abstract terms.[9] In working-class ranks, sharing individual good fortune was often a way to redistribute wealth and social obligations. That Russian workers tended to view *prival'naia* in this light is suggested by vodka "taxes" that laborers imposed on peers who won raises or graduated from apprenticeship.[10] Disseminating the wealth gained by a new job or better wages was a moral imperative, and vodka was an easily divisible substance that could be enjoyed by all. Inasmuch as an individual worker's duty to treat his peers caused him temporary economic hardship, his inclusion in the broader working community meant that he stood to profit repeatedly from any future prosperity experienced by fellow workers. In this sense, his temporary sacrifice was of practical long-term benefit.

Of course, not every laborer wanted to volunteer his pay packet or be a part of drunken company; certainly the working-class press was highly critical of intemperance and the welcoming customs that encouraged it. Enthusiasts of *prival'naia* sometimes resorted to social ostracism, teasing, insults, or threats to pry money from individuals more reluctant than Zinov'ev had been. Most commonly, established workers confronted a miserly newcomer with social isolation, refusing to call him by his given name until he treated the workshop to vodka. Laborers at the Martenov workshop explained to new arrivals, "We will baptize you; we will call you Taras." Only after being taken to the tavern "will we again refer to you as you were christened by your father."[11] But coercion of individuals who stubbornly defied workshop custom occasionally assumed more destructive forms. "Opponents" of *prival'naia* might return to their benches to find their work or their tools ruined. When six new workers at the Main Carriage Workshops refused to buy vodka, for example, the "alcoholics" assigned three individuals to extract the money. The workshop's designated thugs encircled the newcomers. "They didn't skimp on swearing or threats. They even promised to thrash [the six]. . . . The remaining workers stood by and chuckled."[12] Most laborers undoubtedly found it preferable to inaugurate their tenure at a new workplace on a more auspicious note.

Notwithstanding the coercive aspects of social ostracism, an article appearing in a metalworking publication incorrectly insisted that workers abided no opposition to *prival'naia*.[13] In certain cases, laborers who demonstrated that their refusal to purchase vodka was not motivated by uncomradely stinginess could conclude alternative agreements with fellow workers. In 1909, four new lathe turners at the Patronnyi mill refused to spend their money on alcoholic beverages. Initially subjected to "reproaches, sneers and even threats" from fellow workers, the four achieved resolution of the conflict by promising to donate money to an unemployment fund instead. Workers at the Obukhovskii mill encountered a different twist on the problem. A new metalworker's agreement to treat workers there met with some confusion. If he purchased vodka, workshop members who had recently joined a temperance society would be unable to share in the festivities. Laborers agreed that the new worker should treat the workshop to jam, in lieu of the customary vodka.[14]

Despite highly critical tones in the worker press and memoir literature, the widespread practice of *prival'naia* indicates that many individuals appreciated the custom. In failing to condemn his many drunken exploits, Zinov'ev is an unusual memoirist—though he is quite likely a more typical worker than the numerous Social Democratic activists who later felt compelled to denounce their sometimes ribald past. "I am happy myself [to provide *prival'naia*]," Zinov'ev told a fellow printer who had helped him to acquire a position. "Here, I'll give you a ruble and a half; slam down [a few drinks]." Vodka, snacks, and toasts to Zinov'ev's health promptly engulfed the happy print shop.[15] For many workers, self-interested motives doubtless mingled with communal principles in shaping their response to *prival'naia*. Certainly it is not difficult imagine that individuals reacted to the custom differently, depending on their assigned role in the festivities. In all likelihood, some workers who felt burdened when required to treat the workshop became enthusiastic supporters of *prival'naia* when it was their turn to be treated. As Kanatchikov recalled, pattern makers "loved a free drink."[16] *Prival'naia*'s enthusiasts left a less palpable written record than did its critics, but support for the custom was registered through many workers' widespread participation in activities deplored by others. For most workers, *prival'naia* helped to establish and maintain mutually beneficial relations in the pre-revolutionary workplace.

• • •

Just as the collective consumption of alcohol promoted reciprocity among workers, it symbolically affirmed cordial relations between foremen and their charges. Like new workers, new foremen were encouraged to treat the rest of the workshop. Undoubtedly eager to discover whether they now faced a benevolent or a strict taskmaster, workers at the Metallicheskii mill encircled their new supervisor, insisting that he treat them to drinks. If foreman Gel'tman did not disappoint his expectant laborers, he could begin his tenure on a positive note. In addition, his transition to a new workplace might be eased by cooperative behavior from his laborers.

In the pre-revolutionary factory, even established supervisors might treat their workers to alcoholic beverages at certain times. Any important occasion in the life of the supervisor—name days, weddings, and working anniversaries—provided laborers with a potential opportunity to extract free drinks and relaxed time from their superior. Workers quite naturally endeavored to take advantage of such propitious occasions. For mere good wishes and a sign of respect toward the boss—bread and salt, or a pie, for example—laborers might be rewarded with an ample supply of vodka and an unscheduled break in their work routine. These occasions must have been eagerly anticipated by drinking enthusiasts, if only because the relative financial security of foremen allowed them to treat generously. Gel'tman's presentation of twenty-five rubles was a far larger premium than the two to three rubles that new workers typically devoted to *prival'naia*.[17]

It was not simply greater sums of money that distinguished the supervisor's treat from that of other workers. Hierarchical messages embedded in treating by superiors are evident in many ways. For example, supervisors possessed the resources to treat generously, but they—and not the workers themselves—ultimately decided how liberally to treat, if at all. In establishing norms for *prival'naia* expenditures, workers set a price on acceptance into a community of workers. But workers did not exact a particular price for their acceptance of a foreman. The typesetters at Gaevskii print shop had executed their role in the performance well enough: in observance of the shop owner's name day, they showered him with wishes for a long life and good health. But Gaevskii did not offer to treat them in return. Nothing suggests that these disappointed workers did anything other than return to their stations. Workers' usual response to a boss's failure to treat appears to have been grudging acceptance.[18]

In addition, laborers who hoped to procure free drink from superiors followed a script that placed them in a subordinate position. Workers began by expressing their appreciation and reverence for their boss. This might be accomplished by enthusiastically raising him up in the air while shouting "Hurray!" and "Long life!" Signs of homage—never displayed in workers' attempts to convince other laborers to provide *prival'naia*—invariably preceded a treat by the boss. It is of course true that workers could feign submissive behavior, but it would be a mistake to consider their actions nothing more than cynical attempts to elicit alcohol. After all, some laborers gave their foremen extremely costly gifts. On Petr Zhigunov's thirtieth jubilee, for example, workers at the Patronnyi mill presented him with expensive candlesticks and a watch. The promise of drink was not foremost in the minds of these workers. When Zhigunov inquired whether "his children" preferred to drink or to have their picture taken with him—they opted for the photograph.[19] Even if laborers' signs of respect were at times disingenuous, the very act of dissemblance still reinforced hierarchical patterns of domination and subordination.

If everything went according to a mutually satisfying script, treating by supervisors reflected goodwill and respect on both sides. In wishing foremen or directors long life, workers essentially told their bosses, "We respect you and trust you to treat us fairly." In reciprocating with alcohol and relaxed time, a supervisor expressed respect and appreciation for his charges' honest work. As commonly occurs in relations of domination and subordination, however, managers and workers continually tested the boundaries of the relationship between them. The ambiguity embedded in treating by the boss is clearly reflected in the case of Al'bert Ivanovich: things began well enough when workers presented bread and salt to Ivanovich on his twenty-fifth wedding anniversary. Celebrating with his money later in a tavern, they even requested that he join in their festivities. The tension inherent in hierarchical relationships spilled over when Ivanovich insulted the workers by failing to appear at the tavern as they had requested. The next day at the shop, an emotionally wounded worker stormed out of Ivanovich's office, shouting that the supervisor was "not a benefactor" but an "exploiter!"[20] In refusing to drink with his workers, Ivanovich had stripped away the ritual's veneer of mutual respect.

Even intraclass friction was magnified when a supervisor provided workers with drinking money. The opposition that worker activists displayed toward *prival'naia* was muted in comparison with the disputes that arose when foremen or factory directors treated. It is difficult to say precisely why this was true. The greater amount of money involved probably contributed to increased contestation, as did the ritual's ability to make distinctly unequal relationships appear mutually beneficial. In any case, when an administrator presented workers with money for alcohol, there was a greater possibility that some workers would insist on donating the money to a working-class cause—to the unemployed, striking workers, or a workers' paper, for example. Such was the case on 26 November 1912, the annual factory holiday at Westinghouse. As was frequent in such disputes, workers unable to agree on a common expenditure ultimately divided the money: the majority spent its share on spirits, and the smelting workshop donated its portion to "arrested comrades."[21]

. . .

To what extent did these drinking practices, so integral to the pre-revolutionary workplace, revive in the 1920s? In short, not much. After 1914, reports that supervisors bestowed drink in return for workers' good wishes and pies vanished. Given the concentrated attention to alcohol-related issues in the press, especially in the late 1920s, public discussion of these practices would certainly be expected, had they in fact persisted as an important component of work culture. Scattered observances of *prival'naia* are noted in sources from the 1920s, but this once important ritual ceased to be a principal feature of work-centered drinking. As a man named Reingol'd recalled, *prival'naia* had lasted "up to the very end, until the revolution."[22] In the Soviet period, the celebration of *prival'naia* was erratic, and it no longer signaled a potential interruption in the actual workday. By the 1920s, laborers had relinquished these highly scripted rituals. The experiment with prohibition does not account for this change. After all, as previously shown, many of the symbolic and celebratory meanings that pre-revolutionary workers had attributed to alcohol revived during NEP. Explanations for the disintegration of work-centered drinking rituals must be sought instead in the shift in the state's concern with drunkenness in the factory and in laborers' changed attitudes toward working relationships.

Even as it permitted renewed alcohol sales, the Soviet regime loudly proclaimed that there was "no place" for alcohol in the factory. And just as the Communist Party's debates in the late 1920s focused on alcohol's implications for the industrialization drive, literature directed at workers repeatedly emphasized that alcohol threatened productivity through its contribution to high rates of absenteeism, defective production, and industrial accidents. Anti-alcohol literature declared that workers who drank were incapable of devoting their full attention to production; they suffered from lack of coordination, wandered about the factory, interfered with the work of others, showed up at work exhausted, and damaged machinery. Again and again, publications emanating from the Soviet apparatus claimed that inebriated workers grossly interfered with industrial efficiency and growth. By comparison, the tsarist regime had expressed little concern about how workers' drinking practices affected the productivity of labor.

Complaints about drunkenness appearing in factory newspapers in the 1920s show that a great many of the laborers found drunk in factories had arrived at work in an intoxicated state. Numerous newspaper articles complained about individuals who "[came] to work tipsy" or who "began work already 'under the influence.'"[23] Archival sources reinforce this picture. Registers of worker dismissals and reprimands reveal that workers were cited for "insobriety" or for "coming to work drunk" far more often than for "bringing spirits into the factory" or "drinking spirits at work."[24] Laborers were being forced to fulfill consumption requirements by smuggling alcohol into factories or by drinking during regularly scheduled breaks in the work routine. Removed from the immediate purview of the employer, workers thwarted the rules of factory discipline—in some cases by drinking immediately outside factory gates.[25]

Workers' most auspicious opportunity for drinking during the workday was provided by the lunch break. "I drank at the Gosspirt shop during lunch," confessed a man named Konovalov. When metalworker Kuleshov similarly returned from lunch too intoxicated to work, a sympathetic coworker at the Krasnaia Znamia mill stuffed him into a clothes chest, where it was hoped Kuleshov would avoid detection until quitting time.[26] Many other workers joined in the actions of Konovalov and Kuleshov. Especially after 1925, the Soviet press relentlessly published reports of long lunchtime lines at drinking outlets, and closing down drinking establishments during the lunch period became a chief focus of the anti-alcohol movement in the late 1920s.[27] Laborers had of course left the factory to drink during lunch prior to 1917, but drinking away from the factory became a much more pronounced feature of working-class life during NEP.

But the Soviet state's concentrated attention to alcohol's effect on production did not eliminate drinking in the workplace. Indeed, what is particularly striking about workers' use of alcohol in the 1920s is the continued prominence of insobriety in the Soviet workplace—despite the disappearance of work-centered drinking rituals. Workers smuggled spirits past gatekeepers charged with ensuring a sober workforce; they purchased moonshine from coworkers; wives brought alcohol into the factories for their husbands.[28] Laborers at certain mills adapted out-of-the-way places to suit their consumption needs. At Krasnaia Zaria, for example, workers constructed a "tavern" along a passageway to a storehouse. According to the factory newspaper, laborers sat on boxes to "chit chat," and they hid behind boxes when gulping down alcohol.[29] The "secluded corners" where cleaning women found empty bottles may also have served as drinking sites. Perhaps the most favored location for drinking within the factory was one removed from the immediate surveillance of supervisors—the lavatory. The restroom was clearly a social center of sorts, with drinking, relating of anecdotes, and general loitering.[30] Throughout the 1920s, workers managed to consume alcohol within factory walls.

Despite a shift in consumption practices, laborers in the 1920s did not look back to the work-centered drinking practices of the pre-revolutionary years with nostalgia. Given the revival of celebratory drinking away from work and the vigorous support displayed for work-centered drinking in the past, it initially seems odd that laborers gave up those drinking customs so easily. But in light of revolutionary ideals, it is not so surprising that practices symbolizing reciprocity between laborers and their supervisors disappeared in the Soviet era. As privileged members of society, at least in theory, workers in the 1920s deserved their boss's respect without the presentation of pies and shouts of long life. Benevolent treating by supervisors symbolically reinforced a hierarchical relationship that was deflated in the Soviet context. Even workers who had once appreciated the alcohol that was provided courtesy of the boss were probably content to abandon their formerly servile behavior when informed that they were now the most important people in the state. Factory management had been stripped of an ideological basis for dominating workers; in this context, workers could not have been keen to hand power back to their oppressors. (See Chapter 6 for more on the revolution's ability to empower workers).

Accounting for the death of *prival'naia* is more complicated, since a number of factors seem to have contributed to altering workers' attitudes. First of all, in the pre-revolutionary period, laborers had frequently been hired upon the recommendation of an acquaintance, and a newcomer's provision of *prival'naia* was one way to clear this debt. After 1917, the Soviet state made efforts to rationalize the labor market, and more workers began to locate employment by queuing through trade unions or labor exchanges. Employers unhappy with the official channels continued to hire workers in the traditional ways, but securing employment became a more impersonal process for many laborers in the 1920s.[31] Workers who obtained jobs through the labor exchange were merely taking advantage of state services to which they were entitled; those who acquired employment via the trade union had already paid for the privilege of a recommendation in dues. *Prival'naia* was no longer a necessary expression of appreciation and reciprocity. In the 1920s, the Soviet state also paid increased attention to vocational training. Schools organized by trade unions provided instruction in modern machinery and production techniques, making workers who endeavored to improve their job skills less dependent upon fellow workers for training. When the assistance of peers was no longer critical to finding a job or learning a skill, the pragmatic importance of *prival'naia* was greatly reduced. Indeed, when workers acquired jobs or skills through state-sponsored institutions, the ritual could not serve as an affirmation of symbiotic relationships between protégés and mentors.

In the Soviet era, labor exchanges and technical schools extended the equality of opportunity within the working class, even as traditional approaches to hiring and training continued to coexist alongside the new practices. In this connection, Kathy S. Transchel has pointed out the tendency of skilled workers to demand vodka in return for on-the-job training in the 1920s. But the exchange of vodka in these cases was less an expression of reciprocity and the promise of future good relations—as *prival'naia* had once been—than an overt bribe. Transchel notes, for example, that skilled laborers often failed to invite the trainees to drink with them.[32] An unwillingness to include newcomers in the drinking community estranged workers from one another, making these practices quite unlike the pre-revolutionary custom of *prival'-naia*. As one of baker Ivanov's acquaintances noted, pre-revolutionary workers had not considered things to be "in order" if a newcomer merely purchased the vodka for *prival'naia;* it was important that he actively participate in the celebration.[33]

As important as new methods of hiring and training were to the Soviet state's mission of rationalizing industrial production, the position of many skilled workers was jeopardized by such innovations. No longer did the favor of a recommendation or the mastery of technical skill endow established workers with the influence they had once held in the mills. Indeed, as William Chase has observed, the expertise and willingness of technical school graduates to accept the intensification of production was a threat to previously privileged experienced workers.[34] As the Soviet economy improved in the 1920s, the shop floor became the site of increased conflict between experienced older workers and an influx of inexperienced workers who struggled for upward mobility. But these intraclass tensions do not imply that, in general, laborers were worse off after 1917 than they had been before the revolution. Ironically, greater *actual* equality of opportunity in the Soviet workplace made it less important to maintain the appearance of equitable relations. *Prival'naia* suffered in the 1920s because it had become unnecessary and counterproductive. For unskilled laborers, reliance on the experienced worker was no longer the only way to improve their situation. As far as skilled workers were concerned, participating in a ritual that reinforced an ethic of mutuality was at odds with their interest in protecting their expertise.

The demise of ritualistic drinking in St. Petersburg's factories also illustrates that the close integration of work and leisure characteristic of pre-revolutionary factories was breaking down in the 1920s. Albeit fitfully, workers began to adapt to a stricter work regimen. They still dawdled and spent time socializing with coworkers, but they increasingly nutured friendships outside normal working hours—in collective outings to the theater, the movies, or museums, for example. At some factories, special events were scheduled for lunch breaks to substitute for the drunken sociability once intertwined with work hours.[35] The response of workers to the separation of work and leisure deserves more detailed study, but we can infer that laborers may have found it beneficial to accept a clearer distinction between work and nonwork time because they could take advantage of a number of leisure opportunities previously unavailable to them. For example, in the Soviet period, theater tickets distributed through the workplace and trade unions allowed many workers to attend performances that had once been prohibitively expensive. In addition, developments in communications technology led to the emergence of new leisure forms, including film and radio, while shorter working days made it more feasible for the laborer to enjoy these new opportunities. The demise of *prival'naia* is one indication that the importance of the workplace as a social center, at least during working hours, greatly diminished after 1917.

• • •

Even after the drinking rituals that pre-revolutionary laborers had intertwined with their working lives ceased to hold much meaning, insobriety in Soviet factories persisted. Clearly something continued to prompt workers to work when they were inebriated. Despite the disintegration of ceremonial drinking connected with work, for most laborers the consumption of alcohol remained a collective act, a way of cementing friendships and social obligations. In post-revolutionary years, workers' lunchtime outings to the beer hall continued to be group events that reinforced social ties, often among individuals from the same workshop. In part, group solidarity was promoted by certain "organizers of drunkenness," who were perhaps greater champions of drink than the others.[36] A drinking group's cohesiveness was reinforced by the economic benefits to be derived from drinking together;

pooling resources made it possible for workers "to buy a little more forty percent."[37] This was important, since an individual worker's monetary resources could fluctuate significantly from week to week. Drinking with companions was thus a way to accumulate social insurance for difficult days that might lie ahead. A tradition of "comradely mutual aid for drinking" among workers at the Karl Marx mill compelled laborers there to provide drinking money to acquaintances suffering from hangovers whenever possible.[38]

Furthermore, years of custom and folk wisdom had taught workers that—far from constituting a detriment to physical toil—alcohol complemented it. "To your health" was a common toast, and workers in certain industries maintained that there was "no possibility" of managing without drink.[39] Indeed, workers' understanding of "drunkenness" was completely at odds with the conception of it adopted in Soviet anti-alcohol literature. In France and Germany, temperance activists were content to strive for moderation in workers' consumption habits, but anti-alcohol tracts in Soviet Russia repeatedly argued that even small amounts of alcohol severely compromised one's working ability, and they admonished workers to give up drink entirely.[40] Russia's laborers advanced a very different test to determine whether a man was sober enough to work: if he could remain on his feet, he was able to work. Workers who had consumed alcohol often admitted to being "tipsy" [navesel'e], but mere tipsiness certainly did not prevent them from working. As one Korotkov retorted, "After all, I am not falling down, but staying on my feet." Similarly, a Krasnyi Treugol'nik worker detained by the factory gatekeeper attempted to reassure her: "I drank a quarter of a liter . . . And you say that I'm 'drunk'. . . I have drunk a [whole] liter and worked!. . . Don't you worry." The metalworker Ruslov cleverly demonstrated his sobriety by taking off his hat and standing on his head; he doubted the factory director's ability to do the same.[41]

In addition to workers' high threshold for insobriety, many early twentieth-century laborers professed beliefs concerning the physical benefits of drinking. The wisdom most commonly reiterated by laborers was that alcohol reinvigorated the weary, thus enhancing a man's ability to work. According to Sazhin, workers continually repeated a familiar chorus: "'With our hard work you can't manage without drink,' 'drink and work goes faster,' 'if one doesn't drink, he won't endure such difficult labor.'" Statistical surveys also show that about 9 percent of respondents claimed to drink primarily because of "difficult work, tiredness, and for strengthening [ukrepleniie]."[42] Workers' assertions that alcohol complemented physically demanding labor were not simply an attempt to justify unnecessary levity in the workshop, although this possibility undoubtedly entered some calculations. The belief that a bit of alcohol relieved fatigue was common wisdom not only among workers in Russia, but also among laborers in other industrializing countries.[43] Nor can workers be indicted for naïveté in this regard: factory inspectors, contemporary social commentators, and even doctors in Russia championed the restorative powers of alcohol. Highly critical of the claim himself, Sazhin admitted that "many doctors" affirmed the "'strengthening,' nutritive properties of alcohol." Indeed, a 1926 investigation of Moscow physicians found that nearly one-half prescribed alcohol for their patients, often for "exhaustion" [istoshchenie].[44]

Laborers did not need to rely on sophisticated data: the evidence grounding their belief in alcohol's restorative properties was abundant in their daily lives. Laborers in the audience at temperance lectures objected that doctors themselves drank, that drinking relatives had lived long and healthy lives, that they themselves looked perfectly healthy, whereas the abstinent lecturer looked quite "frightful" [pliugaven'kaia].[45] The healthful properties of alcohol were self-evident. Beer prepared from grain was "liquid bread," and people who drank tended to gain weight.[46] Alcohol's strengthening effects were also shown in other ways. One day the lathe turner Sadovnikov, who came to work with a terrible hangover, "[lay] down by the bench, not [having it] in his power to stand on his feet." When his supervisor arrived at the shop that morning, Sadovnikov dragged himself up from the floor and pleaded, "Ivan Petrovich, yesterday, on the occasion of Sunday, I drank a little. Now I have a splitting headache. I can't work. I need to drink a little—lend me enough for a shot." Sadovnikov's request was granted, and he immediately "cheered up, became stronger, and got to work." As anticipated by laborer and supervisor alike, alcohol revived the turner's capacity for work. In another establishment, when packers and gluers needed to work at night, the owner himself ordered vodka and appetizers for all. By drinking and singing, the workers overcame their fatigue and continued to work until morning.[47]

In addition to asserting alcohol's ability to enhance human strength, working-class Russians maintained that alcohol benefited individuals who worked in unusually cold or hot conditions. Anti-alcohol tracts repeatedly emphasized that people were mistaken in thinking that alcohol warmed a chilled body. The illusion of warmth was real, they explained. By bringing blood to the surface of the skin, alcohol did help one to feel warmer; but the internal temperature of the body fell, making the drinker even more susceptible to cold.[48] These physiological explanations aside, behavior based on a belief in alcohol's warming abilities persisted. According to Tiapugin, people who worked in the cold—including cabbies, peddlers, and draymen—"usually consider it necessary to run from the cold to the tavern and drink, in order to 'warm up.'"[49] Men laboring in hot, stuffy conditions drank alcoholic beverages to quench their thirst. Foundries were so hot in the summer, said workers, that they would surely "suffocate" if they did not "wet [their] throat[s]."[50] Again, Russian workers were not alone or irrational in their conviction. In blistering conditions, the body metabolizes alcohol quickly. Even temperance activists admitted that workers exposed to extreme heat did not become intoxicated: despite the "incredible amount" of alcohol consumed by workers in brickworking mills, *Vestnik trezvosti* observed, "drunkards are almost not seen."[51]

With less frequency, contemporary observers claimed that alcohol mitigated certain other sources of discomfort at the worksite. Dust from metal, stone, wood, and glass reportedly contributed to high rates of consumption among grinders, bricklayers, carpenters, woodcutters, and masons. The "atmosphere of dust" characteristic of such occupations was a source of "constant irritation" to workers, especially when they labored without good ventilation. With a "gulp of vodka," the worker could remove the "unpleasant sensation of dryness in his throat." When cement factories did install satisfactory ventilation systems, workers' use of alcohol "noticeably diminished."[52] Drinking also helped break up the monotony of certain jobs. Cabbies and *dvorniki* [caretakers], for example, were both notorious for their high rates of alcohol consumption; as one *dvornik* explained, "it is boring without drink."[53]

Observers today might object that water would have provided workers with far better relief from these work conditions. If factory owners in early twentieth-century St. Petersburg had been willing and able to ensure a healthful alternative, Russian workers might have followed the example of German workers and curtailed their intake of alcoholic beverages.[54] But that was not the case: many turn-of-the-century workers in Russia labored without access to potable drinking water. In 1909–1910, a series of complaints about dirty water, water polluted by gas engines, and the unavailability of water appeared in a leading printers' journal. Other professional papers published similar grievances; workers at the Aivaz mill included the provision of hot water for tea in their strike demands.[55] Even in the 1920s, workers at huge factories, including Putilov and Skorokhod, suffered from a basic lack of water.[56] Without a viable alternative, workers continued to drink alcoholic beverages to meet their presumed physiological needs.

Workers' assumptions about alcohol's healthful properties may help to explain why members of certain occupations seem to have imbibed more than others. There were of course many other factors that shaped individual drinking habits: most conspicuously, women laboring in physically difficult conditions did not justify taking a nip in the same way that men did. Although workers' beliefs about alcohol's physiological effects may not provide a full explanation for the relatively high rates of drunkenness characteristic of certain professions, these beliefs at least furnished laborers with a justification for drinking on the job. A closer look at a few occupations known for prodigious drinking is illustrative.

Metalworkers—especially those who labored in high temperatures—stood out for their use of alcohol. As one named Reingol'd recalled, "blacksmiths especially drank." Aleksei Buzinov seconded Reingol'd's opinion. "Of [all] the strikers [*molotoboitsy*] and blacksmiths," Buzinov wrote, "I don't remember one abstainer. A good one-third [of them] were drunkards in the full sense of the word."[57] Bakers were also exposed to the elevated temperatures that encouraged alcohol use. The memoirs of Ivanov are rich in describing the ubiquitous drunkenness among bakers, especially during night work and in the dormitories where many bakers lived. Ivanov emphasizes the physical hardship endured by bakers at work: intense heat from burning ovens mixed with vanilla to produce a "stench" that made their eyes tear; ventilation was lacking; "clouds of flour dust" caked with sweat on workers' bodies. The need to have fresh bread in the store by morning meant that bakers worked long hours at night. At least in some bakeries, night work was not closely supervised; while the bakery owner slept, workers drank and availed themselves of prostitutes' services.[58] When the legal acquisition of alcohol became difficult, bakers' access to sugar and yeast may well have simplified their production of home brew.[59]

Thanks to the relatively high rate of literacy among printers, a good deal of written evidence leaves little doubt that drinking was a pervasive part of printer culture, especially among compositors. As a history of the printers' union put it: "'Indulging oneself with vodka and beer' became a fundamental habit of printers, and of typesetters in particular."[60] The work process contributed to compositors' profligate drinking. First, unlike the press section, where workers were separated by large, noisy machines, work in the typesetting department was conducive to sociability. In addition, typesetting duties were more irregular than was press work: according to one report, compositors did little more than loaf until 3 P.M.[61] Further, because many printing establishments were located in the central areas of the city, near drinking establishments, it was easy for printers to participate in "tavern civilization."[62]

Cab drivers were also notorious for their high levels of alcohol consumption. In combination with the public nature of the profession, concerns about safety may have led to exaggerated claims about the drunken cabby. Nonetheless, the evidence evokes an image of a profession racked by drinking.[63] In addition to enduring inclement weather, boredom, and long work hours, cabbies suffered from a lack of free time and poor living conditions. Ivan Privalov, who moved from the village to St. Petersburg in the 1890s, recalled that his work as a cabby had been far more burdensome than factory work. The work itself was not harder, he admitted. But at factories, "you finish work and are free. You can go where you want. At cabstands, I'm sorry to say, there is no relaxation, no holidays, nothing. . . . I lived at the cabstand one month, then I went to the factory."[64] Other commentators similarly suggested that drivers' long hours and poor living conditions contributed to their reputation for drunkenness.[65] Though it is likely that laborers at other jobs also justified a nip on the basis of their working conditions, in St. Petersburg, metalworkers, bakers, printers, and cabbies were especially prominent consumers of drink.

. . .

Given most workers' positive assessment of the social and physical effects of drink, it makes sense that the vast majority proved stubbornly impervious to the anti-alcohol movement's emphasis on the social ostracism of drinkers. Activists hoped that individuals who dared to work drunk would be subjected to a social boycott, "like a thief, a strikebreaker, or a saboteur."[66] To achieve this end, factory newspapers printed the names and worker numbers of individuals detained for drunkenness, and public courts summoned drunkards to appear in judgment before their peers. These tactics failed to have the desired effect, primarily because workers tended not to view an intoxicated man with the same scorn, derision, and alarm that cultural activists did. Certainly cultural activists in the 1920s overestimated the effect of shame in a community in which alcohol was largely accepted.

True, a strategy of embarrassment humbled some individuals. A clearly pained Vasil'ev, hauled before a public court and forced to pose for a photograph with other ne'er-do-wells, shielded his face with his hand.[67] There also seems to have been some sincerity behind the Komsomol's effort at Putilov, where for several months the paper printed announcements from youths who swore off drink.[68] But the repentant Vasil'evs were few, and those who agreed to forsake drink were not always steadfast in their commitment. Within weeks after Putilov worker Tarasov vowed to give up drink, he was cited twice for drunkenness.[69] Public pledges notwithstanding, it is difficult to escape the conclusion that workers seldom held acquaintances to their oaths of sobriety. In depending on an indignant public to enforce a culture of sobriety, anti-alcohol activists sorely misjudged their intended audience. As *Pishchevik* noted in 1929, cultural activists hailed the practice of printing drunkards' names in factory papers, but drunkards considered their cameo appearances "a mosquito bite."[70]

Problems plaguing the public courts bared the gulf between activist and audience in particularly striking ways. These courts, not a formal part of the judicial structure, were intended to educate the public about appropriate standards of behavior in the revolutionary state. In 1928, one such court, attended by over three thousand workers, convened to judge laborers found intoxicated at the Krasnyi Treugol'nik mill. Journalistic accounts of the gathering explicitly pointed to the court's effort to embarrass the defendants: "Here they know you inside out." Despite threats of dismissal, some of the laborers indicted for insobriety remained defiant, "I drink and I will [continue to] drink. And to hell with you and the factory!" retorted one of the arraigned.[71] That these gatherings sometimes failed to accomplish the activists' intended mission is also clearly evident in the diary of R. Manevich. Reporting on a trial held at a textile factory in 1929, Manevich observed that workers there did not understand why drinking in the Red Corner and hitting a *dezhurnaia* [orderly] should be considered a "crime."[72] Revolutionary courts depended on an indignant public for their success, but the audiences that gathered often failed to perform their intended role. Instead, viewers protested that the punishments to be meted out were "very severe," "mistaken," and "incorrect," and they applauded to indicate their approval for lenient treatment. At anti-alcohol lectures, too, workers frequently objected to speakers' claims or spoke out "in favor of alcoholism."[73]

In general, workers in early twentieth-century Russia displayed little discomfort about drunken comportment, despite efforts in the media and courts to convince them otherwise. The press printed the familiar refrain again: "No one is embarrassed to appear drunk at the factory"; "The drunkard still does not meet the proper social rebuff"; social disapproval of drunkenness "does not exist."[74] Instead, workers maintained an "indifferent," "encouraging," and "indulgent" attitude toward drunkenness; they "smiled" at drunkards they met on the street.[75] Even party activists sometimes displayed "total incomprehension" about the purposes of an anti-alcohol society.[76] For the vast majority of Russia's workers, inebriation was more often amusing than worrisome.

In the 1920s, efforts to mobilize a mass anti-alcohol movement thus remained elusive. The Leningrad branch of the OBSA officially boasted 350 cells and twenty thousand members in its first year of work, but the organization's actual impact was far more limited than such numbers imply.[77] It is impossible to determine precisely how many OBSA members were truly committed to the organization's goals, but even ardent temperance advocates acknowledged that the OBSA's dedicated membership was "extraordinarily thin."[78] Scattered information about local cells reinforces this impression. The anti-alcohol cell at the Krasnyi Treugol'nik mill, for example, numbered 352 members in March 1929; more revealing is the factory paper's later observation that five to ten activists did not constitute a "mass social organization."[79] There were widespread reports that OBSA cells in Leningrad were inactive. At the Okhta chemical factory, "there was an attempt to create an anti-alcohol circle, but it collapsed." At Rabotnitsa there was an anti-alcohol cell, but "no one knows anything about it."[80]

Individuals committed to anti-alcohol activism faced numerous practical problems in the late 1920s. Though the loss of archival records for the OBSA makes direct information concerning the organization's working conditions extremely limited, the cell at the Putilov mill clearly suffered from a lack of money and literature.[81] In addition, devoted party and Komsomol activists were often overburdened by their many responsibilities. Cultural activists at Krasnyi Treugol'nik noted their preoccupation with a "series of other campaigns" since the anti-alcohol effort waged just one month earlier. A relatively energetic temperance advocate at the Putilov mill failed to immediately address a matter concerning a drunken worker because she had been "very busy" preparing for the upcoming celebration of International Women's Day.[82] Even under the best circumstances, anti-alcohol activists would have found it extraordinarily difficult to persuade workers to eradicate drunkenness from the workplace. Far from seeing harm in the bottle, most laborers considered drinking "a normal characteristic of a normal person."[83]

. . .

Of course, inebriated workers faced another potential source of criticism. Foremen in Russia's factories might have prevailed upon wayward subordinates. However, both before and after 1917, workers' immediate superiors demonstrated little concern about intoxicated workers who managed to make it past the factory gate.[84] Some pre-revolutionary employers had attempted to keep alcohol out of the workplace, as is evident from reports such as that of G. Bol'shakov. He recalled that during his stint at the state printing house, apprentices were subject to the wrath of the administration if they were discovered smuggling spirits into the shop and to the wrath of the masters if they were unsuccessful. According to Bol'shakov, the print shop singled out certain "specialists," dubbed "legs," for their ability to fetch vodka without getting caught.[85] Despite the punishment sometimes meted out to apprentices, pre-revolutionary employers generally maintained rather lax attitudes toward drunkenness in the workplace. We have already seen how supervisors in the pre-revolutionary factory thanked workers by purchasing alcohol for them. An indulgent attitude is also suggested by workers' complaints about the supervisors they deemed to be strict. *Rabochaia mysl'* indignantly reported on a new tyrant at the Putilov mill. When supervisor B. P. Malys smelled alcohol on a laborer's breath, he drove the culprit from the workshop, "despite the fact that, after all, there are many workers who always have a small dose [of spirits] before lunch."[86] Workers' complaints about punishment for insobriety are, in any case, rarer than their observations that factory administrators ignored drunkenness or that laborers were allowed "absolutely freely" to bring "several bottles of beer" into work.[87]

A lenient atmosphere on the pre-revolutionary shop floor is consistent with the attitudes displayed by foremen in the 1920s, a period for which there is more abundant information about punishment for insobriety at the workplace. The high visibility of lunchtime drinking in the Soviet era suggests that there must have been some increased effort to limit workers' egregious habit of drinking openly at the bench, but many individuals charged with oversight of productive efforts—from foremen to the members of conflict commissions—were clearly disinclined to punish workers for drunkenness. In practice, factory administrators routinely adopted an easy solution to the problem of drunken workers: real and professed ignorance allowed them to doing nothing at all. Many factories were unable to report on the number of laborers found intoxicated at work, even in the midst of a highly public anti-alcohol campaign.[88] When a worker's drunkenness *was* brought to the explicit attention of factory officials, they frequently declined to take decisive action. Upon being informed that bookbinder I. Komarov was sleeping off his hangover in the workshop, his foreman replied, "It is not my business to look after drunkards." In a similar case, described as "characteristic," an intoxicated printer who had been asked to leave Pechatnyi Dvor instead went to sleep in the workshop; no one took any further action.[89] Factory administrators frequently either "did not see the drunken worker" or "slapped him on the shoulder and reproached him good-naturedly."[90] Scattered statistical data also suggest that punishing a worker for insobriety was fairly uncommon. Of the more than 12,500 punishments for violations of work discipline at the factories of the Pen'kovyi metalworking trust in 1927–1928, only 168 (1.34%) were for drunkenness.[91] Combined reports for 1927–1929 at Pechatnyi Dvor, Rabochii, Znamia Truda, and Élektrosila show that at those mills insobriety accounted for 3.79 percent of laborers' violations of work discipline.[92] Registers of workers dismissed at Krasnyi Treugol'nik between 1924 and 1929 indicate that only 51 (5%) of 9,905 workers dismissed were cited for drunkenness.[93] Workers were far more likely to be punished for absenteeism or loafing than for drunkenness.

Furthermore, workers who were actually dismissed for drunkenness frequently found their way back to the factory. Reporting on the situation at the Izhorskii factory, Zhelezov noted that several laborers who had been discharged for insobriety were subsequently rehired because "until this incident they had received no reprimand."[94] In other cases, offenders were rehired after a seemingly symbolic dismissal of several days.[95] Reprimands for insobriety were frustrated at many levels. In one particularly egregious case, worker representatives on the conflict commission at Élektrosila insisted that Pavel Volkov be compensated for the alcohol confiscated from him at the mill.[96] More typically, factory administrators allowed workers to continue at the bench despite the orders of the conflict commission (RKK) to the contrary, or else they reinstated workers in view of mitigating circumstances, family position, or long service to the factory.[97] When the factory administration did dismiss workers for drink, trade unions frequently sought their reinstatement. Arguing that the laborers in question were skilled laborers needed for work, or that young workers might still be reformed, union representatives appear to have felt obliged to defend workers' actions. *Leningradskaia pravda* characterized the attitude of trade unions as follows: "They were dismissed—this means [we] must defend [them]."[98] An intoxicated worker might also find an advocate in his foreman. A supervisor's advocacy could simply mean denying that a particular worker was drunk, but his defense could also take more active forms. One foreman attempting to conceal the intoxication of a worker prematurely celebrating payday took it upon himself to work in the subordinate's place.[99]

Their special talents made skilled workers the least dispensable and the most likely to be retained after drunken incidents. In a case called before a conflict commission, for example, foreman Nesterov defended one of the newer members of his crew. Baklanov, having served only two weeks in the workshop, became drunk on his first payday, but Nesterov asserted: "I need him. In the time he worked for me in the shop, from 17 January to 1 February 1929, comrade Baklanov had no reprimand."[100] Concerned with having their workshops run with some manner of efficiency, foremen seem to have concluded that an occasionally drunken worker was a more valuable asset than no worker at all, especially if the worker in question was a skilled hand. "Our administration," complained three women from the Oktiabr' factory, "clearly has the opinion that if a person knows how to work, he will also work drunk, and it is necessary to pardon a specialist even more, because without him it is impossible to turn out production."[101] Skilled workers, well aware of their value to factories, sometimes broke work rules with impunity. One of them, named Evdokimov, said he had been fired and rehired three times. "I am irreplaceable," he announced.[102]

The failure of factory functionaries to take energetic action against drunkenness in the workplace was not, however, solely due to a desire to placate skilled laborers. Like the workers themselves, many supervisors lacked the conviction that drunken workers handicapped production efforts. When a representative of the party cell at the Sokolov print shop was questioned on what measures were being implemented in the struggle against drunkenness, he answered, "Nothing, we allow it," and added, "is it such a pity?—let them drink."[103]

· · ·

The disintegration of drinking customs that had been centered in pre-revolutionary workshop life is symptomatic of laborers' changing attitudes toward working relationships in the 1920s. Although some worker activists had opposed treating by superiors in the pre-revolutionary era, most laborers had welcomed the boss's generosity in providing them with vodka and temporary relief from their normal duties. After 1917, when workers theoretically became the dominant members of the Soviet state, reinforcing the factory administrator's position of authority through the rituals surrounding drink was no longer advantageous for workers, and ritual treating by the boss came to an end. Albeit for different reasons, the custom of *prival'naia* also failed to weather the revolutionary onslaught. As new leisure opportunities opened up to workers, behaviors not directly related to production were increasingly exiled from the factory. The ways in which new leisure opportunities affected workers' attitudes toward labor needs further study, but it is possible that more leisure activities and a shorter workday compensated, at least in part, for the stronger work discipline. Perhaps more directly relevant here, the greater actual equality of opportunity in the workplace of the 1920s obviated workers' need to express respect and reciprocity through shared drink. Workers had once provided assistance to one another in securing employment and mastering work skills. The importance of those personal connections weakened as the socialist state promoted more "rational" means of acquiring jobs and skills through state-sponsored labor exchanges, trade unions, and vocational schools.

The deflation of the drinking rituals did not mean that workers fully accepted the role envisioned for them by the new state. Consumed with the goal of raising the productivity of labor, the Soviet government publicly promoted efforts to eliminate drunkenness from the workplace, especially in the late 1920s. This policy was never effectively enforced on the shop floor. Workingmen continued to assert that alcohol complemented their physiological needs in performing hard labor, and the reputations of drunken workers remained intact within a community accepting of drink. Furthermore, supervisors charged with direct oversight of the shop floor often did not punish intoxicated laborers, even in mills like Krasnyi Treugol'nik, where anti-alcohol efforts in the press were highly concentrated.[104] Although many of alcohol's symbolic meanings persisted through years of social and political upheaval, by the 1920s drink's role in the workplace had changed in important ways.

CHAPTER 4

FUNCTIONS OF THE TAVERN

■ When a laboring man walked into an urban tavern in pre-revolutionary Russia, he was immediately engulfed by the stale smell of old alcohol, a waft of smoke, and noise.[1] But what did he encounter as he made his way through the building? Why had he come to this place, and what did his being here mean? The most important leisure space of working-class males, taverns have been the subject of growing interest since Jon M. Kingsdale published his seminal article, "The 'Poor Man's Club,'" in the early 1970s. But the Russian tavern and its functions have been studied much less than drinking establishments in the West, and no one has previously compared the Russian tavern to its Western counterpart.[2] Secondary works exploring the dynamics of tavern life in the United States, Germany, France, and Great Britain help to place Russian experience in broader perspective: although Russian establishments fulfilled many of the same social functions as taverns in the West, in pre-revolutionary Russia the life of the tavern was marked by an unusual degree of political violence flowing, in part, from the tsarist government's tight supervision of the drink trade. Furthermore, Russia's revolutionary experience generated both continuity and change in tavern social life. After 1917, the diminution in political activity in drinking establishments was part of a broader dispersion of activity formerly centered in taverns. But although post-revolutionary taverns became far less lively and versatile than their imperial predecessors, they remained a central feature of worker culture. Most importantly, revolution did not diminish the tavern's importance as a masculine social space.

• • •

The size and design of prewar taverns in urban Russia were diverse, but most were two-story establishments housing a kitchen, a bar, a water closet, a billiard room or two, and several dining rooms.[3] Since the kitchen itself lacks any important social role for the tavern's clientele, it will not be discussed here. The water closet is also utilitarian and needs little comment, other than to note that the tavern's provision of public restrooms may have attracted some customers.[4] The function and significance of the billiard rooms, the bar, and the dining rooms require more extensive exploration.

In the prewar era it was rare for an urban Russian tavern not to have at least one billiard room, and many had two. An important focus of tavern life, billiard playing contributed to the establishment's general commotion, as the sound of tapping cue sticks and knocking billiard balls rang out. "Ten [ball]. In the middle," competitors announced. "Ace—on the right, in the corner. Five points."[5] The billiard table's indispensability in Russian taverns seems to have far surpassed any importance the game held in Western countries.[6] The role that billiards played in attracting clientele was clearly recognized by the tsarist government and tavern owners alike: closing down billiards frequently constituted the government's punishment for violations of tavern regulations; many owners sought permission to install additional tables during prohibition.[7] The element of sport was probably enough to satisfy some customers, but wagers on the outcome could enhance the importance of a billiard game. Because monetary betting on billiards was prohibited, the extent of gambling is difficult to determine with certainty. There is little doubt, though, that wagers were placed with some frequency and that prohibitions on gambling were subtly subverted by making the drinking bill the stakes.[8]

The bar, the room in which alcohol and food were sold, was also the place from which the bartender—usually the tavern owner—supervised the activity of the establishment. The proprietor's personal participation in the life of the tavern is reflected in ownership patterns: some individuals in St. Petersburg owned two or more establishments, but approximately 85 percent of the private owners maintained a single establishment. Further, the substantial stability in ownership

patterns helped to foster familiarity between owners and frequent customers: over one-half of the taverns that survived three years in St. Petersburg remained in the hands of the same owner; of taverns that did
change hands, over 50 percent passed to family members of the former
owner. It is understandable, then, that workers often spoke of going to
"Gubanov's" or to "Makarych's," referring to the tavern by the
owner's family name.[9] The centrality of the tavern keeper is also evident from pre-revolutionary city directories, where the proprietor's
name is always listed, in most cases preceding the establishment's
name. The tavern keeper's incentive for cultivating good relationships
with customers is clear. Attentive proprietors increased their profits by
courteously putting "one bottle of vodka after another" on the table
and by encouraging friends to have something a bit stronger than tea.[10]
For customers, developing a good relationship with the bartender was
important to establishing credit. One bartender allowed three workers
whom he had known "a long time" to pay their drinking debt every
Saturday.[11] This symbiotic relationship notwithstanding, the Russian
tavern owner kept himself aloof from his clientele. Customers in early
twentieth-century Russia sat with other customers, and conversation
between the bartender and individual clients was not facilitated by
stools at the bar. French publicans promoted interaction with customers by shaking hands with entering patrons, sharing toasts, conversing with lone customers, and providing customers with nicknames
and free drinks.[12] Russians did not consider such social interaction part
of a successful bartender's duties. Shelves of bottles glittering behind
them, tavern keepers in Russia tended the counter while guests con-
versed sitting at tables.[13]

Dining rooms of many different shapes and sizes allowed the tavern
to furnish both private and public atmospheres. Small rooms, which
separated one drinking group from the others, provided the isolation
necessary to conduct private conversations or engage in a variety of illicit activities—gambling, for example.[14] In some establishments, small
rooms were also used by customers inclined to avail themselves of
prostitution services. When an undercover medical inspector inquired
about the possibility of having sexual relations with one of the women
patrolling a drinking establishment on Sadovaia, a waiter nodded: "In
the private rooms, of course it is possible."[15]

Whereas small dining rooms helped to isolate customers from a
public setting, large rooms propelled them into a sphere that fostered
social interaction. Indeed, workers had many practical reasons to seek
out tavern sociability. Like taverns in Western countries, Russian tav-

erns had an important role to play as a labor exchange. At the turn of the century, when Zinov'ev wandered into a tavern on Vasil'evskii Island, he overheard conversations centered around typographic work. A nearby customer soon explained: "This is our [typesetters'] club. We call it 'Maidan.'" Zinov'ev inquired into the club's purpose, and the new acquaintance elaborated, "Let's say, for example, you are without work. If you want, you can find work here through one of the guys."[16] This function of the tavern thus influenced the clientele of individual establishments; as N. A. Kuznetsov recalled, every profession had a tavern where its workers gathered.[17]

Large dining rooms furnished the relaxed social atmosphere that attracted workers to the tavern. Here, laborers found it easy to become acquainted.[18] Indeed, tavern design discouraged isolated drinking and encouraged mingling among patrons. The lack of customer seating at the bar meant that there was no place in the tavern intended to make individual patrons feel comfortable sitting alone. Instead, customers sat at small tables, usually in drinking groups of two to four people. Moreover, in Russian taverns, a cadre of drinkers was not isolated from the social space of other drinking groups, as they were in eighteenth- and nineteenth-century French cafes.[19] Tables were situated close enough to each other to make social interaction possible, and new arrivals were met "cordially and hospitably."[20] For workers who had few alternatives, the tavern was an important meeting place, and one better suited to conversing with acquaintances than the workers' humble apartments. When company called, therefore, workers set out for the tavern, since "there [was] no reason to sit at home."[21]

Large dining rooms were also the site of another important tavern attraction—music. Just as every tavern had a billiard room, almost all had music. What drew people to the local tavern? "The songs! . . . the splendid melody of songs," enthusiastically recalled K. V. Skorobogatov. The organ most commonly provided musical entertainment, but the orchestrion, the piano, the accordion, and balalaika and string orchestras all contributed to the creation of a festive air. The gramophone, a modern mechanical invention that "delighted the peasant," squeaked out songs like "The Little Box" or "Katerinushka."[22] Individuals who worked at factories by day spent their evenings entertaining fellow workers in the taverns. In Skorobogatov's memory, some of these workingmen sang so beautifully that "listeners put aside their vodka, forgot about their mutual hostility, and their faces brightened up." When Vasilii Buianov went from tavern to tavern, singing in his pleasant baritone, the "whole hall" would sing along to popular tunes like "Sten'ka Razin," "Dolaia gor'kaia," and "Ermak." The guests also enthusiastically sang drinking songs on their own.[23]

Nearly all pre-revolutionary taverns provided the basic services described thus far. In some cases, establishments also included a large hall, bowling alleys, balconies, outdoor gardens, or water troughs for horses, but these services were less widespread. Though the presence of a bowling alley might have been of decisive importance for some patrons, the omnipresent billiard room held far broader social significance.

• • •

Historians have recognized the tavern as a vital center of male working-class sociability in many countries, but only recently have scholars begun to explore the ways in which masculinity was mediated within the tavern's walls. Yet the most enduring feature of the Russian tavern was precisely its role in providing laboring men with a public forum for asserting their self-identity as men. An obvious way that men reinforced the tavern's masculine social space was to exclude most "respectable" women, a practice that was not unique to Russia. According to Lynn Abrams, tavern customers in nineteenth-century Germany were "almost invariably male." Similarly, Thomas Brennan maintains that Parisian women who needed to consult with their husbands who were in the tavern did not enter the premises, but talked to their spouses at the doorway.[24] Many Russian women were similarly reluctant to enter the tavern. A wife might, for example, survey the tavern crowd from the doorway or the window or wait outside while a man went in to fetch her spouse.[25] In some cases, women hesitated even to pass by drinking outlets. A woman named Baranova found it "very difficult" to walk past certain taverns in Narva district, where, she claimed, women were "undressed and raped."[26] The exclusion of women from drinking establishments was of course incomplete, but the women who did cross the tavern's threshold entered a social space governed by men.

Of the women who were found within the walls of Russia's urban drinking establishments, prostitutes were most frequently mentioned.[27] The comportment of prostitutes did not conform to the standards expected of "virtuous" women; they acted "indecently, they offended customers with shameless words and actions, they swore loudly and laughed."[28] Inasmuch as women in the tavern adopted these characteristics, their behavior greatly resembled the behavior of drunken men. "Respectable" women avoided the tavern, men discouraged them from entering, and concerns about public morality contributed to formal limitations on the female presence, particularly in establishments selling spirits. Not only did the St. Petersburg city governor ban female servants in establishments selling strong liquor, but city officials routinely prohibited female participation in musical performances in taverns.[29] It is possible that tsarist bureaucrats exaggerated the threat to public morality posed by the combination of spirits and women. W. Scott Haine argues that the presence of women in nineteenth-century French cafes was a sign of "peace and privacy rather than promiscuity or provocation"; and Beverly Ann Tlusty has found that women in early modern Augsburg both shared tables with men and helped to establish drinking norms in public places.[30] Nonetheless, the possibility that any woman frequenting a Russian tavern might be presumed to be sexually available is suggested by a waitress's complaint that women who were "honest and had a sense of proper virtue" served "one week at most."[31] Russian sources do not depict women as casual participants in tavern life. The sole reason Mrs. Braun ever "crossed the threshold of a tavern" was to speak to the bartender about selling alcohol to her husband on credit.[32] In Russia, "virtuous" women generally did not influence the tavern's social space.

There was, however, one category of women connected with the tavern's operation who eluded public comment. Female proprietors, many of them widows, were responsible for the operation of a full 10 to 12 percent of drinking establishments in prewar St. Petersburg (see table 3). Ownership patterns further reveal that the former owner's wife was at least as likely to take over formal responsibility for tavern operations as the former owner's son (see table 4). The lack of public comment on the female owner's presence is an indication that she was not thought to constitute the same threat to public morality that other women in the tavern did. No doubt this was primarily because her income clearly flowed from the sale of drink, and not from the sale of sex. The invisibility of female tavern owners in Russian pictorial and literary sources also suggests, though, that they did not play a critical role in influencing the tavern's public space. Even a male bartender's prerogatives could be limited in this respect, as customers could and did dispute the tavern keeper's right to regulate patron behavior.[33] A lack of evidence about what female owners *did* do makes it difficult to say for certain how important women were to the daily operation of their taverns. It is possible that women, both as wives of owners and as owners in their own right, managed the financial life of the establishment or prepared food in tavern kitchens.[34] But unlike female proprietors in other countries, women in Russia do not appear to have served alcohol at the bar, perhaps entrusting this task to male family

Table 3—Drinking Establishment Owners, 1902–14

	1902		1914	
	N	%	N	%
Male	610	73	1310	74
Female	100	12	178	10
Multiple/Unknown Gender	7	1	39	8
Brewery	116	14	136	8
Total	833		1663	

members instead. Haine argues that female proprietors in France attracted a mixed male-female clientele, but there is no indication that the operation of a Russian tavern changed when its ownership passed to a woman. In fact, the only explicit evidence is to the contrary: in 1926, *Leningradskaia pravda* commented that one woman operated a tavern "in the tradition of her husband," that is, with no less noise or alcohol and with no fewer prostitutes in the establishment.[35] The women normally present in Russian taverns did not challenge men's governance of this public space.

Masculine space in taverns was also affirmed in a more positive manner: male behaviors inhibited in other public arenas found fuller expression within the tavern's walls. David D. Gilmore, Lyndal Roper, John Tosh, and others have argued that manhood must be "won or wrested through struggle." In most societies, manhood is not believed to develop naturally—it must be achieved and constantly reaffirmed before other men.[36] The absence of a female presence in Russian taverns, then, allowed men an unfettered opportunity to exhibit masculine behaviors, an opportunity that found its most prominent expression in drinking, cursing, and fighting.

As workers considered drinking itself an essential element of manhood, so the tavern provided a space in which masculinity could be publicly asserted and defended. In the tavern, men chided for bashful "feminine" abstinence could gain admission to the masculine community by drinking in the presence of other men. Men might even distinguish themselves, their superior physical strength, and their virility and control by prevailing in drinking contests.[37]

Table 4—Transfer of Tavern Ownership within the Family, 1902–14

Second Owner	1902–05		1911–14	
	N	%	N	%
Son	3	8	12	24
Wife	15	39	12	24
Daughter	—	—	—	—
Brother	2	5	4	8
Father	2	5	2	4
Sister	—	—	3	6
Unknown*	16	42	18	35
Total	38	99	51	101

*The high percentage of "unknown" cases derives from the impossibility of determining ownership patterns through patronymics when ownership passed from women to men.

Masculinity was also asserted in taverns through men's use of rough language. Contemporary characterizations of the tavern frequently noted the prominence of cursing, an indication that language within the tavern's walls was coarser than it was in other public arenas. Indeed, in the 1920s, the presence of "foul language" became an indication that an establishment was no longer a "proletarian club, but a beer hall."[38] The use of obscene language was not considered appropriate for respectable women. Swearing and other explicit language, also a source of tension between male and female laborers on the shop floor, rebuffed many women.[39] In an atmosphere governed by male values, colorful language found fuller expression.

Fights that broke out in and around taverns sometimes ended violently, and they were a source of concern to bureaucrats responsible for maintaining order in drinking establishments.[40] Surely many individuals who frequented Russian taverns came and went peaceably, but the tavern nonetheless appears to have been the site of frequent physical disputes. Contemporary Western opinion readily, but incorrectly, attributes drunken aggressive behavior to the inevitable effects of alcohol: anthropological research has clearly demonstrated the tenuous nature of such connections. In a now classic study, anthropologists Craig MacAndrew and Robert B. Edgerton showed that most drunken comportment is learned—it is not the result of the physical effects of alcohol. With regard to aggressive behavior in particular, this assertion has been convincingly reinforced by many other investigations. Summarizing a wide body of anthropological literature on alcohol and aggression, Dwight B. Heath tellingly observed that aggression is not ordinarily considered part of the image of drunken women. The complicated relationships between alcohol and aggression, he concluded, are more diverse "than one would expect (or could account for) on the basis of a pharmacokinetic model alone."[41] The reasons for the belligerence men displayed in Russian taverns must therefore be sought in the social meaning of these contests, a task that is facilitated by stepping briefly outside the tavern.

Historians are aware that fistfights, even those that ended in the death of some participants, were a form of entertainment among Russia's lower classes. In urban areas like St. Petersburg, competitors from different villages, professions, or factories regularly faced off in highly anticipated battles that pitted twenty to four hundred workers against each other and drew huge crowds.[42] The rules governing such fights were sometimes abandoned, but the existence of rules suggests that fighting within certain boundaries was an acceptable way for particular groups and individuals to increase their social status. Claims to enhanced prestige were explicitly expressed in the bragging that followed the fight.[43] Women did not directly participate in these fights.

A desire to enhance and maintain social standing likely also motivated much of the belligerent behavior that men exhibited in taverns. The parallels between planned group fights and the disputes among individuals in the tavern should perhaps not be too tightly drawn, but the suggestion that men defended and enhanced their social standing by fighting is consistent with Brennan's study of tavern life in eighteenth-century Paris. According to Brennan, insults and slander frequently provided the impetus for fights in which participants defended their "honor, status, and power."[44] The possibility that Russia's workingmen sought out the tavern as a place to settle disputes publicly cannot be dismissed. If scores were settled in taverns frequented by coworkers or neighbors, even peers who had not witnessed the confrontation directly were sure to learn the outcome.

. . .

The tavern's provision of private and public space made it an institution well suited to the needs of political movements, both revolutionary and reactionary. The privacy of small dining rooms made them a convenient place to carry on conspiratorial conversations or pass on illegal literature.[45] At the same time, the tavern's public space was crucial to those who hoped to organize the working masses. Drinking establishments were not the only place where Russian workers met in large groups—the workplace, the theater, and the forest all served as forums for political discussion—but the importance of the tavern and its nonalcoholic counterpart, the tea room, has been glossed over by historians of Russia. No doubt this is partly due to the reluctance of the revolution's victors to acknowledge that alcoholic atmospheres were the site of revolutionary politics. In 1928, an impatient Sakharov sought to remind future generations that the "ordinary tea room" played a "huge role" in the revolutionary movement among bakers. "It is impossible to skip this page [in history]," he asserted.[46] A certain Gromov similarly recalled a "small" but "characteristic" detail: agitational work by the leather workers' union frequently had been conducted "in the tea rooms, beer halls, [and] taverns."[47] Those who sought to gain the loyalty of workers—including the Zubatovtsy, Father Georgii Gapon, and trade unions—were compelled to conduct agitational work in the most obvious places where the target population could be found.[48]

Agitational work could be organized or accomplished on an impromptu basis. In 1907, for example, six hundred workers of the Old Lessner mill crowded into a tavern to learn about May Day. Such a large gathering clearly required advance preparation and the cooperation of the bartender, who was "very democratic" and who reportedly put the establishment at the organizers' disposal "with pleasure."[49] Impromptu political discussion was most intense in 1905, when workers went to taverns to find out what was happening in the city.[50] But even at other times, normal patterns of tavern sociability could disguise political activity. For example, during a 1903 strike, workers came in small groups to the Rossiia, where Social Democratic leaders moved from table to table, explaining the strike's aims.

The overtly political function of a few taverns and tea rooms made them the focus of intense political rivalry between working-class groups, who literally invaded and destroyed each other's meeting places. Although the tavern served as a forum for political discussion in all major Western countries,[51] its role as a battlefield appears to have been more pronounced in Russia. During the strike wave in October 1905, armed detachments from the Putilov mill went to taverns near Sennaia Square, a "nest" of the Black Hundreds. Sitting "calmly" in this hostile space, the Putilovtsy engaged in threatening conversations designed to be overheard.[52] Also in 1905, working-class activists' attempts to distribute "good dinners" to unemployed workers of Nevskii mill in Vasilek came to an abrupt halt when a cadre from the reactionary Union of the Russian People burst into the tavern, demol-ished it, and squandered the money they stole at Kitai, a well-known haunt of the Black Hundreds.[53] The next morning, the leader of the operation undertaken by the reactionaries was dead. The situation escalated further in January 1906, when Social Democrats and Union members engaged in repeated clashes near Tver', a tea house providing meals to Union members who "[had] not participated in strikes."[54] The metalworkers' union ultimately retaliated for the loss of Vasilek later that month, when Tver' was itself bombed. Two workers who perished in that blast were put to rest amid whistles and "unflattering epithets" cast by Social Democrats and the Black Hundreds alike.[55]

Political and territorial rivalry between socialists and reactionaries was also played out in another tavern frequented by workers of the Nevskii mill. Like fellow workers, turner V. Sergeevich had gone to Zubkov's tavern every payday.[56] In 1905, trouble began. Not only did the assassin of a Social Democrat find refuge in the tavern, but also Zubkov refused to meet workers' demands that the establishment close during the general strike in the fall.[57] In 1907, *Rabochii po metallu* complained that the Black Hundreds brandished revolvers and knives, refusing to let the metalworkers frequent the tavern. Zubkov himself reportedly saw every worker as a "seditious plotter" and had repeatedly "kicked a guest down the stairs." Workers announced a boycott, which they agreed to lift if Zubkov paid ten thousand rubles to an unemployment fund. The dispute was a contest about the dignity of workers as much as it was about the workers' right to frequent the tavern in peace: the metalworkers' paper took obvious satisfaction in noting that Zubkov's requests to have the boycott lifted used "the polite form of address."[58] Differing reports and recollections on the conflict with Zubkov make the outcome of the conflict murky, but its intensity is obvious.[59] As with the rivalry over Vasilek, competing political groups clashed sharply over the right to control the public space provided by Zubkov's tavern. The most intense contests appear to have pitted Social Democrats against the Union of the Russian People, though in 1917 the Red Guard did confiscate munitions at the Mar'ina Roshcha, a Socialist Revolutionary hangout.[60]

The political violence present in the Russian tavern was rarely matched in other countries. Gareth Stedman Jones has argued that in turn-of-the-century London, working-class institutions like the pub were inward-looking, defensive, and part of a "culture of consolation." He states that conversations in British pubs were more likely to be about sports and entertainment than politics. In the course of the

American Revolution, David Conroy indicates, men used taverns as a "public stage," where they expressed disdain for royal officials through aggressive speech and posture. Similarly, Haine argues that the French café became a forum for ritual insult of the police and government authority in the wake of the French Revolution and, especially, the Paris Commune. Café habitués grumbled about "aristos," and thousands of individuals suffered arrest for dubbing the Paris police "scum," "cows," and "idlers."[61] As important as the posturing and verbal assaults perpetrated in American and French taverns were, these contests were less lethal than those occurring in Russia. The greatest similarity to the Russian experience is found in Germany. James S. Roberts has described the German tavern as an "organizational center" of the labor movement—a role that was particularly important during the antisocialist laws. Recent research on the tavern's role in nineteenth-century Germany has shown how effectively the labor movement developed an opposition worker culture by organizing gymnastic, singing, and sports clubs in the tavern.[62] In the early 1930s, when the storm troopers began to make inroads into taverns formerly controlled by Communists, shootings and political assassinations reminiscent of those earlier played out between socialists and reactionaries in Russia became a part of tavern life in Hamburg and Berlin.[63] Yet Germany never experienced the large-scale political violence directed against drinking establishments as a whole that was characteristic of Russia's revolutionary crises.[64]

W. Arthur McKee has nicely shown the varieties of anti-alcohol protest that occurred across the Russian empire during its revolutionary moments. In some cases, revolutionaries plundered drinking outlets as a source of income; soldiers looted them to subvert closure of alcohol trade during mobilization; peasants protested the commune's loss of licensing fees; in western provinces, ethnic minorities lashed out at a Russian institution.[65] When huge general strikes engulfed Russia's capital in 1905 and 1914, socialist activists mindful of the income that the regime derived from the alcohol monopoly promoted sobriety as a way to deprive the tsarist government of revenue and uphold the integrity of demonstrators' demands.[66] A strong political statement was made when large groups of workers avoided the taverns en masse, for in so doing, they dramatically altered their normal behavior patterns and hit the government directly in the pocketbook. Even more tellingly, workers dissatisfied with government policy pillaged and destroyed state property at alcoholic outlets run by the state.

In 1905, boycotts against drinking establishments in St. Petersburg were precipitated by Bloody Sunday. Though workers' initial reactions to a boycott were unenthusiastic, Aleksei Buzinov reports that many ultimately agreed "not to drink vodka, and to manage without the state shops and taverns." During another strike wave in the autumn, the laborers at some mills, including Putilov, passed resolutions to punish workers who violated alcohol boycotts, and volunteers enforced boycotts by setting up pickets around drinking establishments.[67] Archival sources make it clear that liquor boycotts were accompanied by a substantial degree of violence directed against state-run shops selling alcohol for takeout. Angry crowds destroyed alcohol supplies by hurling stones at shelves of bottles, smashed glass windows, assaulted proprietors, and committed arson by overturning lamps. In the course of 1905, crowd violence against more than two hundred state-run alcohol outlets in St. Petersburg province produced material damages in excess of thirty thousand rubles.[68]

In wide-scale strikes that again engulfed the empire in the days immediately preceding the outbreak of World War I, discontent with the government again found a target in drinking establishments. *Gazeta kopeika* carried daily inventories marking the crowd's progress in closing alcohol outlets: on 7 July, drinking establishments were closed on Sampsonievskii Prospect, Raz'ezzhaia Street, Nevskii Prospect, and Ligovskaia; the following day, taverns were reportedly closed in all districts of the city; on 9 July, the focus of strikers' discontent became drinking establishments on Shlissel'burgskii Prospect; by the tenth of the month, "hooligans" were breaking tavern windows and destroying government monopoly shops.[69]

Precisely because the government depended so heavily on liquor revenue, attacks on alcohol outlets were a highly effective way for workers to express their dissatisfaction with the regime. Judging by the action that St. Petersburg's workers directed against drinking establishments, protest patterns were more destructive and more systematic and constituted a greater threat to the regime's survival in 1914 than they had in 1905. By the time a revolutionary mood again engulfed St. Petersburg in 1917, the government had closed its alcohol outlets of its own accord. Had it not done so, there is every reason to suppose that workers would have again expressed their frustrations by attacking them during revolutions in February and October.

. . .

Just as government supervision of the drink trade made liquor outlets an appropriate target for the expression of working-class discontent, it had an important impact on patterns of working-class sociability. In fact, the government monopoly on alcohol had been designed with certain social objectives in mind. Tighter regulation of the alcohol trade, the regime hoped, would moderate the population's consumption patterns by compelling lower-class individuals to drink at home, thereby abandoning their more gregarious public drinking. When new laws regulating the sale of alcohol came to St. Petersburg in 1898, the majority of the taverns selling drink for consumption on the premises were shut down. Rather than fulfilling its intended objectives, though, the monopoly system propelled many lower-class drinkers onto the streets. "Street drunkenness" became especially concentrated around state shops, which sold spirits for takeout only. Hoping to profit by renting drinking glasses to the liquor outlets' customers, stakanshchiki facilitated drinking on the street by setting up stands around the shops.[70]

Bureaucrats in the Ministry of Finance soon lamented the appearance of street drunkenness. In the ministry's view, if the masses insisted on drinking in public, it was preferable that they drink in a regulated atmosphere. The result was a steady and dramatic increase in the number of drinking establishments that permitted alcohol consumption on the premises, particularly in outlying and working-class districts of the city. Between 1902 and 1914, the number of beer halls and taverns listed in St. Petersburg's city directory doubled, from 833 to 1663 establishments, and the rate of increase in working-class districts generally outstripped that for the city as a whole. The rapid expansion in drinking facilities meant that wherever laborers worked or lived, they were more likely to find drinking establishments conveniently located in 1914 than they had at the turn of the century. At the same time, the formation of stable drinking communities was facilitated by the persistence rate for drinking establishments. Of 833 drinking establishments in St. Petersburg in 1902, 70 percent remained in operation through 1905; almost half continued in business through 1908. Not only that, but in the years leading up to World War I, particular taverns and beer halls were increasingly likely to stay in business.

Thus, workers could develop regular consumption patterns; they could set out for the same establishment every payday or drink with the same group of companions every week. Sergeevich's faithful attendance at Zubkov's tavern on paydays has already been mentioned. Laborers at the Trubochnyi mill went to nearby establishments on Vasil'evskii Island's Seventh and Twelfth Lines. Putilovtsy also went to "definite" taverns: the Mar'ina Roshcha, Kitai, Novo-Petergof, and Rossiia, for example.[71] Although affinity based on place of employment seems to have been the most important source of cohesion reflected in tavern society, it was not the only one. The drinking establishments that functioned as labor exchanges or as outposts for specific political groups discussed earlier, for example, expressed craft and political affinity. Certain establishments were also distinguished by their atmospheres. Krasnyi kabachok was reputedly the most "lively" establishment in Putilov district, whereas one Mikhailov's tavern, where "old men gathered," was "one of the quiet taverns."[72] Affiliations based on geographic origins may also have provided a source of tavern sociability. The practice of *zemliachestvo*, a well-developed support network based on region of origin, eased peasant migrants' transition to the city. The possibility that migrants made and sustained connections with fellow *zemliaki* in drinking establishments is suggested by tavern names. In 1914, ten taverns in St. Petersburg bore the name Tver', and fourteen were called Rostov or Iaroslavl. These areas also provided a large proportion of St. Petersburg's in-migrants.[73] Parallels between regional patterns of in-migration and geographically based tavern names are not unambiguous—no tavern was named Pskov or Vitebsk, for example—but they are suggestive.[74] Even migrants from Ul'ianovskoe village, Rzhev, Podolsk, Tikhvin, and those from many other regions may have found their compatriots most easily in the drinking establishments bearing those names. Cohesive drinking groups could thus form on the basis of multiple identities and circumstances, but workers appear to have imbibed most often with coworkers in establishments situated near their place of employment. This pattern of sociability likely forged relationships that reinforced working-class solidarity during moments of political unrest, since workers who drank together presumably faced similar difficulties at work and in their communities.

Any habitual drinking patterns that workers developed in the early twentieth century came to an abrupt halt with the outbreak of World War I and the concomitant prohibition on the sale of spirits. Public drinking did continue, but it became considerably more haphazard and difficult. Some proprietors engaged in the illegal sale of alcoholic drinks; others chose not to notice customers who brought their own alcoholic beverages into taverns and tea rooms.[75] But restrictions on drink nonetheless disrupted workingmen's patterns of sociability. In any case, many of them had been called upon to serve in the war. Circumstances no longer allowed groups of workers to casually set out from the factory to the tavern after getting paid on Saturdays. Workingmen who remained in the cities and who chose to drink together were compelled to be much more resourceful in order to find both alcoholic beverages and a place in which to consume them. Few individuals made such strenuous efforts in the midst of war.

When the sale of wines was reintroduced by the Soviet government in 1921, the drink trade in its previous incarnation no longer existed. The number of taverns and beer halls listed in St. Petersburg's city directory did climb throughout the decade, from 76 in 1923 to 294 in 1928, but the collection of drinking establishments during the 1920s never again rivaled the more prolific tsarist days. Constriction in the number of genuine drinking establishments prompted workers to carve out new social spaces for drink. Indeed, one of the most telling aspects of drinking culture in the NEP years is the way in which male laborers inexorably brought alcohol into the very institutions that revolutionary activists had created with the intent to reduce the tavern's attractiveness. Working-class men compensated for the tavern's relative absence in part by appropriating public space in Soviet-era dining halls and workers' clubs.

The creeping tentacles of alcohol first grasped at newly opened dining halls in the early 1920s. A dining hall in Volodarskii district opened propitiously enough in 1923, with portraits of Lenin and Mikhail I. Kalinin adorning its walls. Two months later, "attributes of the old uncultured life" had emerged. *Krasnaia gazeta* complained that patrons smoked and gambled in the billiard room, itself an obvious inheritance from the pre-revolutionary tavern. Patrons ignored a sign imploring them to refrain from cursing, and a bottle of beer—"if not two or three bottles"—reportedly sat on almost every table. Within weeks, the Volodarskii establishment had been transformed into "an ordinary tavern."[76] Persistent reports about alcohol consumption in dining halls reveal that the situation in Volodarskii district was far from unusual. In 1924, *Vestnik profsoiuzov* complained that the "majority" of dining halls were being converted into beer halls.[77] Activists had intended for dining halls to become "hearths" of the "new way of life," without the drunkenness, cursing, and other "similarities" to tavern life; nonetheless, many halls mutated into taverns and beer halls.

The same was later true of the worker's club, an institution that labor activists also promoted as a sober center of the new way of life, "a school of Communism."[78] By the mid-1920s, consistent reports began to surface that "of late," particular clubs in Leningrad were selling beer. The Russkii Dizel club did not attract "all" founders, complained *Krasnaia gazeta*, but only "the enthusiasts of drink." When laborers in clubs spit and threw their cigarette butts on the floor and when the billiard playing, card games, and gambling so characteristic of the pre-revolutionary tavern resurfaced in clubs during the 1920s, the distinction between the tavern and the club was inevitably strained.[79] As was true of dining halls, not all workers' clubs were converted into virtual taverns. Yet many male laborers endeavored to create a social space more inviting and flexible than that which prevailed in model clubs. In exaggerated form, the club's atmosphere of excessive constraint was expressed in a 1925 cartoon in *Krasnaia gazeta*. Two workingmen entering a club were visibly taken aback by a host of admonishing signs: the bookcase was not to be touched, reading the wall newspaper was prohibited, drinking water from the samovar was forbidden, and smoking was not permitted.[80] With their presence and their pocketbooks, male workers demanded the provision of less structured, more "tavern-like" atmospheres. Numerous clubs and dining halls in the 1920s offered alcoholic beverages as a fiscal imperative; they could not otherwise compete with the easy camaraderie of the beer hall. The social preferences of workingmen explain why there was sometimes very little difference between a "beer hall" and a "beer-hall club."[81] It is impossible to determine precisely which clubs and dining halls in Leningrad offered alcohol for consumption on the premises; but despite the presence of these alternatives to the tavern proper, the number of drinking establishments in Leningrad was dramatically lower in the 1920s than before the war.[82]

Other structural changes in the drink trade also affected the social life of workers. First, the persistence rate for drinking establishments was significantly lower in the 1920s than it had been before prohibition, partly because of the Soviet government's effort to transfer the drink trade from private owners to cooperative establishments: by 1928, only 1 percent remained in private hands. Even when private ownership was not at issue, facilities offering alcohol for consumption on the premises led a precarious life in the 1920s. Any drinking establishment faced capricious elimination by a state that simultaneously monopolized alcohol production and condemned drunkenness. During the late 1920s, haphazard repression of alcohol outlets lent a thin veneer of credibility to the state's professed commitment to eliminate drunkenness from Soviet life. As if to chronicle the anti-alcohol movement's steady progress, *Pravda* proudly reported in 1928 that seventy places selling alcohol in Leningrad were to be closed; *Trezvost' i kul'tura* added the demise of twenty-seven beer halls in January 1929; later that year a leading OBSA representative claimed that the organization had eradicated 20 percent of the establishments selling drink in the city.[83] But there is little reason to suppose that such repression had much effect other than to encourage the creation of new drinking centers; in certain cases, centers of drunkenness survived despite orders to the contrary. The highly popular Gorshok, for example, repeatedly reopened under different names.[84] Yet even erratic suppression of drinking establishments could have its impact on working-class sociability.

The structural eccentricities in the drink trade during the 1920s—fewer facilities offering alcohol for consumption on the premises, the elimination of private ownership of taverns, the high rate of turnover in the alcohol industry, and the capricious suppression of alcohol outlets—had important consequences for tavern sociability. Perhaps most predictably, the relatively sparse set of beer halls in Leningrad in the 1920s seems to have made the composition of any one institution's clientele more heterogeneous, bringing together workers from a variety of backgrounds. When sources in the late 1920s reported that there were no longer any taverns near the Putilov mill, it did not mean that workers from that stalwart citadel of revolution had given up public drinking, but that they now traveled farther to do their drinking. Rather than sharing public space with fellow Putilovtsy in taverns situated directly across from the mill, as they had in the past, in the 1920s the mill's workers sometimes frequented more distant establishments, such as Gorshok, on the Obvodnyi Canal, where they drank with rubber workers from Krasnyi Treugol'nik, spinners from Sovetskaia Zvezda, and workers from other factories.[85] Because of the greater diversity in tavern clientele, probably patrons in the 1920s were less likely to understand neighboring conversations that centered on work, a phenomenon that may in turn have led to less social interaction between groups of drinkers or to a change in the types of discussions carried on within the tavern's walls.

On the one hand, such diversity may have facilitated the development of a more uniform worker culture in the Soviet period; on the other, bringing together laborers from a variety of working situations may have hastened the depoliticization of tavern life. No longer did laborers sharing public space in the tavern have the same boss, or trade, or working frustrations. Changes in tavern culture thus may have affected the political cohesion of Russia's working class in several ways, none of which can be confirmed on the basis of available evidence. It is clear that in the Soviet period, there simply was less room for individual occupational groups to command their own public space in a beer hall. Nonetheless, increased diversity in the beer hall's customers does not mean that homogeneous drinking publics had vanished entirely.

Exclusive gatherings of workers from particular occupations or mills seem to have occurred less often in the limited collection of beer halls, however, than in the dining halls and clubs that offered drink. Such institutions often did not admit a self-selected public, since trade unions and factories sponsoring dining halls and clubs intended them for members' use. The preference that many workers continued to display for overcrowded beer halls may thus have been motivated, at least in certain cases, by the beer hall's presence as a public place open to all men. In a beer hall, workers could easily include nonmembers in their drinking circle.

As the constricted number of drinking establishments in the 1920s gave rise to a more commingled drinking public, workers also began to drink at home and on the street with increased frequency.[86] Certainly it is not difficult to imagine that some individuals who might have stopped by a beer hall on their normal route home from the factory were less inclined to set out for an establishment three kilometers away. For working-class youth in particular, parties held at the homes of friends provided a substitute form of sociability in the 1920s (see chapter 5). Another alternative to the tavern, street drinking, had developed in tsarist Russia in the wake of the government's effort to suppress taverns in the 1890s; the practice revived when public drinking facilities were again threatened in the 1920s. In a few cases, street drinking may have been intended as an overt sign of defiance, arising as it did in the very places where drinking establishments had been liquidated. Both before 1914 and in the 1920s, a characteristic location for street drinking was near shops that sold alcohol for takeout only. In the 1920s, the most infamous of the so-called "no-entry signs" [kirpichniki] were situated near the Putilov mill. The streets around these tumbledown buildings reportedly became a "lively place" on paydays.[87]

The high degree of uncertainty and instability in the alcohol trade during the 1920s complicated male sociability based on drink. Fans who approached Gorshok in 1926 were among those many workers who directly encountered a fickle drink trade. How might this beer hall's patrons have responded to finding the institution's doors unexpectedly closed? And what would drinking companions do who had intended to rendezvous there? Gorshok's patrons, like many other workers faced with the suppression of particular establishments, were compelled to adopt some alternative, whether abandoning their intention to drink, drinking at someone's home, opting to drink in the street, or setting out for a different beer hall. Alternately faced by closures and opportunities to "test" the strength of beer at new establishments, workers who enjoyed public drinking likely found it difficult to develop predictable routines in the 1920s.[88] Yet workingmen continued to seek out public space for drinking, even after some of the attractions that had drawn their brethren to pre-revolutionary taverns had faded or virtually disappeared.

・・・

The "traditional green on yellow sign" that distinguished drinking establishments in tsarist days continued to grace the exterior of Soviet beer halls.[89] Inside, a good deal had changed. Like so many other Soviet institutions, the drinking establishment of the 1920s was a far more austere, generic institution than its pre-revolutionary counterpart had ever been. The bartender had played a central role in the life of the pre-revolutionary tavern, but the overseer in Soviet establishments became a less visible personage.[90] The billiard room, an indispensable center of pre-revolutionary tavern sociability, failed to assume the same significance in the 1920s. A state that hoped to make "sensible" leisure more attractive than beer halls discouraged the game that so clearly attracted clientele. The billiard table at the Volodarskii dining hall mentioned earlier, for example, was removed within two weeks of press complaints that the establishment was degenerating into a tavern. By the second half of the 1920s, the Soviet beer hall appears to have been divested of this once-beloved attraction.[91]

Two additional features critical to pre-revolutionary tavern life were largely expelled from drinking establishments by the 1920s. First, the tavern's importance as a source of information about employment possibilities diminished significantly. Construction workers—members of an itinerant, poorly organized profession—did continue to find work through connections made in the tavern; but in general, trade unions and labor exchanges were now assuming formal responsibility for the distribution of manpower.[92] Whether or not unions were successful in creating a more rational labor market, the demise of labor exchange functions in post-revolutionary taverns made drinking establishments more barren institutions. The previously rich versatility of tavern space was also diminished in the 1920s as drinking facilities were stripped of their overt political functions. Here, too, other institutions were replacing the tavern. A host of new and newly legalized avenues were now available to channel worker discontent, facilitate political organization, and promote political education. Trade unions and factory committees, for example, addressed problems centered on the workplace. These organizations had their own venues and did not require the public space once provided by the tavern. Political lectures were far from the most popular form of club work, but the club still provided an important alternative to the beer hall for some elements of the working class. Although discussions among laborers frequenting taverns in the 1920s could range from high politics to the expense of water and electricity,[93] workers seeking serious political engagement or redress of grievances could turn to a wide array of formal institutions. Factory committees, trade unions, party cells, and local soviets—all illegal or nonexistent in tsarist Russia—now promised to address working-class concerns. The tavern's primacy as a site for working-class political organization significantly diminished as a result. Divested of many formerly important attractions, the Soviet beer hall was a far more circumscribed institution than its pre-revolutionary counterpart.

Had the once vibrant life of the pre-revolutionary tavern, then, been transformed at last into a "culture of consolation?" Certain elements of pre-revolutionary tavern sociability that remained in the 1920s might suggest that it had. Most significantly, music and song in beer halls continued to command workers' affection. In a "good tavern," one reportedly could always hear either "a raucous 'machine,' or a quartet of wandering musicians, or a cabaret."[94] In this respect, the culture of Soviet beer halls would seem to be similar to the late-nineteenth-century English music halls that Stedman Jones describes.

Nonetheless, one element of tavern sociability critical to both pre- and post-revolutionary establishments, though consistent with Stedman Jones's conception of a "culture of consolation," suggests that workers in the 1920s continued to have complex motivations in seeking public drinking space. In the face of significant obstacles, working-class men in the 1920s strove to uphold the tavern as a distinct masculine preserve. In addition to alcohol consumption, the obscenity and physical aggression characteristic of prewar taverns persisted in Soviet successor institutions. It was still "uncomfortable" for women to enter these premises. Prostitutes speaking "indecent words" still sought clients in establishments where drink was sold, but most working-class women remained reluctant to frequent public space in which alcohol and cursing were prominent components.[95] Of the thousands of female workers who might have benefited from the dining hall at Krasnaia znamia mill, a female correspondent reported, only a brave few could face the drinking that occurred there.[96] At least one dining hall attempted to compensate for the anxiety beer sales caused women by forbidding alcoholic beverages in a section specially designated for women and children. But male imperialism could and did conquer this oasis.[97]

Men's ability to intimidate women into abandoning social space through their comportment should not be interpreted solely as evidence of misogyny. Not only had working-class men used taverns as a place for the free expression of masculine behaviors prior to 1914; their occupation of gendered space became more difficult—indeed, defensive—in the wake of the 1917 revolution. The tsarist regime's support for a patriarchal ideology in which authority clearly descended from God the father, to the (male) tsar, to each male head of a household[98] was directly challenged by the Soviet state's affirmation of the primacy of class over gender. After 1917, workingmen were empowered by virtue of their class, but the authority attributed to them by virtue of their sex—whether in work, in politics, or in family life—was threatened.

Indeed, many of the behaviors that workers associated with masculinity in the pre-revolutionary tavern—drinking, cursing, physical belligerence—were frowned upon by the Soviet state. In subjecting such comportment to censure, revolutionary activists were essentially asking workingmen to refrain from masculine behavior. In other words, worker activists urged rank-and-file workingmen to voluntarily consent to what they would have perceived as their own emasculation, if not outright feminization. The same message was sent through the state's alcohol policy. Connections that working-class language made between masculinity and the consumption of strong alcoholic beverages are discussed in chapter 2. In terms of gender expectations, it is therefore highly significant that many establishments offering drink for consumption on the premises in the 1920s legally could sell only wines and beer—beverages that most workingmen had considered appropriate only for women and children. Restaurants and dining halls could sell any type of alcoholic beverage, but after March 1927, clubs and other "cultural establishments" could satisfy the Russian worker's preference for "masculine" spirits only by subverting the law.[99] In the late 1920s, then, workingmen whose public consumption of alcoholic beverages conformed to the letter of the law could easily become "red maidens," "*babas*," and "babies." In practice, proscriptions against the consumption of spirits were undermined by proprietors who sold spirits under the table and by customers who smuggled spirits into public places and mixed them with their beer. The resulting concoction, *ersh*, was a distinctively Russian adaptation. Though illicit, *ersh* permitted working-class men to conform to their own expectations concerning gender and alcohol. This undoubtedly explains why the use of spirits in prohibited places was widespread and, frequently, open.[100]

Activists' efforts to limit the amount of alcohol that workers consumed were similarly ineffective. Some clubs and dining halls adopted formal limits on alcohol consumption, but drinkers who had reached their quota in one establishment could set out for others or ask non-drinking friends to purchase beer for them. Rules limiting consumption could be inconvenient, but they did not impinge on the drinking styles of committed men.[101]

Even when public drinking space had been stripped of almost every other formerly important function, then, it persisted as a gendered forum. Although revolutionary leaders had promised to supplant identity based on gender with identity based on class, male workers in the Soviet state defended a public space in which to affirm their identity as men. That they attempted to retain such a deeply rooted part of their identity in a period of social crisis is certainly understandable. In the 1920s, men no longer sought work or planned strikes in the tavern. They might have been required to travel farther to drink, or they might have suffered through finding their favorite watering hole closed or overcrowded, but by sneaking vodka into the club, by cursing in ways that repelled women, and by managing to drink more than they were allowed, they could affirm that they were still men. Indeed, it seems possible that many workingmen felt a greater need to affirm their masculine identities in the 1920s than they had before the socialist revolution. Assessing the validity of this hypothesis would require systematic study into expressions of masculinity in various aspects of life, a task beyond the scope of this study. The investigation of drink does show that laboring men in the 1920s endeavored to safeguard drinking establishments as a masculine forum and that they did so in the face of considerable difficulty.

• • •

Some observers argued that the tavern's popularity was rooted in a lack of alternatives. In recalling pre-revolutionary leisure options, a man named Andreev mused: "How did the majority of workers relax? They played cards and billiards, drank, beat [their] wives, and so forth. There was absolutely no other culture among workers." Questionnaires conducted by worker organizations before the 1909 temperance congress brought back similar answers. Workers went to the tavern because "there [was] no other amusement," because they did not have clothes appropriate for the theater. Whereas other establishments kept workers out, in the tavern "they always admit [workers]."[102] Working-class activists may have regretted the tavern's prominence in the lives of Russia's laborers, but the bulk of the working-class rank and file was more inclined to get the greatest enjoyment and advantage that they could from this public space. The continuing importance of the tavern in the Soviet era, when other leisure opportunities for workers were more widely available, leaves little doubt that many laborers had an essentially positive view of the tavern and the time they spent within its walls.

That the beer hall in the 1920s remained a crucial site of male sociability is testimony to the importance men placed on the preservation of their gendered identities, for the revolutionary state had greatly weakened the tavern's vitality as a multidimensional institution. Laborers could now find work through trade unions; the customer's relationship with the bartender became depersonalized; and the all-important billiard table was gone. The tavern's importance as a highly charged political arena also dissipated in the 1920s, when other institutions served as avenues for gaining political education and expressing political grievances. The political history of the Russian tavern was nonetheless a rich one, since the Russian government's liquor monopoly made alcohol outlets an opportune target for the politically disfranchised.

CHAPTER 5

WOMEN, CHILDREN, AND SOBRIETY

■ Despite important limits to its accuracy, the image of sober women and children held significance, both for women and children themselves and for Russian society more broadly. At a rudimentary level of analysis, the "temperate" woman illustrated the behavior that laboring men saw as most appropriate for women. More deeply, the equation men made between workers and drinkers conceptually excluded "abstinent" women and youth from the working class; as far as most workingmen were concerned, women in particular remained outsiders in the workers' state. Furthermore, throughout the early twentieth century, temperance activists considered the "nondrinking" women and youth their logical supporters. The revolution of 1917 did give rise to a distinctive youth culture, but sobriety was not its hallmark. And working-class women demonstrated no categorical antipathy toward drink; instead, women's complex reactions to alcohol generally included the acceptance of a male prerogative to drink and an attempt to limit the impact that expenditures on alcohol had on their own family's economic well-being. Women normally used limited, individualistic methods to defend the family economy, engaging in vociferous, collective action against drink only during moments of revolutionary unrest. The clear and vigorous messages that women sent during mass demonstrations were, however, marginalized by the revolutionary state, which failed to incorporate women's family-centered objectives in a substantive way.

• • •

The pervasive presence of drink in the working-class culture meant that even infants consumed small quantities of alcohol. In most cases, of course, babies and very young children who imbibed alcohol did so on the initiative of their parents. Mothers added alcohol to the baby's milk or prepared a cloth pacifier soaked with spirits as a way to get the child to stop crying or to go to sleep. This simple solution allowed a mother to accomplish her work rather than hover over a discontented child.[1] In this respect, mothers probably dealt with male and female infants similarly. In addition, temperance literature repeatedly complained that lower-class adults entertained themselves, on occasion, by watching the antics of drunken children.[2] The evidence is indirect, but adults who sought entertainment in the intoxicated child may well have focused on the behavior of drunken girls as often as on the behavior of little boys.[3] Although physicians and temperance activists advised parents that even small quantities of alcohol were dangerous for children, that message appears to have had little effect. Given their beliefs about the physical benefits of alcohol, working-class parents probably saw little harm in amusing themselves by making children a bit tipsy. In 1929, three-year-old Kolia Korotkov died from alcohol poisoning, but his parents and communal neighbors had foreseen no harm in providing the child with alcoholic beverages. Kolia's mother claimed not to understand why the child had died; Kolia's father pointed to the healthful properties of drink: "Wholesome grains go into beer—barley, for example," he asserted. Other residents in the Korotkovs' communal apartment echoed similar themes: "'Well, I don't have a stone heart. . . . Can I really turn down [the request of] a child?' . . . 'Let him drink, at least he will be healthy.'"[4] None of the adults caring for Kolia Korotkov understood alcohol's ability to threaten the youngster's life.

Clear gender distinctions began to emerge when a child advanced beyond infancy. We have already seen how working-class fathers prodded their sons to drink. There is no evidence that girls were similarly encouraged. The divergence is explicable, perhaps, in the adult workers' conviction that children who learned to drink while young would be immunized against alcoholism.[5] At least in theory, only male children would have required protection against adult alcoholism, for little girls were destined to mature into abstinent women.

When working-class youngsters entered their teens, the decision about their alcohol consumption was increasingly made outside the parents' sphere. Young men inducted into the working world became part of their coworkers' drinking circle; fellow workers could thus greatly influence the drinking habits of young males. Furthermore, in the 1920s, the working-class youth created a distinctive social niche for themselves. The political power and self-awareness of the youth grew as old hierarchies based on *sosloviia* and age crumbled along with the tsarist regime. No evidence suggests that working-class youth held special drinking parties in the prewar era, but such gatherings clearly became an important part of adolescent culture in the second half of the 1920s. Indeed, an investigation into leisure pursued by the working-class youth in Leningrad's Vyborg district revealed that young workers were more likely to drink at a party convened in a friend's home than in a pub.[6] Meeting in the home of a friend was probably one way that young adults responded to the shortage of taverns in the Soviet era. Young workers, who had come of age after prohibition, may have been more willing than their elders to accept alternate drinking sites. In any case, the consumption of alcoholic beverages was a central feature of the youth parties held in the 1920s. "Not one" party was held without drink, asserted a twenty-one-year-old founder from the Metallicheskii mill. When investigators inquired whether he might find parties interesting without drink, he replied negatively: "Without drinks it is boring."[7] Well-intentioned plans to satisfy guests with tea reportedly led to melancholy gatherings; only when the inevitable bottles of vodka appeared did a party turn merry.[8]

In the 1920s, working-class youth also sought a special niche in public drinking space. As *Leningradskii rabochii* observed, "Youth do not like to carouse with old men on payday." Bored with the old sounds of the accordion, young people preferred to frequent taverns that hosted jazz bands and foxtrots.[9] Drinking establishments patronized by the youth—rather than by workers from particular factories, professions, or regions of the country—were a new phenomenon reflective of youth's enhanced status in the 1920s. Liberated by revolution, young adults became more autonomous actors in Russian society; in the 1920s, they were relatively free to pursue leisure independent of their elders' protective oversight. Although working-class youth in the 1920s preferred different forms of leisure than their parents had, there is nothing to suggest that their diversions were any more sober. In 1928, the Vyborg district Komsomol found that 96 percent of the young men continued to consume alcoholic beverages.[10]

• • •

The dearth of women's voices in historical literature prohibits any attempt to critique workingmen's feminization of abstinence through an analogous analysis of workingwomen's linguistic conventions. Women's behavior nonetheless reflects their approach toward alcohol. Contrary to the assumptions embedded in male discourse, most women in the working community did not have a categorical antipathy for drink, viewing it instead as an ordinary part of working-class life. In many cultures, women act as suppliers of alcohol, a practice that was in some ways also characteristic of worker culture in early twentieth-century Russia.[11] It was the working-class mother, after all, who quieted her infants with spirits, and working-class women certainly prepared and served alcohol in the home. One woman implicitly condoned her husband's drinking through her efforts to invest his beverage with a pleasant citrus flavor, a task she accomplished by soaking orange rind in a bottle of vodka. The wife in a fictional sketch was reluctant to proscribe her husband's celebration of payday, since she knew this was his reward for a week of hard work on behalf of the family. Perhaps most tellingly, in complaining that female workers were "indifferent" to drinking in the shop, a 1929 article in *Rabotnitsa i krest'ianka* demonstrated that working-class women often were not opposed to alcohol consumption per se. "To drink," the women asserted, was not "a sin."[12]

Furthermore, statistical material on female drinking makes it clear that the image of women as nondrinking was not a true reflection of many women's lives. Taken collectively, a wide variety of indices—including arrests for drunkenness, death by alcohol poisoning, and treatment rates for alcoholism—show that both before and after the revolution of 1917, women accounted for about 5 to 15 percent of the populations with alcohol-related problems.[13] Largely because investigators assumed that problem drinking by women was not pervasive enough to warrant special study, the only major investigation between 1900 and 1929 in which St. Petersburg's working-class women appear to have been questioned directly about their consumption patterns was conducted in the late 1920s by the Vyborg district Komsomol. According to the published report, 35 percent of female youths drank either "occasionally" or "regularly"; the remaining 65 percent were apparently nondrinkers. The representativeness of a lone study should not be overestimated, but the essential integrity of its findings is suggested by scattered statistical data, which indicate that about one-third of the working-class women in early twentieth-century St. Petersburg drank, at least on an occasional basis.[14]

Impressionistic evidence and narrative accounts detailing drinking practices among working-class women are far more sporadic than are such descriptions of male customs. That is partly because women drank less, but the thin source base is also attributable to lower female literacy rates, which made women less likely than their male counterparts to leave written records. The memoir of Z. I. Zapechina, an unusually rich descriptive source penned by a female worker, is therefore worth examining at length. In her midteens in 1914, Zapechina worked at the Okhtenskaia spinning mill. According to her account, the week before a young woman working at the factory was to be married, female coworkers "gather[ed] around her machine and [sang] songs" during lunch—a custom that Zapechina found very pleasing. The main celebration, however, took place the Monday after the wedding, when the newlywed was obliged to appear at work

> in her housecoat, in order to show that she was [now] not a girl, but a woman. She brought vodka, beer, candy, cookies, and nuts . . . and treated [everyone]. The foreman did not protest. All this she hid by her machine, and she treated [everyone] at lunch time: some [women] drank vodka, some [drank] beer, girls nibbled nuts and ate candy, but some [of the women] also drank vodka. The merriment, songs, and dances began, until it looked like the machines would collapse. . . . Suddenly the foreman appeared out of nowhere. . . . 'What is this?' [The women] explained and he congratulated the bride, and he took out ten rubles to give [her] for refreshments. And [the women] complimented the worker: the foreman is a good [boss]. . . . Sometimes they didn't work more after lunch.[15]

The evident fondness with which Zapechina recalls these events illustrates that alcohol's function among workingwomen was celebratory, just as it was among workingmen. Furthermore, her casual tone implies no condemnation of women who drank alcohol; on the contrary, it suggests that the celebrants and the foreman alike recognized that workingwomen deserved their moments of merrymaking.

Zapechina described another female drinking custom, albeit with greater brevity. She reports that on the Thursday before Whitsun [Semik], women came to work tipsy. They then gathered twigs, which they decorated with colored paper, and, singing and dancing, set out for the forest, where they continued drinking.[16] This custom had its roots in the Russian village: unmarried rural women convened in the forest during Whitsun to drink beer, sing, decorate birch trees, and learn their fortunes by tossing wreaths into a stream. A wreath that sank into the water forecast a young woman's impending death or continued maidenhood; the lucky women whose wreaths floated were sure to marry soon.[17] Zapechina does not link Whitsun festivities with maidenhood, but participants in the celebrations she describes do appear to have been exclusively female. Except for the foreman, who happened through the shop, no men are present in her account.

On at least one occasion, Zapechina and her cohorts shared the celebration of *Semik* with workers from the Neva and Shtiglits factories.[18] The uniqueness of her memoir makes it difficult to judge how widespread these practices were among the women workers. It seems likely, though, that women like Zapechina, similarly delighted with these celebrations, would have carried the traditions with them as they changed jobs—just as their forebears had transported festivities from village to city. Fleeting evidence bearing on the persistence of such customs into the revolutionary years shows that some women attempted to revive the celebration of *Semik* early in the 1920s. In 1922 *Krasnaia gazeta* reported on festivities at the Severnaia weaving mill, where women marked the occasion by adorning themselves with ribbons and flowers, drinking, singing, and generally raising "a racket" in the factory. The same newspaper also reported on a celebration by seven Putilov women in 1923, the last identifiable time that the holiday was observed by working women in St. Petersburg.[19]

Attempts to revive Whitsun celebrations in the early 1920s show that people living through revolutionary times seek to sustain favored cultural traditions. By the second half of that decade, the most important opportunities for female drinking had shifted from *Semik* to new holidays instituted by the revolutionary state. In the late 1920s, Russia's working-class women began raising their glasses to the revolutionary holiday that extolled the virtues of women, International Women's Day. There are several reports of women coming to work on 8 March "three sheets to the wind," or bringing vodka into work with them. At the *Leningradskaia pravda* print shop, for example, "many" women workers came to work drunk, and a few were taken home unconscious.[20] Drunken celebrations of this holiday also pervaded more private spaces in apartments and communal homes. Natalia Nikolaeva, a worker at Krasnyi Treugol'nik mill, greeted the day with generous quantities of alcohol and vigorous dancing, thus disturbing her neighbor who lived downstairs. Reportedly fearing that the ceiling was about to cave in, he requested that she restrain her festivities. But Nikolaeva would accept no interference in her celebration of this distinctively female holiday. "This is none of *your* business," she told him. "Today is a *women's* holiday; I will drink and carry on—and no one will forbid [my doing so] or do anything [about it]."[21] For other men, the drunken celebration of Women's Day seems to have provided a fortuitous window of opportunity. In one communal home, I. Zhiga reported, women smuggled in vodka by concealing bottles in their skirts. Soon the "drunk, disheveled, brazen" women were singing in the street. Men followed on the heels of this vulnerable prey like "wolves after meat."[22]

A shift over time in the specific occasions appropriated for female drinking is less important than it might at first seem. To be sure, by the 1920s, workers of both sexes were making adjustments to a revolutionary holiday calendar: as workers agreed to substitute observance of May Day for the celebration of Easter, women shifted their festive observances from now proscribed religiously based ceremonies such as Whitsun to officially sanctioned secular holidays for women. Of greater significance is the overall pattern of female consumption that remained constant throughout the revolutionary years. Men made use of the weekend, especially the weekends when they got paid, to spend time drinking with companions, but similar female festivities were far more scattered.[23] Whether the occasion was Whitsun or International Women's Day, such a holiday came only once a year, and the celebration of an acquaintance's marriage was more fortuitous than routine. Relative to men, women had far fewer opportunities for socially sanctioned drinking. But their appropriation of those infrequent drinking occasions allowed them occasional opportunities to drink without posing a substantive challenge to the drinking privileges of men.

Although not unequivocally accurate in attributing abstinence to the feminine realm, then, the language of working men correctly pointed to the relatively restrained use of alcohol among working-class women. Neither women nor youth can be said to have strictly adhered to a temperate way of life, but the image of abstinence was more consistent with the actual behavior of working-class women than it was with the behavior of youth. Further, there was a striking discrepancy between the consequences of imbibing for these two "temperate" groups. When an "abstinent" youth consumed alcohol, no inevitable negative repercussions were said to follow. Women who stepped outside the abstinent ideal, however, promised to unleash domestic distress and sexual licentiousness, bringing great harm to their families.

"[When] a husband is a drunkard—the floor of the home rots," a Russian proverb maintained. But it was even worse when the wife drank, for then, "the whole home rots." A woman who consumed alcohol likely became inattentive to her domestic responsibilities, a mere "addition to the pigs."[24] In a different context and many years later, the same sentiment was reflected in *Rabotnitsa i krest'ianka's* description of the plight in the Varvar household. After her husband left for work, Kuz'mina Varvara frequently drank and locked the couple's small children in the apartment, finally returning home in the early morning hours. Mr. Varvar also drank, but, the journal noted, "to fault [him] is impossible. He comes [home] from work, and the apartment is cold; the children are ragged [and] dirty—and he takes up alcohol in order to escape all this."[25] The responsibility for the unfortunate plight of the entire Varvar family lay squarely upon the shoulders of the drunken wife. Her drinking caused her to ignore the family's needs, and she was at fault for the disheveled home that remained. As one pamphlet observed, when the mother joined the father in drink, no one was left to tend to a child's cries for bread.[26] The workingwoman's domestic responsibilities made it imperative that she lead a temperate life.

Injunctions against female alcohol consumption were also invoked in the name of women's chastity. In literature designed to resonate with working-class audiences, drinking girls and sexual promiscuity were systematically portrayed as inevitable companions. In a prerevolutionary story by S. Zhivotskii, for example, the innocent young Aniutka leaves her village to take employment as a domestic worker in St. Petersburg. After drinking with new city friends, she awakens with a headache, unable to remember the events of yesterday—and with Ivan, one of her new acquaintances, sleeping at the table next to her bed. Her uncle's warning to "guard her honor" has been in vain; doubtless a sober Aniutka would have successfully resisted Ivan's advances.[27] In the 1920s, the presence of alcohol at youth parties reportedly created a prime environment for young women to lose their virginity. Among youth in the Vyborg district, parties were an even more important drinking occasion for young women than they were for young men. The threat that such parties posed to female chastity was therefore all the more obvious.[28] Drinking by women—apparently the intoxication of young men was a less salient contributing factor—was the prelude to kissing, kissing games, and the foxtrot. Normally modest young women reputedly started hugging one fellow after another,

and couples "dispersed to the corners [of the room]."[29] "I was fourteen
. . . It happened at a party, after drinking," confessed one young
weaver.[30] Women's access to alcohol needed to be limited, lest the
working-class family fall apart and female sexuality run amok.

The divergence between the alleged consequences that drinking
women, as opposed to drinking youth—both considered "abstainers"—brought to working-class life is reflective of important power relationships within that community. As Barbara Alpern Engel so aptly
observed in her recent monograph on lower-class women in late tsarist
Russia: "While few historians say so outright, the proletarian is gendered. When they use the word 'he' they almost never mean 'she.' . . .
[Women are] omitted from this discourse."[31] In large part, this is precisely because historians of working-class Russia have tended to focus
on the experience of male laborers, who themselves marginalized
women in their discourse and cultural life. Rank-and-file laboring men
identified workers closely with the consumption of alcohol, and since
women and children were defined as nondrinkers, laboring men
dubbed them nonworkers, conceptually excluding them from full
membership in the Russian working class. And yet, men could consider youthful drinking acceptable in practice, because young boys, at
least, would one day become workers. The privileges bestowed upon
fellow workers, including the right to drink, would one day be conferred upon them. Rank-and-file workingmen did not extend the same
flexibility to women. Had male workers accepted female drinking as
routine behavior, they would have implicitly recognized women's
right to equal status as workers. This they were not prepared to do.
More than youth, women posed a potential challenge to masculine
dominance of working-class life. It was consequently of greater importance that their access to alcohol, a symbol of inclusion in the working
community, remain limited.

Of course, women's "abstinent" character was not the sole factor
preventing laboring men from accepting them as full-fledged workers.
Historians are already aware that women living in Russia's working-
class communities often did so as wives and mothers of workers but
were not themselves employed in factories, mills, or domestic service.
Even women who were engaged in wage labor generally earned less
than their male counterparts, were less likely to be employed in
"skilled" occupations, and were presumed not to have families relying
on their income for vital support.[32] This investigation of drink adds to
that already familiar picture by showing that the marginalization of
women in Russia's working-class communities extended beyond their

irregular employment, low pay, "limited" skills, and "supplementary" income—women were also culturally excluded from a masculine social milieu. Anne Gorsuch has similarly observed that male workers—in many ways understandably—were loath to endorse a feminization of working-class culture.[33] In his decided avowal that "girls are not comrades," a fictional worker simply and succinctly demonstrates that a female presence spoils male camaraderie.[34] For rank-and-file working-class men, acceptance of a female prerogative to drink would have constituted symbolic self-emasculation. The close associations that most laboring men made between "men" and "workers" would help marginalize Russia's working-class women well after the 1917 revolution formally ushered in legal gender equality.

• • •

Intermittent consumption of alcoholic beverages among women and youth notwithstanding, the relatively restrained drinking by the two groups encouraged temperance advocates to believe that they could tap into a natural constituency. Whether before or after 1917, anti-alcohol activists, recognizing the difficulty of changing the habits already ingrained in older generations, endeavored to foster a "completely sober Russia" by devoting special attention to the drinking practices of the youth. Russia's children would turn away from alcohol, activists believed, because they would be reared as nondrinkers.[35]

Pre-revolutionary temperance activists had advocated temperance education in schools and in the church, but they never proposed a topsy-turvy world in which mere children were encouraged to inculcate proper social values in their elders. In the 1920s, though, an adolescent state beckoned young men and women, who had come of age in "new conditions," to smash the negative remnants of working-class behavior "inherited" from the tsarist regime. In effect, children were encouraged to become teachers, a transformation plainly evident in a poster of the time: standing before a blackboard and facing his audience, a Young Pioneer demonstrates how to "correct" mistaken lifestyles by crossing out the letter "i" in the word *spirt* [alcohol] and replacing it with an "o"—forming *sport* [sport].[36] Anti-alcohol literature exhorted young people to expose their fathers who drank, thereby subjecting the private conduct of adults to the unremitting scrutiny of youngsters. Prescriptive short stories and plays depicted model Soviet children who scolded drinking adults and who vowed to report family members' drunkenness to the factory paper or the comrades' court.[37] These narratives contained compelling didactic messages for adults as well as for youth: in the Soviet state, adult values clearly could be misplaced, grown-ups could be appropriately reprimanded by their own children, and there was no legitimate separation between private behavior and public reputation. The revolutionary state's emphasis on collectivity meant that the temperance movement applauded mass anti-alcohol demonstrations by youth with even greater enthusiasm than it displayed for precocious tattletales. Mass manifestations of anti-alcohol sentiment were not themselves new in Russia; prior to World War I, church-sponsored "Temperance Days" had been marked by public prayers, anti-alcohol lectures, and processions throughout St. Petersburg.[38] The anti-alcohol demonstrations staged throughout the Soviet Union in 1928–1929 were distinguished by their youthful composition. Fathers tramping well-worn paths from factory to beer hall unexpectedly encountered their children bearing posters that demanded "sober parents" and the purchase of textbooks instead of vodka.[39] These protests would seem to have epitomized the very heart of cultural revolution in Russia: self-conscious youth apparently battled a stubborn enemy that prevented working-class resources from being used in more productive ways. Other historians have noted the cultural revolution's emphasis on the creation of a truly "proletarian" culture as well as the youth's importance to that endeavor.[40] The children's anti-alcohol demonstrations of 1928–1929 were an expression of those trends.

In their anti-alcohol battles, temperance activists also hoped to tap into the latent army of "abstinent" women. As with youth, more than women's status as "nondrinkers" attracted the anti-alcohol activists to this constituency. Throughout the early twentieth century, temperance literature reiterated two refrains ad infinitum: drunken husbands beat their wives, and the money that men spent on drink threatened the fragile family economy. Anti-alcohol activists repeatedly advised young women to be cognizant of a potential spouse's drinking habits: could a woman truly love a man who went drinking, left her home alone, returned swearing and fighting, wasted money, and fathered sickly children? If drinking was a fiancé's only weakness, one journal advised, a young woman should submit her betrothed to a two-year test of sobriety.[41] Women who had not possessed the foresight to marry non-drinkers were, nevertheless, obliged to stop the use of alcohol in the home. Above all, women must not drink themselves; they should not give alcohol to their children or send youngsters out to buy vodka.[42]

Moreover, temperance advocates encouraged by foreign example argued that the sequestered domestic sphere was not the only arena in

which women could make a significant contribution to the detoxification of the working class: Russian women should also endeavor to influence alcohol-related public policies.[43] As might be anticipated, activists in the pre-revolutionary era tended to stress the responsibilities
of "educated" women, but some believed that working-class women
were also important to the success of temperance movements. At a
1908 Russian women's congress, for example, R. R. Boduén-de-Kurtené
emphasized that educated women in other countries worked alongside
"barely literate women from the people" who had been instrumental in
evicting men from taverns. Numerous pre-revolutionary publications
directed at an unsophisticated reading audience suggested ways that
women could influence male drinking behavior; a public health journal
specifically recommended Dr. A. Korovin's *Obligations of the Russian
Woman in the Struggle with Alcoholism* as material appropriate for the
"simple reader."[44] Even political conservatives such as N. N. Shipov argued that women's potential contribution to anti-alcohol efforts justified granting them the franchise and the right to serve in institutions of
local self-government.[45] After 1917, of course, working-class women
were depicted by the self-consciously "proletarian" state as logical
standard-bearers in anti-alcohol crusades. This clarion call became particularly pronounced after March 1927, when Sovnarkom allowed local
government organizations to prohibit alcohol sales via popular referen-
dum. Pointing to the latent power of the female voice, Larin assured
women that their efforts in this direction would not be wasted: there
were certain districts and factories, he noted, where women themselves
constituted a majority.[46] In these areas, working-class women assumed
a numerical position that theoretically allowed them to prevail over the
collective will of men.

The actual contribution that women and youth made to the struggle
for sobriety never matched the activists' expectations. Broad general
support for temperance among youth certainly cannot be inferred from
a handful of well-publicized demonstrations. Fictional children vowed
to write to the factory paper about their fathers' drunkenness, but
there is no indication that real children ever did so.[47] Organized youth,
who should have been the most sympathetic to the goals of temperance activists, proved neither consistent nor energetic in their endorse-
ment of a sober culture. In 1928, several Komsomol activists at Krasnyi
Treugol'nik argued against their "collective repudiation" of drink, on
the grounds that not everyone would be able to adhere to such a
pledge.[48] As historian A. I. Bukharev concluded, anti-alcohol activities
sponsored by the Komsomol consisted of episodic actions taken by

individual cells.[49] Komsomol women at one factory agreed *"not to kiss drunken fellows,"* and the Young Pioneers' cell at Putilov demanded that a nearby beer hall be closed, but these were unusual—not ordinary—accomplishments.[50] Significantly, in attempting to instruct youth about comportment appropriate in the Soviet state, Komsomol activists resorted to subterfuge, vaguely inviting those fond of drink to discussion of "a question that interests you personally."[51] A 1929 meeting of Soviet Russia's leading anti-alcohol activists starkly illustrated the weakness of anti-alcohol efforts among Soviet youth. Even more telling than Larin's observation that few youths were attracted to temperance efforts was the assembly's reaction to the remarks of the Komsomol leadership. When Komsomol representatives attempted to list their organization's recent accomplishments, they were assailed by hostile comments from the floor: "Not enough! [The Komsomol] isn't doing anything!"[52] As consumption patterns among youth suggest, "new" conditions of life in the 1920s did not make young workers any less accepting of alcohol than their elders had been.

Women also proved disappointing allies in the struggle against drink. Women in Russia's working community responded to male drinking in complex ways, but they never became a vital force in organized anti-alcohol efforts. During the height of anti-alcohol efforts in the late 1920s, for example, women reportedly accounted for 15 to 20 percent of the membership in Leningrad's OBSAs.[53] This might appear to be a respectable figure; after all, working-class women were more reluctant than men to participate in any aspect of public life. But female constituencies greater or comparable to that of the OBSA were also characteristic of many other voluntary organizations at that time, including the Down with Illiteracy Society, the Friend of Children, the Society for the Promotion of Defense and Aero-Chemical Development, the International Organization for Aid to Revolutionaries, and the League of the Godless.[54] In short, women exhibited no greater enthusiasm for anti-alcohol organizations than they did for groups connected with a wide variety of other matters. Disappointed temperance activists consistently described female participation in their endeavors as "insignificant," "rare," and "weak," and delegates at a 1929 gathering devoted considerable discussion to the reasons for inadequate female participation. Unceasing appeals in the press that summoned women to "active participation," to form the "first ranks of fighters" and stop "cry[ing] in the pillow" tellingly reveal that this call rang hollow.[55]

Working-class women's indifference to organized temperance efforts shows that they did not share the anti-alcohol movement's strong antipathy to drink per se. Not only did working-class women provide alcohol to family members and drink themselves; in addition, the link that the pre- and post-revolutionary temperance movements made between male alcohol use and wife-beating found little resonance among working-class women, despite a large body of general and specific evidence supporting the allegation that many intoxicated men indeed subjected women to physical discipline.[56] As other scholars have shown, lower-class men in early twentieth-century Russia widely employed physical force as a way to gain their wives' obedience and respect. Perhaps, then, working-class women did not respond to the temperance movement's appeal to the physical insecurity of the family because they did not perceive a link between their husbands' drunkenness and being beaten.[57] In McKee's view, alcohol was a "facilitator," rather than an "actual cause" of spousal violence.[58]

The failure of working-class women to flock to anti-alcohol organizations does not mean that they sanctioned male drinking practices in their entirety. For most working-class women, the struggle against male alcohol consumption was normally a mundane, personal fight, one that centered on circumstances peculiar to their individual households. The element common to women's particularistic struggles, the one that was central to women's concerns, was the maintenance of a sound family economy. The primacy of this goal is illustrated by a petition that a certain Fedotova wrote to the Second Psychiatric Hospital in the late 1920s. Her husband, she complained, was being held by the hospital for treatment of alcoholism.

> And for some reason they aren't releasing him. . . . When my husband was around, *although he drank, he fed his family*. Now I beg you to give an order to the hospital so he will be released *in order that his family will not die from hunger*. I have three children between the age of one and five years. And one of the children is very ill. . . . I cannot come to discuss with you how under Soviet power [you] must not leave children to die from hunger. Again I ask that you release my husband *so that he can feed his family*.[59]

Fedotova clearly believed that her spouse's main responsibility was to provide for the family's material needs. He fulfilled this mission to her satisfaction, and she therefore condoned his drinking practices.

Women found drinking spouses most troublesome when alcohol expenditures interfered with the family's financial well-being. That a sound family economy was the predominant concern of many working-class women was evident not only in Fedotova's petition but also in the most common form their anti-alcohol battles assumed: waiting for the pay packet by the factory gate. When the ending bell rang on payday, women huddled outside mills were determined to see their spouses come home with pay packet intact—or at the very least, they demanded that husbands relinquish money to cover essential purchases before there was any opportunity to set out for the tavern. Women faced some clear disadvantages in this assignment. Successfully spotting a wayward husband within the crowd exiting the plant was not always easy, especially at large factories, where workers commonly used more than one exit, or when groups of men conspired among themselves to evade their wives. As one woman outside Krasnaia Zaria complained, it was impossible to discern much in the exodus, since men in the crowd "continually hinder [things], and some intentionally push and shove, in order that attention will be turned to them."[60] Even women who managed to locate their husbands had accomplished only part of their mission: the task of securing money from the man who earned and possessed it was a delicate assignment. As the family's main breadwinners, male workers could try to claim that "their" money should be spent according to their own discretion. Following a dispute with his wife, the bookbinder Dudyrkin bellowed to his drinking companions, "Who earns the money—me or her? I [do]! This means I am also the master of the money. I will spend it as I want. And she [will not give me] an order."[61] A woman who endeavored to obtain a portion of the pay packet needed to use persuasion as a means of inducing the male wage-earner to transfer part of his pay to her.

Despite unpleasant obstacles, this female mission was by no means destined to fail. If generations of women had been systematically frustrated in their attempts to acquire money from their men, surely they would have had little incentive to persist in their semimonthly sojourns to the factory. Indeed, women in working-class communities faced the task before them with enough fortitude and inventiveness that men called them "tugboats."[62] When confronted with multiple exits, women relied on the assistance of children and relatives. As one woman in the crowd outside the Krasnyi Treugol'nik mill advised another: "Here is what I do. I stand here, [I send] one daughter to Petergofskii [Prospect], a second [daughter waits] on Tarakanovka."[63] Women whose husbands proved elusive at the factory gate might continue their searches, peering into their spouses' favorite haunts and confronting a wayward man in the tavern itself.[64] If all else failed, when an inebriated man finally collapsed in bed at home, his wife rummaged through his pockets in hopes of finding and salvaging the remaining resources.[65]

Most importantly—and of course not by accident—the argument most frequently advanced by women intent on procuring funds from their husbands centered on a principle accepted by working-class men and women alike: the wage-earner had a responsibility to provide for the material requirements of the rest of the family, and for the needs of children in particular. Youth were not ardent anti-alcohol activists themselves, but children did have material requirements that prompted their mothers to take action against their drinking fathers. "Six children need to be fed," and "Hungry children are waiting," women insisted in a refrain intended to demonstrate that their vigilance was not motivated by selfishness. Even the delinquent husband's coconspirators were not immune from prosecution. "Aren't you embarrassed to drink with a family man," one woman scolded.[66] Anti-alcohol activists pored over investigations of working-class budgets in an attempt to assess the percentage of household income that workers devoted to alcohol, but the concerns of working-class women were far more direct. In a story housewife Karaseva wrote for *Rabotnitsa i krest'ianka*, the protagonist's actions were likely indicative of her own: she determines precisely what she needs to buy and how much money she needs before ever setting out for the factory on payday.[67] Similarly, bookbinder Dudyrkin's wife refused her husband's request for fifty kopeks to spend on drink because, she said, son Mit'ka needed shoes and daughter Katiusha a coat.[68]

Working-class men were not insensitive to the financial hardship that unbridled drinking could bring to their families. In 1929, the Krasnyi Vyborzhets factory paper noted that many workers voluntarily sought "to provide for their family for [the next] two weeks, and they transfer the money to their wives, who are standing by the gate."[69] A detailed report on spousal interactions at Putilov in early 1927 depicts one worker handing his earnings to his spouse; another gave his wife only a small portion of his earnings but reportedly relinquished the rest after receiving a negative response to his hopeful inquiry, "Is it enough?"[70] Portraits of men who resolved to surprise their wives by coming home with the pay packet intact or who vowed to hand over the week's earnings to their wives are also contained in short stories.[71] As shown earlier, men drank because sharing alcohol with others was a way to demonstrate friendship and goodwill; it was a way to thank acquaintances for assistance with finding employment and acquiring job skills; it was a way to celebrate the arrival of the weekend and to affirm their identity as men. The fact that men drank did not automatically entail neglect of their responsibility for the economic health of their household.

Nevertheless, because of fluctuating and often limited monetary resources among Russian workers, men frequently confronted two competing desires: celebrating payday by drinking with companions, thus reaffirming comradely relations with their male companions, and providing for their family's welfare. Only occasionally could both objectives be satisfied at once. As a worker from the Baltic mill noted, a small but happy minority of the mill's workers earned enough "for living and for drink."[72] In 1911, employees at the Gesler mill gladly accepted overtime, because extra earnings enabled them to cover essential purchases and still have money left to drink.[73] Working-class families continued to experience the same financial pressures in the Soviet era. Competing demands on the workers' pay packet thus contributed to a considerable degree of contingency in encounters between spouses. It is impossible to reconstruct precisely the complicated interpersonal relationships and highly variable circumstances that influenced the outcomes of particular negotiations between partners at the factory gate: perhaps one day a wife was more insistent because her spouse had spent too much on drink last payday, or maybe he believed that Katiusha's worn overcoat would last a bit longer. Maybe he believed that he knew best how much could be spent on drink and how much was needed for household necessities.[74] Or perhaps a husband merely hoped that his wife would trust him not to bring economic disaster to the family: "The money is ours: it will be yours," a male worker chimed to his wife in a play from the late 1920s.[75]

In any case, the dialogue between couples was complicated by the presence of the crowd. By meeting her husband outside the factory, a woman had the potential threat of social embarrassment on her side. The street was, after all, a public arena—and one that was more heavily populated on paydays than other days. Throngs of people milled about making plans for the holiday, perusing the wares of vendors, and simply hanging out. On the one hand, a wife could attempt to publicly embarrass her husband if he refused to provide money commensurate with the family's needs. Likely few men were happy to become beleaguered spectacles in the presence of their peers. "Stop whimpering, I tell you!" an annoyed fictional worker admonishes his wife, "All the money will be [brought home]; I won't drink it up. Go home, I will drink only a couple of beers and then I will come home. Truly I will. Go away and *don't put me to shame* before my comrades."[76]

On the other hand, the presence of a crowd only provided the potential for embarrassment—it did not ensure disgrace. Public sympathy could just as easily turn to the side of the "oppressed husbands."[77] The social dynamics in certain crowds generated atmospheres antagonistic to feminine goals. In a story that Anna Gol'dberg wrote for *Za novyi byt*, for example, the father "cursed and pushed the mother aside. A crowd gathered around them. Some urged the couple to calm down, others amused themselves by egging them on: "Give in to the *baba*," some spectators teased.[78] What these disparate examples powerfully suggest is that the ultimate fate of individual families varied from week to week under highly contingent circumstances, a conclusion contemporary observers also drew. According to a certain Vesnin, turn-of-the-century men responded in a variety of ways when met by their wives at the factory gate: "Part [of the men] went home; but some, having given their wife part of the money, went with comrades to the tavern, where they drank up the remaining money and [later] returned home to their wife for a supplement."[79]

Working-class women normally displayed concern about male drinking only insofar as they perceived alcohol as a threat to their own household's current economic health. In the context of working-class life in the early twentieth century, this individualistic, limited approach made sense. Whether before or after 1917, most working families lived on the margin: women who appeared at the factory gate could thus influence the household's financial well-being in tangible, decisive ways. The ability of women to influence the funds that spouses devoted to drink is a sign that women possessed some authority in the working-class family. But women's choice of individualistic strategies, their need for constant vigilance in the oversight of the family economy, and their persistent appeal to principles with which men already agreed also point to women's comparatively weak position in working communities. Women subordinate to masculine authority and dependent upon a family wage were understandably reluctant to directly challenge the drinking prerogatives claimed by their husbands. Given the importance of drink in the male worker culture, men might well have marginalized women who persisted in taking more ambitious positions as too extreme, exposing such women and their families to increased financial danger.

Joining organized anti-alcohol efforts or quixotically demanding that a husband renounce drink was more risky for women than attempting to affect male behavior in less programmatic ways. This explains, perhaps, the apparent popularity of remedies that promised to cure the unwitting drinker. In the prewar era, a host of commercial advertisements explicitly directed at a female audience promoted odorless, tasteless concoctions to be sprinkled on an unsuspecting man's food. Women continued to attempt surreptitious treatment into the 1920s.[80] Such solutions offered women the hope of altering male behavior without engaging in a direct confrontation with the family's main wage-earner.

. . .

In exceptional circumstances, the moderate aims and methods women normally adopted in pursing a sound family economy could be replaced by open, vociferous collective action challenging not only men's right to drink but the state's right to sell alcohol. It is true that the working-class demonstrations in 1905 and 1914 were marked by actions directed against drinking establishments. But the full significance of these boycotts becomes clear only when women are brought into the historical picture. According to Buzinov, the boycott effort in early 1905 originated in St. Petersburg's textile mills—establishments whose workforces were predominantly female. Hearing news of the campaign, one man burst into his workshop to alert his male coworkers: "There's trouble, brothers, women have proclaimed a war on the alcohol monopoly!" Most men, though, seem to have initially greeted news of the "women's campaign" with ridicule, as if it was a bit of a joke.[81] During a second strike wave in the autumn of 1905, the "wives and relatives of striking workers" convened a "grandiose women's demonstration" on Vasil'evskii Island to demand that drinking establishments be closed for the course of the strike.[82] Scattered evidence suggests that anti-alcohol action was once again initiated by women during labor demonstrations in the summer of 1914. When male workers from Novyi Aivaz began their strike on 5 July by spending payday in the beer halls as was their custom, a group of about fifty female coworkers entered a number of drinking places, broke bottles over the tables, and compelled the men to quit the establishments.[83] The women of Novyi Aivaz were not alone in taking decisive measures against drink in 1914: an article appearing in *Novoe vremia* noted that a "crowd" containing "many women" destroyed beer shops and taverns in Vyborg district on 9 July; though he failed to elaborate, a British contemporary fleetingly referred to "riots" that occurred in St. Petersburg at this time "because women tried to destroy the vodka shops."[84] As other scholars have noted, the Russian language complicates efforts to define the nature of women's participation in strikes by privileging masculine vocabulary: government and newspaper reports rarely identified the gender of striking workers, employing the masculine form *rabochie* to refer to male and female workers [*rabotnitsy*] alike.[85] Nevertheless, in light of the anti-alcohol initiatives that Buzinov and others explicitly attribute to women, it stretches credulity to suppose that women were not active in the "crowds" closing drinking establishments along Ligovskaia, Malyi Posadskaia, Bezborodkinskii, and other St. Petersburg streets in 1914. In both 1905 and 1914, the proclivity that some of these crowds displayed for destroying liquor supplies—by hurling stones at shelves of bottles or by spoiling wares in the street—is consistent with the "rumbustious and noisy" attributes of female protest identified by historian Steve A. Smith.[86] But the historical record is silent about the motivations of women who participated in these events.[87]

In her important study of women's protest in early twentieth-century Barcelona, Temma Kaplan suggested that lower-class women who engage in collective action are motivated by "female consciousness," that is, an understanding that they have the "right to protect and feed their communities."[88] Given the central concern that working-class women in St. Petersburg normally demonstrated about alcohol's effect on the family economy, Kaplan's investigation suggests a sensible explanation for the anti-alcohol actions taken by Russian women in 1905 and 1914. Drink potentially threatened the economic health of working families, and women who promoted boycotts or smashed bottles of alcohol in the street were acting in the family's economic defense. And yet the situation must have been more complex. Kaplan also notes that female solidarity is welded by a "common antagonism," by a "shared outrage"—but the common enemy in this case was not a new antagonist.[89] Working-class women in pre-revolutionary Russia regularly attempted to limit the economic impact of alcohol expenditures by cajoling, coaxing, and scolding their men; they returned to this approach in the 1920s. Why, then, did they so dramatically alter their behavior during the general strikes in 1905 and 1914?

First of all, the prospect of a general strike undoubtedly changed the calculation of risk for many members of the working class, including women. In an era when most working families lived on the margin and had no access to strike funds, the economic danger presented by a potentially prolonged strike was very real. Male laborers from Novyi Aivaz who went to the beer hall on an ordinary payday had a reasonable expectation that they would receive fresh funds two weeks hence, but the men who went on strike in July 1914 had no such assurance. As shown earlier, women did not normally impose themselves on the male camaraderie in the tavern. This invasion of male space by working women was highly unusual, and it suggested that the stakes were high. With the family economy placed at greatly increased risk, there was a corresponding diminution in the perceived gamble that women took in adopting overt actions to prevent their husbands from expending money on drink. Alcohol's threat to the family economy was not new; but during a general strike, women in working-class communities had a heightened sense of its potential danger. Furthermore, the importance of the revolutionary moment that women faced in 1905 and 1914 must be appreciated. Here was a rare opportunity for them to advance their own proposals for a better society, including the unusual demand that husbands, sons, and brothers renounce drink entirely. According to the theoretical work of James C. Scott, the ambiguous way in which subordinate groups (such as women) advocate their interests in daily life can be transformed into more open and unequivocal confrontations in highly unusual situations.[90] During the revolutionary crises of 1905 and 1914, when unrest in St. Petersburg's streets made it plainly evident that social norms were in flux, there was a real possibility that women's family aims could be written into a new social contract. If the goals of the family were successfully advanced, the household economy would no longer be periodically endangered by husbands' drinking patterns, and women's sojourns to the factory gate could come to an end. Under such highly elastic yet threatening circumstances, women who normally showed little enthusiasm for formal temperance organizations did not hesitate to take energetic action against alcohol.

Although historians of Russia have accepted a link between women's collective action and their familial concerns in some contexts, they have been reluctant to acknowledge explicit political aims as a component of protest among women of the lower classes.[91] As Kaplan suggests, however, "everyday life" can become a "political process," and women defend their right to feed their families "with the support of government or without it."[92] Historians of Russia once held their assumption that lower-class women were essentially "apolitical" in common with scholars in other fields, but this premise is increasingly challenged outside of Russian history.[93] It is therefore appropriate to examine the possibility that women participating in St. Petersburg's mass demonstrations dovetailed familial and political goals.

As we have seen, the pre-revolutionary Russian tavern was not only an important political meeting place for working-class men but also an institution that excluded respectable working-class women. One important development entailed in shutting down drinking outlets during mass demonstrations, then, was the immediate inclusion of women in the political process. If taverns were closed and political protest moved into the street, workingmen no longer ruled an independent political forum, for the street could belong to women as well as to men. It is not unambiguously clear that women intended to create an alternative political forum by closing the taverns, but it is also unclear that this effect was merely fortuitous. Women probably understood, at least intuitively, that their interests were more likely to be considered if men found themselves without their normally exclusive masculine forum. Another aspect of women's anti-alcohol demonstrations is also suggestive of women's political concern: even untutored women undoubtedly knew that alcohol sales produced important revenue for the tsarist state. By simultaneously damaging the state's fiscal interests and calling for political reform (1905) or criticizing the autocracy for its harsh treatment of laborers (1914), many demonstrating women surely realized that their acts could be viewed as evidence of hostility toward the regime. It is hardly self-evident that women who hurled stones at drinking establishment windows and smashed bottles of spirits hoped that by perpetrating such highly charged acts they were only challenging drinking husbands. It is just as likely and far more credible that they were angry with a government that profited by undermining the family economy they tried so insistently to defend. As Kaplan puts it, "The government was not aiding" women in their endeavors.[94]

It was in February 1917 that Russian women stepped most dramatically onto the modern political stage. By 1917, prohibition had mitigated specific concerns about alcohol's impact on the family economy, but working-class women were no less worried about the difficulty of sustaining their families than they had been in 1905 or 1914. Indeed, when the tsarist government proved unable to provide adequate supplies of bread to the city, women in St. Petersburg unleashed demonstrations leading to the autocracy's demise. Women's objectives during early twentieth-century Russia's manifestations of revolutionary unrest, whether in 1905, 1914, or 1917, deserve more serious scholarly attention than they have received. The fact that there is as yet no adequate investigation into women's goals or patterns of mobilization in February 1917—in spite of the prominent role that they played in those demonstrations—is symptomatic of the scholarly neglect. Future studies of mass protest in Russia during this period must not reflexively dismiss women's potential for political activism. After all, it was women who sewed the banners reading "Down with Autocracy."[95] When women in February marched *for* bread, they necessarily marched *against* ineffective government.

• • •

Revolutionary changes in the government in early twentieth-century Russia gave greater independence and visibility to working-class youth. Judging from their experience with alcohol, youth theoretically subject to the authority of their elders generally did not constitute an autonomous stratum of society in pre-revolutionary Russia.[96] In contrast, the Soviet state empowered working-class youth, calling on them not only to serve as model citizens but also to teach generations tainted by "pre-revolutionary" habits a "new" way to live. But as Gorsuch has shown, youth could "challenge as well as champion" the Soviet state's cultural norms.[97] If the model Komsomolets abstained from alcohol, many working-class youths attended parties centered around the availability of drink, and adults ensured young boys' future inclusion in the laboring community by encouraging them to adopt normal worker behavior, including drinking.

Unlike youth, women, supposedly abstinent, were not empowered by revolution. Despite the revolutionary changes in government, investigation of women's relationship to alcohol suggests a remarkable continuity in the shape of most working-class's lives. The temporary disruption brought about by prohibition aside, before 1914 and in the 1920s women of Russia's working community responded to alcohol's pervasive presence in the working community in a highly consistent way. Although they did not display an actual intolerance for drink per se, they could and did contest the expenditures that their spouses devoted to alcohol when they believed their own household's economy to be in imminent danger. Women pursuing the path to economic well-being did not always find the road clear, obstructed as it sometimes was with husbands intent on celebration, alternate factory gates, meddling crowds, and Katiusha's old overcoat. But their efforts were often rewarded: by reminding her spouse of the family's material needs, a woman could sometimes compel him to relinquish his earnings.

The constrained, individualistic methods by which women defended the family economy were transformed into overt collective action during moments of extreme unrest. By removing the normally fragile assurance of immediate future income, massive general strikes increased the threat that unwise expenditures posed to fragile family economies; moreover, by disrupting the ordinary course of social and political life, the strikes raised the possibility that women's family concerns might be addressed in new and more responsible social agreements. Scholars outside the Russian field have observed that the normally "muffled" voices of women "ring with a startling, sharp clarity" during mass labor actions and that subordinate groups normally absent from the public stage have "so much to say when they finally arrive."[98] Certainly a great deal was "said" when St. Petersburg's working women announced alcohol boycotts and destroyed alcohol supplies during mass labor demonstrations in 1905 and 1914. When working-class women determined that no money should be devoted to drink, they took an extraordinary step that explicitly privileged family goals over men's cultural prerogatives. And by damaging the state's interests through their anti-alcohol actions, they indirectly asserted that government had no right to impede their efforts to feed their families. But however energetically Russia's women sent these messages during rare flashes of labor unrest, their need to resume the use of less overt, individualized, and seasoned techniques for defending the family economy in the 1920s shows that the goals of "female consciousness" did not find substantive expression in the revolutionary state. Women's consistently limited opportunities for socially sanctioned drinking and the alleged threats that drunken women posed to domestic and sexual harmony in working-class communities ensured that women could not become full partners in a distinctly masculine worker culture.

CHAPTER 6

WORKER CULTURE AND REVOLUTIONARY LEGITIMACY

■ In October 1917, the established social order in Russia was uprooted in favor of "workers' power." The revolutionary government's effort to establish and enhance its political legitimacy necessarily continued long after October; that was due in part, as historians have recognized, to the inherent theoretical and practical difficulty of sustaining authority for a workers' government in a predominantly agrarian, peasant land.[1] Yet historians of early twentieth-century Russia have failed to sufficiently appreciate the importance of another, perhaps greater obstacle to the successful perpetuation of a workers' state: a tenacious cultural fault line that ran directly through the revolution's main constituency: urban male workers. Although working-class women played critical roles in early twentieth-century Russia's major manifestations of revolutionary unrest, on a daily basis the main battles over the soul of revolution were waged among working-class men. As expressed in the sharply polarized political discourse of revolutionary Russia's worker activists, two kinds of workers faced each other across a deep cultural divide. One of these worker types, the "rank-and-file" or "backward" worker, has been discussed extensively in the preceding pages. His was a world in which heavy drinking, fighting, womanizing, and cursing were accepted, even esteemed, forms of comportment; he was allegedly uninterested in books and politically apathetic. The "backward" worker's counterpart, the "conscious" or "advanced" worker, is better known to historians of the 1917 Russian revolution: he is understood to have been sober, tidy in dress, sexually restrained, and committed to political and educational improvement.

The stark polarization embedded in the rhetorical construction of "conscious" and "backward" laborers grossly oversimplifies the real possibilities within a range of worker comportment. Applying and interpreting these discursive inventions too literally fails to illuminate not only the murky space between the two extremes but also the worker's facile ability to parry between the world of the "conscious" and the world of the "rank and file." The permeability of the territory separating the two milieus was a critical factor in allowing the workers' revolution to succeed in the first place: workers who did not fit neatly and consistently into either cultural category were vital catalysts in the revolutionary process.

The discursive construction of "advanced" and "rank-and-file" workers was nonetheless fraught with profound political implications, particularly after 1917. Defining working-class culture was, of course, an issue intimately connected with the legitimacy of a workers' state. The cultural models represented by "conscious" and "rank-and-file" workers did reflect, albeit in distorted form, a myriad of behaviors deeply rooted in the Russian working class, and disputes over culture were conducted through the prism of these discursive conventions. In a workers' state, which of these two cultures—that of the "advanced" worker or that of the "rank and file"—could rightfully be endorsed? Which was the "true" workers' culture? Making the correct choice was a political imperative, for a workers' state could not justly endorse an alternative culture, whether it was "bourgeois," "peasant," or some other type.

• • •

Although debates over the appropriate way of life for workers assumed new significance in a workers' state, the essential outlines of the argument were present well before the October revolution. Prior to 1917, publications controlled by labor activists continually reiterated how senseless it was for the worker to waste his wages on an evening of drunkenness when those funds could be committed to books, to the trade union movement, to the aid of striking workers, or to unemployment funds. Labor activists believed that consuming alcohol was inimical to a "conscious" worker's emphasis on reason, that working-class resources could be more profitably directed toward the long-term political interests of Russia's workers. Over and over again, the working-class press urged St. Petersburg's laborers to stop drinking and join the union, to stop reading sensational, gossipy daily newspapers like *Gazeta kopeika* and turn instead to trade union publications.[2]

The personal experience of politically active workers firmly grounded their belief in an inverse relationship between drunkenness and commitment to working-class causes. When "conscious" laborers begged their coworkers to pay union dues or assist the unemployed, shortsighted members of the rank and file reportedly responded as if they did not have ten extra kopeks—though the very same "scoundrels" could be observed spending three to five rubles in the tavern "with pleasure."[3] Workers at San Galli explicitly affirmed activists' convictions that working-class causes suffered because of the money "backward" workers squandered in the tavern: "[It is] better to spend [money] on drink than to pay the union," they maintained.[4] Workers derived tangible benefits from drinking with their friends, as we have seen, but one skeptical laborer could discern no practical advantage in union membership. He would join the union, he declared, when he paid fifty kopeks in dues and received a ruble in return.[5] For activists attempting to gather dues, it was disheartening to see compatriots so happily spending money in the tavern when their requests for support were solidly rebuffed: "50 kopeks is not a joke, brother."[6]

"Advanced" workers also deemed drinking men unreliable allies in strikes and political battles: "For a bottle of vodka [a drinker] is sometimes ready to go against his comrades and to impede their struggle. In case of danger, he is the first to run and the first to betray the common cause of the people."[7] An activist at the Ofenbakher mill complained that drunkenness was a "huge obstacle" to the development of consciousness there; the worker who drank and played hooky from work, he went on, must be "quieter than the water, lower than the grass, and agree to the conditions that the capitalist proposes."[8] A need to remain "lower than the grass" forbade workers' energetic participation in collective action against employers. At least on occasion, the activists' general fear that drinking men were unreliable allies in strikes appears to have been borne out. In 1912, for example, a strike at the Stasiulevich print shop reportedly ended after the administration reached an agreement with workers who had been previously dismissed for drunkenness.[9] For working-class activists, there was no clearer proof that a successful economic and political struggle required a sober working class.

In short, labor activists believed that workers who drank had neither the desire nor the commitment necessary to protest their lot in
life. There was one path out of the worker's "beastly" existence: a
"sober" life and work in the trade union would lead to a "human"
life.[10] An article appearing in *Trezvost' i berezhlivost'* in 1902 noted that
foreign, especially German, experience showed a distinct correlation
between sobriety and worker participation in public life. The more organized the working class, the greater the number of workers who abstained from alcohol and urged their peers to do likewise.[11] "Conscious" workers who wrote memoirs therefore typically included
testimony about the far-reaching changes in personal behavior that
had accompanied any newly acquired political savvy. Representative
are P. A. Tiushin's reminiscences about the growth in his "consciousness": after coming under the influence of "good comrades" at work,
he began to participate in a discussion circle and "completely
changed" his way of life. "I stopped drinking," he reported. "I
stopped being attracted by games of chance and fights."[12] Even if the
conversions described in accounts such as Tiushin's are often exaggerated, it is apparent that many workers altered their personal conduct
in response to growing political consciousness. In other instances,
workers with an aversion to alcohol were inexorably drawn into the
"conscious" world. G. Sharshavin, for example, sought employment in
a place where laborers did not spend their leisure in the tavern but
were interested instead in the "events of the country."[13] It makes sense
that laborers like Sharshavin, who held the diversions commonly pursued by their brethren in disdain, sought out environments more hospitable to their own proclivities. In expecting their comrades to read
books, attend lectures and the theater, and work to improve the situation of the working masses, "advanced" workers supported a nondrinker's sensibilities by demanding alternative uses of time. In the
public view of Russia's labor activists, "consciousness," sobriety, and
progress in the workers' movement went hand in hand. As Mark D.
Steinberg and Stephen Frank have pointed out, labor activists hoped
that all workers would adopt the "conscious" workers' standards of
"cultivation, morality, and . . . political radicalism."[14]

After 1917, the Soviet state incorporated the main tenets of this culture into its official ideology. Since revolutionary leaders of working-
class origin had been reared within a cultural milieu that favored "conscious" behavior, this was only natural.[15] Working-class activists, who
now assumed positions of control within the state apparatus, continued to champion rational, self-disciplined behavior and to maintain

that drunkenness was incompatible with the goal of advancing the interests of workers. The temporary adoption of prohibition during world and civil war and the Soviet state's desire to mitigate the harmful effects of drinking on labor productivity also influenced attitudes toward alcohol in the 1920s, but the continuity between the concerns expressed by working-class activists in pre-revolutionary Russia and the values propagated by the revolutionary state is nonetheless clear. *Rabochii bumazhnik* illustrated in concrete terms how workers who drank could use their funds more wisely: the money Soviet citizens spent on drink in 1928 alone could have more profitably purchased either 720,000 tractors or apartments for 1,200,000 workers. Similarly, *Pechatnyi dvor* asserted that "every kopek" should be spent "rationally and deliberately." In the wake of the "great proletarian revolution," workers must not "foolishly" waste their wages on alcohol.[16] Nor were they to spend time engaged in frivolous pursuits. As previously discussed, worker activists advocated organized, rational leisure activities that emphasized educational improvement and political activism. In his study on leisure patterns among working-class youth, A. G. Kagan helpfully suggested schematic outlines for using one's time sensibly— outlines that plainly did not countenance young workers' frittering away their time and money in the beer hall. Though he left little room for playfulness or spontaneity, N. Amosov explained that the Soviet state was "not against" holidays, only against "senseless" holidays. Instead of "days of savagery, drunkenness, bloody beatings [and] a huge loss of resources and power," he proposed "intelligent relaxation, intelligent entertainments," which would revitalize the worker, restore his strength, and educate him about "the ideas of communism."[17] Reading good books, visiting museums, and attending lectures were means to these goals; drinking decidedly was not.

In its self-conscious promotion of the cultural values of "advanced" workers, the Soviet state purposefully legitimized a way of life that tsarist authorities had often considered revolutionary. Given the close link between "consciousness" and sobriety in the minds of Russia's labor activists, it is hardly surprising that tsarist officialdom had tended to distrust temperate workers, suspecting them of participation in the revolutionary movement. The imperial police, for example, had searched for clues into dangerous political attitudes by studying specific aspects of worker behavior. In questioning a landlady at the turn of the century, one gendarme learned of a well-behaved tenant who did not drink or contemplate marriage. "Aha!" the officer intoned meaningfully, "this means it is necessary to watch him."[18] Dmitri G.

Bulgakovskii expressed the same suspicious attitude toward non-drinkers in his pre-revolutionary short story *Zhizn' Kass'iana*. After witnessing the deleterious effects of drink in the factories, the well-intentioned Kass'ian founds a temperance society at a factory near his village. Kass'ian's activities nevertheless bring him to the attention of authorities, who suspect him of distributing "revolutionary proclamations" among factory workers."[19] Certainly working-class activists repeatedly complained that employers preferred to hire "alcoholics" over "abstainers," since "alcoholics" were less likely to challenge an employer's authority.[20] Factory administrators had not been concerned with drunkenness in the factories, one Bauman claimed, because "of the two evils for production—drunkenness and revolution—the first was nevertheless better than the second."[21]

In tsarist Russia, the perception of temperate workers as troublemakers was pervasive enough that revolutionaries sometimes posed as drunkards in order to evade detection. Fedor S. Tikhomirov, an activist in the textile workers' union, secured factory work by informing the director that he had recently arrived in St. Petersburg from Moscow—after having argued with his wife over a two-week drinking spree.[22] In his memoirs, Skorobogatov recalled his coworker Svistunov, a "first-rate" drunkard. Much to Skorobogatov's surprise, when the revolution came, Svistunov turned out to be the "main ringleader" in the factory. "This underground Bolshevik played the role of the profligate drunkard so wonderfully that a professional actor might envy him!" Skorobogatov enthused.[23]

Whereas tsarist authorities had been suspicious of the motives of workers who remained sober, participated in workers' organizations, and emphasized educational improvement, the Soviet state explicitly endorsed this way of life. The legitimation of a "conscious" way of life was expressed most prominently through the Communist Party and its youth group, organizations designed to represent the culture of the "conscious" in its purest form. In principle, the party was to be composed of "advanced" workers, who were "obliged to serve as an example" for the rest of the population.[24] That intoxicated members could not fulfill this obligation is vividly expressed in stories designed to portray the conduct of conscientious Communists. A 1924 sketch in *Iunyi kozhevnik*, for example, depicted Aleksei, a former drinker who now wishes to join the Komsomol. Aleksei's boss, Pavel, could provide a recommendation but for some reason does not broach the subject. One day, however, Pavel "tests" Aleksei: staggering and carrying a bottle of moonshine into work, he encourages Aleksei to take a swig.

The astonished Aleksei quickly seizes the offensive bottle from his companion, at which point Pavel, laughing, hands over the coveted Komsomol application. In taking resolute action against drunkenness, Aleksei has proven himself worthy of membership in the youth organization. A vignette appearing in *Golos kozhevnika* similarly suggested that drinkers are useless to the party: deep in his heart, the drunken protagonist realizes that "he is not a Komsomolets, not a worker." But there was perhaps no more explicit expression of the party member's responsibility to remain sober than a cartoon appearing in a 1929 issue of *Krasnyi putilovets:* in its depiction of an intoxicated worker vomiting on his membership card, the comic sketch graphically illustrated how the drunken worker "soiled" the party's reputation.[25]

Given the transformation in state power effected in 1917, the legitimation of a previously revolutionary cultural model was an intended, logical outcome. But the import of the new state's cultural predilections was more far-reaching than this. Just as it promoted the values of "advanced" workers as appropriate to life in the Soviet state, Soviet officialdom publicly discarded as wrongheaded the culture of the majority of Russia's laborers. The overwhelming majority of male workers did drink, for what they believed to be sound reasons. Scattered suggestions that modifications in drinking habits might allow alcohol to fit into official culture generally were not very favorably received by the cultural leaders of the revolution. The only difference between "cultured" beer halls and a regular beer hall, L. Zheleznov scoffed, was that cultured establishments had "checkers, chess and newspapers, and beer is sold not in bottles, but in mugs." A certain Fridman agreed that the worker would not "drink less" in cultured establishments than in a simple beer hall.[26] Even when forced to permit renewed alcohol sales and to consent to limited facilities for public drinking, the state's public rejection of rank-and-file values was firm.

Furthermore, in its public discourse, Soviet officialdom denounced the cultural values of workers who did imbibe by equating drunkenness with counterrevolution and drunkards with the enemies of the state—an equation that had its roots in the pre-revolutionary past, when labor activists had associated "alcoholics" with politically passive workers and strikebreakers. The most prominent identification of drinking with counterrevolution is presented by reports on the alcohol pogroms that visited Petrograd in the wake of the Bolshevik coup. A stain on the dignity of revolution, the raids on liquor supplies throughout Petrograd in November and December 1917 were represented as a conspiracy by "bourgeois," "counterrevolutionary," and "monarchist" elements to create disorder among "nonconscious" elements of the Russian working class; true revolutionaries and genuine representatives of the Russian working class—especially Red Guardists—were credited with dispersing the crowds and pouring the offensive liquor into Petrograd's canals.[27] But evidence of the link between alcohol and counterrevolution hardly ends with the untoward events of late 1917. In 1925, *Golos kozhevnika* denounced drunken workers as the *"enemy . . . of the whole working class."* In 1928, the factory paper at Putilov condemned the wayward worker Turkin, who drank and "curse[d] the Communists." According to *Rabochii bumazhnik,* the worker who drank alcohol committed *"a crime"* against "himself, his family, production, and the state." *Krasnovyborzhets* dubbed drunkards "deserters" from "the laboring front"; Kovgankin associated "alcoholism" with "old, petty bourgeois" life. Workers in the beer hall, asserted *Leningradskii metallist,* were "insufficiently educated in the proletarian spirit."[28] When alcohol was linked to crime, counterrevolution, and the worker's class enemies, the cultural values of the working-class rank and file were thereby morally, socially, and politically impugned. Perhaps the most far-reaching statement condemning the behavior of drinking workers was penned by B. S. Kovgankin. "Laborers of the USSR," he asserted, *"do not have the right* to poison their strength, body, and brain—which are needed for collective work, socialist construction, and the proletarian state." Here Kovgankin claimed for the state jurisdiction over the daily disposition of the worker's corporal being. A worker's insistence on rendering anything less was inherently antistate.[29]

• • •

Although the Soviet state was steadfast in publicly asserting the superiority of the "conscious" worker's cultural values, revolutionary leaders in the 1920s were hardly in a position to anoint the "advanced" worker as the sole, or even the primary, representative of cultural propriety. "All workers," writes Stephen Kotkin, "were enveloped in extensive publicity about their importance."[30] The 1917 revolution indeed had been a revolution wrought in the interest of every worker. However negatively the future development of that revolution affected some of its intended beneficiaries, in public discourse and iconography, the ordinary laborer remained an exalted member of the Soviet state. "Backward" though he might be, the rank-and-file worker was still a worker, and the workers' revolutionary victory in 1917 had quite logically led many laborers whose comportment deviated from "conscious" norms to conclude that their own values should, nonetheless, command respect; they believed that they should have a role to play in deciding what behaviors were or were not appropriate to life in a proletarian state. And Russia's "backward" workers determined that the revolution was not endangered by alcohol consumption; if anything, the opposite was true.

Workers did not express this conclusion through strikes, political manifestos, or mass demonstrations but through sustained daily resistance to unwelcome encounters with the officially sanctioned culture of sobriety. This was a highly contextual political arena, one in which challenges to authority were frequently—though not always—indirect or purposely left open to alternative interpretations. Away from work, the working-class rank and file's opposition to the cultural model embodied in the image of the "advanced" worker was manifested in their "improper" celebration of holidays, their refusal to use public space as the new regime intended, and a variety of other forms of passive resistance; at the factory, ordinary laborers expressed their cultural preferences through increased combativeness and appeals to legal rights; in all aspects of their lives, ordinary workers invoked the language of revolution in order to affirm the legitimacy of their own cultural choices.

We have seen that a strong equation between drink and celebration made it "impossible" for many workers in early twentieth-century Russia to celebrate a holiday without drinking and that drinking on revolutionary holidays was a way for workers to sustain festive customs in modified form. But celebrating revolutionary victories with alcohol was also a way for drinking workers to assert the essential legitimacy of their behavior, to deny their critics' charge that drinking was in any way "counterrevolutionary." After all, were they not celebrating May Day, the October Revolution holiday, or production victories? Activists supporting the sober life epitomized in the "advanced" worker disapproved of the rank and file's mode of celebration, but surely not even they could argue that a desire to celebrate was itself inappropriate.

Rank-and-file workers also expressed opposition to the behavioral standards of their "advanced" brethren by refusing to use public leisure space as cultural activists intended. As we have seen, though worker activists had designed workers' clubs to serve as places of "sensible relaxation and amusement for workers," many clubs were frequented by drunken patrons.[31] Workers displayed considerable combativeness about their right to visit cultural institutions while intoxicated. In one case, two metalworkers who had been excluded from the trade union's holiday house occupied the premises, drank vodka, ate, and threatened to shoot anyone who disturbed them. That menacing action was exceptional, but many laborers asserted their right to use the public space provided by the club in ways that "advanced" workers would have deemed inappropriate. In 1925, *Rabochii bumazhnik* observed that drunken workers from the Zinov'ev mill "not infrequently" argued about their right to enter the club; in 1929, *Krasnyi treugol'nik* similarly noted that drunken youths in the club started fights when they were asked to leave.[32] A cartoon published by *Leningradskaia pravda* summed up the situation: as a sad-faced moon looked down on a holiday home and its environs, men drank in the bushes, and a couple sitting on a park bench embraced.[33] Workers continued to claim that their actions were compatible with revolutionary convictions. When the intoxicated Markelov arrived to attend a performance at the club, for example, the ticket collector informed him and his companions that drunken individuals were not permitted in the establishment. "Not allowed?!" Markelov exclaimed, "[but] we are summoned to a new way of life [*byt*]." And then, consoling his friends, Markelov ironically suggested, "[Hiccup] . . . Let's go, friends, we'll [go] drink out of grief."[34] Other forms of passive resistance were also present in working-class diversions. To note but one example, workers acting in dramatic roles involving alcoholic beverages sometimes employed the real thing, "for effect."[35]

A similar struggle to promote and defend values attributed to the "rank and file" was conducted at the workplace. Throughout the early twentieth century, as we have seen, many Russian laborers viewed alcoholic beverages as an integral part of their working lives. We have also seen that both before and after 1917, workers' immediate superiors exhibited little concern about the drinking practices of their subordinates. But more importantly here, in an apparent departure from pre-revolutionary practice, by the 1920s those laborers who were cited for drunkenness at work frequently failed to accept reprimand. Instead they turned on their accusers with profane language, fought with the guards, argued that they were indeed capable of work, or expressed indifference.

In 1929, reminded by coworkers of the large number of recent reprimands for drinking, an employee at Élektrosila shrugged: *"Soviet paperwork accepts anything."* Other workers reprimanded for drunken absenteeism argued that, since deductions for lost time would be duly taken from their pay, their superiors had no reason to complain.[36] Laborers endeavored to rid themselves of their critics by pulling rank. "I have worked here longer than you," one worker retorted to a factory committee delegate, "and I will do what I want."[37] The lack of similar evidence for the pre-revolutionary years—particularly when considered in conjunction with Soviet workers' avowed right to enter the club while intoxicated—suggests that workers in the 1920s were wielding a new assertiveness and self-confidence about their status in society. From their point of view, the revolution had provided them with a means to justify their behavior, even if the puritans of the Social Democratic movement did not approve. For example, the drunken Kol'ka Leshii informed his foreman, "*No one* has the right to remove [me] from work."[38] Although no direct evidence has been encountered to indicate that intoxicated laborers in the 1920s referred explicitly to their legal privileges, surely *Vestnik profsoiuzov* would have had no other reason to observe that "[workers] drink because they don't experience any fear, because Article 47 of the Code of Laws on Labor involuntarily defends their 'interests.'"[39] Some workers even seem to have viewed their willingness to work while drunk or hung over as a concession to their bosses, since labor laws gave the worker "the right to be absent 72 days per year."[40] In a fictional account, when a Komsomol activist approaches Petr Asmolov, who has come to work on unsteady feet, Asmolov explains that he is tardy because he has a headache. Adding that he could just as well have been sick that day, Asmolov suggests that the activist thank him for coming in at all.[41] Although some "backward" workers expressed interest in learning the special skills associated with "cultured" drinking, they "utterly support[ed] and even salut[ed]" their right to drink. For them, drinking was a personal matter of little legitimate concern to the state.[42]

Whether at work or at play, workers in Russia employed the language of revolution in defense of their right to drink. Much as the protagonists in Edward P. Thompson's classic article on the development of time discipline in early modern Europe had learned "to fight, not against time, but about it," by the mid-1920s Russian workers had mastered revolutionary discourse and used it to further their own ends.[43] Many scholars, including David L. Hoffmann, Sheila Fitzpatrick, and Boris I. Kolonitskii, have observed that Soviet citizens exhibited great flexibility in their use of language, that workers could "contest official discourse, subvert intended meanings, and pursue their own interests." In Stephen Kotkin's felicitous phrase, by the 1920s workers had learned to "speak Bolshevik."[44]

In one fictional account, when a worker who has been reprimanded for drunkenness arrives at the dining room for lunch, his friends invite him to join their table by hailing him, "Hey, parasite of production!"[45]

Joking about drunkenness by appropriating the revolution's language clearly made a mockery of the cultural values promoted by the state, and it implied that individuals accepting of drink held more reasonable views. When celebrants at a youth party in 1928 drank toasts "to cultural revolution," the ironic use of language was also apparent.[46] Under normal circumstances, a drink and a toast were signs of agreement, respect, and celebration. This toast took on an entirely different meaning, because drinking and the principles of cultural revolution so obviously contradicted each other. Such a gesture could only have been meant either as a sign of defiance or ridicule or as a recognition of the inability of mere humans to live up to such lofty norms. Yet the satirical use of language made any intention to subvert the wishes of the state relatively easy to deny. Context and tone were as important to expressing meaning as were the words; precisely because of this, the worker's words could be used to profess compliance even when his comportment conflicted with the expectations of the state. In 1924, for example, *Pechatnyi stanok* reported on a conversation in which a worker expressed a preference for state liquor over moonshine out of "patriotic feeling."[47] Surely no one would argue that the money spent in the state shop did not benefit the state. How, then, could anyone question his desire to drink in the first place? Similarly, in a meeting at Krasnyi Treugol'nik, a certain Burilov suggested that "fighters" against alcoholism should "[drink] a bottle a day, drink 30 bottles a month" in order that 30 alcoholics would remain "without vodka."[48] As long as the alcoholics went without, surely there was no harm in others having a bit to drink.

The rank-and-file worker's satirical manipulation of revolutionary language was accompanied by labeling. Just as labor activists called drunkards "enemies" and "counterrevolutionaries," drinking workers conferred counterrevolutionary epithets on their cultural opponents. In a 1926 story printed in *Pechatnik,* Ivan Kapustin's attempts to drink are repeatedly thwarted by his clever wife. Yelling in frustration, he finally condemns her efforts by designating her a "White Guard devil."[49] In a direct challenge to the life of "conscious" workers, drinking companions detected an "intellectual odor" emanating from individuals reluctant to join their drinking circle.[50] An example centering on the issue of attire rather than drink also makes clear the rank and file's linguistic attack on the culture of "advanced" workers. A certain worker at Krasnyi Treugol'nik always came to work "dressed decently" and always changed out of his work clothes before leaving the mill. Other laborers found such an emphasis on cleanliness odd and snickered that this smart dresser had become "infected with bourgeois psychology."[51] The White armies, the intellectuals, and the bourgeoisie—these were the enemies of the revolution and the working class. In thus labeling their cultural opponents, the working-class rank and file asserted that it was the "advanced" worker who represented a way of life alien to a workers' state.

No less than working-class activists, rank-and-file workers saw the 1917 revolution as their victory. As such, they expected their values to command healthy respect in the Soviet state. That some laborers became discouraged with the way the revolution had developed was plainly evident in barroom grumblings overheard by I. Zhiga in the late 1920s. As a group of workers discussed how one of their comrades had been fired—simply for calling the factory director a "clumsy devil"—a young man held forth:

> This friends, is what we have come to. . . . *What kind of workers' power is this*, friends? Huh? Don't talk, don't miss work—and what if I am not in the mood to work? I can't work, and that's it. Am I obligated to unburden my heart? Maybe tomorrow I will shoot myself, or no—I will throw myself in the Neva [River]; but they wouldn't give a damn, right? Let the worker die, right?

A second member of the group agreed. "They have persecuted the worker, completely persecuted [him]," he complained, "and they're all Jews, Jews—now they, the damned [Jews], command everyone. Power is in *their* hands."[52] In the eyes of these companions, something had gone dreadfully wrong with the workers' revolution: the power that should have been invested in the worker had trickled instead into the greedy paws of the factory directors and Jewish intellectuals prominent in the revolutionary leadership. As Sarah Davies has similarly argued of the 1930s, Jews were often associated with the Bolshevik Party, and the Soviet public perceived that power rested not in the people but in "an elite of officials, Jews, and so on."[53] How could workers' power mean anything, if it did not mean that the worker could call the boss "clumsy," skip work when he wanted, or, by implication, get drunk when it suited him?

Many laborers did more to uphold their perceived rights in the workers' state—including, as we have seen, their prerogative to drink—than these comrades who sat complaining in the beer hall. Contestation in the 1920s over drinking practices suggests that rank-and-file workers exhibited more self-confidence about their status in society and greater boldness in meeting everyday challenges to their cultural values than they had before 1917. Whereas laborers in the pre-revolutionary era often avoided leisure institutions such as the theater because of its expense or because their attire was too shabby, workers in the 1920s argued about their right to frequent the club—even if they were intoxicated. Signs of increased combativeness over the right to work while intoxicated have also been mentioned. Prior to the success of the workers' revolution, laborers could neither cite the law in defense of their right to miss work nor employ the language of the state in support of their right to drink. But in the 1920s, they were able to interpret the law to their own advantage, and the language of the revolution became a versatile instrument in a worker's hands. Workers expected Soviet authorities to listen to them, argues Fitzpatrick.[54] In comparison with his pre-revolutionary counterpart, the rank-and-file worker of the 1920s was a more confident figure, more sure of his rights in society, and ready to point to his privileged status as a way to support actions deemed unacceptable by others. According to a 1925 article in *Pravda,* when policemen attempted to evict intoxicated men from public places, the drunkards asserted that no one should "dare to touch" a "citizen of the Soviet state."[55] The victory of a workers' revolution empowered ordinary laborers, enabling them to insist that their values be reckoned with—even if their wishes were not compatible with those of working-class activists. Though the Soviet historians Aleksandr Z. Vakser and V. S. Izmozik did not believe it a healthy phenomenon, they were quite correct in observing that some workers in the 1920s "demanded respect toward their lack of culture [*nekul'-turnost'*]."[56] In effect, the workers' revolution had legitimated two incompatible visions of life. Working-class advocates of both the "sober" world of the "conscious" worker and the "drunken" world of the "rank and file" had in fact made the revolution; proponents of either could legitimately claim that their values were appropriate to life in a workers' state.

• • •

As constituted by labor activists, the "conscious" worker was sober, frugal, purposefully committed to education, and engaged in political life; the "backward" worker was inebriated, wasteful, occupied with mere diversions, and politically short-sighted if not entirely apathetic. Real workers were of course more complicated than this, and the polarized images prominent in revolutionary discourse fail to describe the more ambiguous position of the majority of Russia's laborers.

Though the range of working-class behavior included all of the characteristics attributed to both "conscious" and "backward" laborers, few working individuals exhibited behavior that permanently and incontrovertibly enrolled them in the ranks of the "conscious" or the "rank and file" as discursively defined. In the lives of real workers, elements of both cultural constructs could be expressed simultaneously. For example, to which category should we assign an anonymous worker who voluntarily donated two kopeks in exchange for a book on temperance—but reserved his more valuable twenty-kopek piece for drink? How are we to understand workers who went to the beer hall to "disperse boredom" after attending a lecture? What is to be made of the "old men and drunkards" who read an upstanding labor publication like *Rabochaia mysl'*? Or the fictional protagonist who sleeps "like an innocent child" after he "consciously suggest[s]" putting names of frequent absentees on the factory blackboard—only to find his own name heading the list posted the following morning?[57] And where does comrade Paranin belong, whose only expressed reason for leading a sober life had nothing to do with his political attitudes but merely reflected his desire to save money?[58] When one Khaidin suggested that a Soviet dining hall offer beer *and* books, L. Sokolovskii asked rhetorically, "Where is the logic here . . . ? Are tar and honey compatible in one dish?"[59] Though it would not be the answer for which Sokolovskii hoped, the behavior of many laborers suggests that they found nothing particularly odd about such a concoction. In their everyday lives, Russia's workers rarely acknowledged that there was anything at all strange about their penchant for mixing cultural practices attributed to divergent sectors of the working class.

Just as many women and children did not conform to the image of abstinence reflected in the discourse of working men, many workers who might be considered "advanced" by virtue of their political attitudes, reading choices, dress, or other behavioral characteristics did not maintain the temperate life publicly championed by labor activists. Many did not even attempt to do so. When Komsomol youth at the Morozov mill were encouraged to combat drinking, smoking, and cursing, they demurred: "Is this really for us to do?" or "I'd like to reform, but I can't."[60] At the Lenin mill, the "majority" of youths on the club board reportedly used the facility for drinking themselves.[61] Some of the same activists who spoke in public meetings against drunkenness and smoking took up those very vices upon adjournment; others assured rank-and-file workers that "cultured" drinking was "not too bad" [*nichego*].[62] One Sobolev, not only a long-standing member of the party but also a recipient of the Order of the Red Banner, puzzled aloud during a meeting that touched upon drinking, "But who among us doesn't drink?"[63]

Workers who drank but otherwise "fulfilled the criteria of 'consciousness'" thus greatly resembled "mass" workers in their ability to take what they wanted from the revolution while dispensing with the rest.[64] The comportment of actual workers, whether advanced or backward, fell along a hazy and highly flexible continuum. And yet the implications of drinking by advanced workers were not so nebulous. If drinking women posed a potential threat to a male-dominated worker culture, an advanced worker's intoxication posed a potential threat to the integrity of the revolution. Indeed, the "advanced" worker who periodically imbibed alcohol arguably posed a greater danger to revolutionary principles than did the "backward" worker who only intermittently devoted his attention to books. In theory, the "conscious" worker was distinguished by everything from political attitudes to clean fingernails. Judging by the attention paid to drunkenness, however, sobriety was one of the more important indications of "consciousness." Many worker activists may not have believed that their enjoyment of a "couple of beers" compromised the workers' revolution. Whatever they thought, though, the "revolution," in its publicly idealized form, was endangered by their comportment. Whether one considers drink or other important areas of cultural life, disparity between the actual revolutionary course and the ways in which "revolution" is idealized in discourse can have important consequences, as the events of 1991 clearly remind us. When public discussion becomes too patently at odds with social, political, and economic life, something has to change.

At the same time, if early twentieth-century workers had not easily combined elements of working-class life that were incongruent with discursive conventions, the revolution of 1917 may not have succeeded in the first place. Just as workers found it natural to merge elements of "consciousness" with elements of "backwardness," they also found it relatively easy to emphasize adherence to the values of one milieu or the other, contingent upon the circumstances in which they found themselves.[65] At critical junctures in the political life of pre-revolutionary Russia, laborers who oscillated between diverse segments of the working class appear to have emerged as key arbiters in the struggle for power. As Wynn has argued, workers who were not loyal members of working-class organizations "gave the revolutionary movement its power" during general strikes in 1905.[66] Among these workers were envoys like the baker Leshka Krasil'shchikov, who reportedly spent his time at the turn of the century drinking, whoring, and playing billiards. Nothing in Krasil'shchikov's earlier, "backward" life seems to have foreshadowed the role he would play as one of the "fighters" in 1905, when Bloody Sunday compelled him to urge his former drinking buddies and card-playing companions to shed their image as "drunkards [and] riff-raff, for whom life—real life—is inaccessible."[67] In his efforts, Krasil'shchikov was joined by his fellow baker, Pskovskii. Tired of his "swinish" way of life, Pskovskii "went out on strike and didn't want to drink at all." "Enough," Pskovskii declared, "I have drunk enough, [and] it is time to come to my senses."[68] Within the political context of early twentieth-century Russia, Krasil'shchikov, Pskovskii, and many other unnamed laborers modified their conduct as a way to demonstrate their personal support for a new social charter that would incorporate greater respect for workers. Particularly between 1905 and 1907, workers intermittently abandoned drink in order to deprive the government of revenue and to maintain "revolutionary discipline" during strikes; temporary vows of abstinence were enforced by the members of individual work shops, who voted to fine drunken workers in favor of strike committees or the unemployed.[69] During general strikes in 1905 and 1914, huge numbers of workers stopped drinking and closed the taverns in order to signal their deep dissatisfaction with the tsarist regime. As demonstrators in 1914 proceeded down the streets of Russia's capital city, they closed and destroyed establishments selling alcohol; in at least one symbolically suggestive case, boxes of beer were used to construct barricades.[70] The sheer number of individuals involved and the frequently violent conduct of demonstrators clearly affirm that "sober" labor activists alone could not have been responsible for the initiatives against drinking establishments. In mobilizing workers who normally did imbibe to undertake actions like this, the arguments of individuals like Krasil'shchikov and Pskovskii were, in all likelihood, more convincing than the entreaties of unfamiliar nondrinking workers could ever be.

Recognizing both the vital political role performed by unorganized workers and the difficulty of casting laborers like Krasil'shchikov and Pskovskii into an exclusively "conscious" (or "backward") mold, Joan Neuberger has recently advanced the concept of "hooliganism" to help explain the dynamics of working-class protest in Russia—particularly the strikes that engulfed St. Petersburg in the summer of 1914. Though familiarity with hooligan codes of conduct assists in illuminating the cultural significance of overturned trams, thrown rocks, and an escalation in political violence, as Neuberger argues, other aspects of worker protest remain unbounded by hooliganism.[71] "Hooligans," for example, were associated with drunkenness, but—whether in 1914 or earlier in the century—workers employed sobriety as a weapon against the tsarist state. Like "hooligans," workers threw rocks; unlike "hooligans," many workers renounced alcohol.[72] Thus, whether historians discuss working-class comportment in terms of "consciousness," "backwardness," or "hooliganism," most laborers clearly did not adopt any of these codes of conduct in full; rather, they displayed a remarkable ability to pick and choose from the behavioral menus before them, a talent that compels historians to continue seeking more satisfying ways to make "tar and honey" compatible in one dish.

A healthy appreciation for context will be fundamental to any better understanding of working-class comportment. The commitment to sobriety displayed by workers during social upheavals in tsarist Russia was clearly governed by peculiar circumstances, and many workers who gave up drink in support of political demands—in 1905, in 1914, or during a strike—undoubtedly had no intention of changing their drinking practices permanently. Even in the heady days of 1905, Putilov workers famed for their revolutionary enthusiasm agreed only to renounce drink for a specific period of time.[73] Whether Krasil'shchikov and Pskovskii again took up drink may never be known—but thousands of workers clearly reverted to their old ways. Furthermore, workers did not continue to use collective sobriety as a political weapon against the Soviet state, notwithstanding the Soviet government's resumption of the old tsarist government's monopoly on spirits. In the 1920s, it was drunkenness—not sobriety—that indicated workers' dissatisfaction with certain elements of state governance. Collective manifestations of political opposition that were exhibited by workers (via sobriety) in the pre-revolutionary era were replaced in the 1920s by acts of (drunken) defiance that were often more oblique, more individualistic.

To explain these modifications in worker behavior, we should return for a moment to the alcohol boycotts of 1905 and 1914 and to Scott's theory of domination and resistance. Scott argues convincingly that truly revolutionary situations are rare; most political protest is thus based on the "realistic expectation" that the "central features" of domination in a given society "will remain intact."[74] Scott's work would suggest that St. Petersburg's workers adopted alcohol boycotts as a method of political protest during an extraordinary times, when the state's inability to maintain order in the street plainly demonstrated that tsarist authority was highly vulnerable. In that situation, uncharacteristic acts of overt collective protest made sense to workers, because they perceived a real and rare opportunity to recast the workers' place in Russian society. By the mid-1920s, however, it is quite likely that Russia's workers were adopting the more common forms of protest that are the focus of Scott's study. In other words, Russian workers no longer believed that they were participants in a revolutionary situation: they knew that a civil war had been fought and won, and they now assumed that the Soviet state was there to stay. Moreover, workers' demands were purported to be an integral part of the Soviet state's own political agenda. As Jeffrey J. Rossman has similarly observed, the claim that Soviet Russia was a workers' state gave workers "motive to express dissatisfaction when they perceived that their interests had been betrayed."[75] In this political context, resisting unwelcome portions of the state's cultural prescription made more sense than did collective attempts to undermine the whole system.

• • •

The October revolution empowered Russian workers—though not always in ways its leaders had anticipated. Throughout the early twentieth century, as we have seen, two conflicting visions of working-class culture were expressed in Russia's highly polarized political discourse. In practice, the line between the culture of "advanced" workers (with its emphasis on educational improvement, sensible leisure, and sobriety) and the culture of "rank-and-file" workers (with its acceptance of drunkenness and other "coarse" behaviors) was a fluid one. In their individual comportment, workers often exhibited elements of both cultures or alternated between them, depending on the circumstances in which they found themselves. Indeed, workers who oscillated between cultural extremes proved critical in mobilizing the working community during Russia's major political crises. But the existence of two distinct cultural models—both of which encompassed behaviors indigenous to the working class—carried profound political implications, because these models ultimately offered conflicting interpretations of the workers' revolution. Perhaps it was precisely because large segments of the working population had adopted sobriety as a political weapon against the tsarist state that working-class activists in the 1920s seemed astonished to find even the "hereditary, esteemed proletariat" in the lines outside liquor outlets.[76] "What is this, comrades!" implored an article appearing in *Verstatka*. "Is this really the life of the worker in the Soviet state? From the workbench to the beer hall, from the beer hall to the workbench, and . . . [that's] all!"[77] Yet the "sensible" culture represented in the construction of the "advanced" worker was just as incomprehensible to those many laborers who found alcoholic beverages an indispensable element of sociability, celebration, and physical toil—that is, an essential element of their very identity as workers.

In the 1920s, many common laborers defended their drinking practices with an assertive confidence about the worker's new place in society, employing the language of revolution in defense of their interests. The victory of a workers' revolution ultimately empowered both rank-and-file and advanced workers, for proponents of either cultural model could legitimately argue that a workers' state should respect their fundamental values. The inherent conflict between working-class cultural strata revealed through the study of drink does not mean that the Soviet state was doomed to fail from its very inception. The tension between two incompatible visions of working-class culture and the legitimacy that both could claim does mean, however, that building a workers' state was destined to be a far more difficult task than any of its architects had imagined.

CONCLUSION

■ In 1927, L. A. Gabinov observed that drunkenness was so embedded in working-class life that "even the October revolution . . . was not able to destroy it."[1] As far as it went, his statement was certainly correct. By the end of the 1920s, workers' alcohol consumption again rivaled prewar norms, despite the period of prohibition and the inauguration of a new political apparatus. But workers' use of alcohol directs us to deeper threads of continuity running through the cultural life of early twentieth-century Russia. In three broad areas, Russian culture proved particularly impervious to revolutionary change: in the meaning attached to cultural symbols, in leisure forms and associations, and in gender relations.

The durability and utility of cultural symbols, especially those connected with religious belief, has been noted in other contexts. Steinberg, for example, has shown that working-class authors—many of whom had no personal attachment to theism—used metaphors of suffering and redemption to explain workers' plight and social salvation. Bernice Glatzer Rosenthal has similarly pointed to the "scientific" Bolsheviks' use of occult symbols to express their ideas in ways that would resonate with the Russian population.[2] Even beyond religious imagery, though, the social life of Soviet Russia remained heavily imbued with cultural symbols inherited from the pre-revolutionary past.

Many symbolic meanings that workers had attached to alcohol prior to revolution reemerged intact, even after years of world war, prohibition, revolution, and civil war. Before and after 1917, workingmen viewed alcohol as a mechanism for distinguishing the masculine from the feminine realm, the world of adults from that of children, and "real workers" from interlopers. Sociability, goodwill, and inclusion in the working community were all signified though men's sharing of drink. It is certainly understandable that workers wanted a way to express something as important as friendship toward others; it is equally understandable that they would turn to already familiar ways to do this. The tenacity of cultural symbols in the early Soviet period suggests that the icons retained after the more recent revolution in 1991 should perhaps not seem so incongruous. Lenin's continued presence outside Smol'ny, for example, could still symbolize his diligent work on Russia's behalf; shiny buttons sporting hammer and sickle could likewise express pride in Soviet Russia's imperial might, even though armbands now identified recruits as members of the armed forces of "Russia." The resonance of cultural symbols is stubbornly impervious to change; they do not yield easily to mere revolution.

Other significant strands of continuity have also emerged in the course of this study. Just as the pre-revolutionary symbolic meanings of drink reemerged in the Soviet era, the basic character of pre-revolutionary leisure and sociability also resurfaced in the 1920s. Many laborers did find it advantageous to adjust to the revolutionary calendar imposed by the Soviet state, but drink steadfastly retained its festive connotations, for traditional as well as for revolutionary holidays and, albeit less frequently, for women as well as for men. And although certain leisure forms—cinema and the theater, for example—became more accessible to the victorious proletariat, many old patterns of sociability were not displaced, despite the state's obvious disapproval of them.

The preservation of pre-revolutionary leisure forms suggests that the relationship between state and society by the late 1920s had been shaped through protracted negotiation and compromise. The modus vivendi, always subject to additional arbitration, was not perfect for either side, but likely it did meet both parties' most urgent concerns. The state concentrated its attention on transforming culture where it seemed most imperative to revolutionary success: in Russia's factories. Workers in turn retained a great deal of autonomy in the time they spent away from work. Since the history of leisure in Russia has been little explored, it is difficult to say exactly how the population envisioned this trade-off. The social history of drink nonetheless suggests that it is in recreation, diversion, and entertainment that historians might expect to find the greatest affinities in Soviet and pre-revolutionary traditions.[3]

Any study of alcohol's societal role naturally produces a highly gendered view of life. In this realm, some particularly striking continuities emerge. This study reinforces the findings of several recent investigations that have emphasized the Russian working class's "masculine" construction, both in practice and in the historical understanding of Russian labor.[4] Whether before or after 1917—and despite the Bolsheviks' theoretical emphasis on the primacy of class as the key to social identity—sex consistently proved an important determinant of experience and relative power in Russia's working communities. In the 1920s, both rank-and-file workingmen and the Soviet state implied that women did not quite fit into "worker" culture. Most laboring men did not really consider women workers at all, purposely excluding them from their conception of "worker" and from male camaraderie. Even after the Soviet state ensured that public drinking establishments were stripped of many pre-revolutionary attractions, male workers continued to carve out distinctive masculine space in the tavern and its alternatives; women continued to avoid or feel uncomfortable in this atmosphere. In innumerable ways, the Soviet state, too, sent subtle messages that it valued "feminine" attributes less than "masculine" qualities: the Zhenotdel was marginalized within the Communist Party; the revolution of February 1917 was depicted as the less important, "feminine" revolution, whereas "masculine" status was reserved for "Great October."[5] Women useful to Soviet society, such as Dasha, the heroine of Fyodor V. Gladkov's novel Cement, often assumed masculine characteristics: she wore a "man's blouse" and her appearance was "not womanly."[6] Instead of reaping benefits from the workers' revolution, the workers who were women coped much as they had before: coaxing and cajoling without substantively challenging male prerogatives.

Notwithstanding the strong continuities expressed through cultural symbols, leisure forms, and gender relations, Gabinov's remarks do not tell the whole story—for the revolution of 1917 also changed life in important ways. Indeed, the languid pace of cultural change and workers' dogged determination to hold onto favored traditions make any disjunctures in revolutionary Russia all the more intriguing.

The revolution of 1917 did not destroy pre-revolutionary leisure forms, but it did significantly impact work and working relationships. As the production-conscious state endeavored to eradicate alcohol from the labor process, the ritual drinking that had been closely integrated into the life of pre-revolutionary workshops dissipated. In the 1920s, workingmen continued to proclaim the physically beneficial effects of alcohol and to labor under the influence, but their consumption of alcoholic beverages was increasingly accomplished outside the factory. Previous signs of reciprocity and equality among workers, along with the signs of respect between workers and their supervisors, faded. In the workers' state, respect for laborers was assumed, expressions of hierarchy no longer made sense, and workers availed themselves of new opportunities for job placement and training. In addition, as drinking customs—and, presumably, other nonproductive behaviors—were exiled from the factory, the distinction between work and leisure became more pronounced than it had been in pre-revolutionary days. This separation, already well under way in other industrialized countries, was given a definite shove by the Bolshevik state's emphasis on economic modernization. Perhaps the concentration of large, modern factories in Leningrad made these processes more advanced there than they were elsewhere in the Soviet Union by the late 1920s, but significant changes in work must be anticipated in other industrial areas as well.

Furthermore, even though the overall framework of gender relations remained intact throughout the revolutionary years, in the 1920s a significant fault developed in that once-sturdier frame. Investigations that emphasize the Soviet state's "masculine" character arrive at their conclusions through consideration of state policy, administration, and the law. In contrast, investigation of workers' drinking practices suggests that Soviet values posed a substantial threat to many workingmen's own conceptions of masculinity. Indeed, when viewed from the perspective of rank-and-file workingmen, the revolution of 1917 may not have seemed like a "masculine" revolution at all, but an excessively "feminine" one.

In a broader European context, some scholars have suggested that there was a "crisis in masculinity" in the years surrounding World War I.[7] Although the gendered aspects of the world war have not been similarly explored by historians of Russia, workers' attitudes toward drink suggest that in revolutionary Russia, masculinity as most male workers understood it was under attack from "feminine" intellectuals who admonished laboring men to behave in "feminine" ways.[8] According to labor activists, working-class men should no longer drink, curse, fight, or womanize. The Soviet state prohibited and discouraged the public consumption of strong spirits—the only appropriate "masculine" beverage. Instead, it urged working-class men to support "feminine" abstinence or to satisfy their misplaced desire for alcohol with "weak, women's" drink. Prior to 1914, the omnipresent tavern had provided workingmen with a distinctive masculine forum. In the 1920s, such space as remained was severely limited and continuously subject to erratic suppression by the state. Unlike proponents of the labor movement in other countries, worker activists in Russia never successfully advanced the idea that drunkenness was "unmanly."[9] On the contrary, the Soviet state's cultural priorities potentially threatened rank-and-file working men with emasculation.

With such a fundamental, and a formerly empowering, part of their identity at stake, it is no wonder that many male workers attempted to extend their masculine space, as best they could, into dining halls and clubs. Many scholars have commented on the trend toward cultural conservatism and the restoration of "traditional" values in the 1930s. By the early 1930s, the Soviet state may have been similarly compelled to give workers their "masculinity" back. As activists in the 1930s no longer badgered men about drinking, as women were encouraged to procreate and men were relieved of burdensome paternity suits, many rank-and-file working-class men and women probably believed that gender roles had been restored to their proper relationship.[10] Perhaps, too, it is no accident that the state seems to have accepted cultural values that workingmen more commonly considered masculine in the 1930s and 1940s, years that consumed Russia's men in terror and in war.[11]

Finally, if the role of drink was a matter of political disagreement between different strata of the working class throughout the revolutionary era, the significance and implications of such disagreement mushroomed to new heights after 1917. Russia's workers understood that the 1917 revolution had been accomplished in their name, but they were not a uniform mass that consistently experienced common problems, dreams, and goals. Thus, this study strongly underscores the contested meanings attributed to the 1917 revolution and demonstrates how Russian laborers interpreted and vigorously endeavored to capitalize upon their revolutionary victory.

Their efforts were indeed vigorous. Though there is little scholarly disagreement that the revolutionary state energetically—if sometimes haphazardly—promoted its objectives, the actions of rank-and-file workers are often seen as more defensive, reactive, and cowered. For example, Hoffmann's study of Moscow acknowledges that peasant in-migrants creatively blended elements of "peasant" and "urban" culture. His concentration, however, is on migrants' retention and adaptation of rural institutions, especially village networks and artels. Peasant adoption of urban cultural practices, he concludes, was "superficial and ostentatious." Although workers' drinking practices reflect a similar blending of cultural practices, the blending is more progressive than Hoffmann's study of peasant migrants suggests. St. Petersburg's workers eagerly adopted new cultural practices—when they believed them to be advantageous. Similarly, although many scholars share my interest in various uses and understandings of revolutionary language, workers' proactive stance vis-à-vis drink suggests that they were not always as servile or unquestioning as Orlando Figes has recently argued. Since workers who "spoke Bolshevik" often advocated a view of revolution despised by the state, they were even more assertive than Kotkin's study of Magnitogorsk would allow. Nor did workers have particularly limited goals—the upward economic mobility encapsulated by Fitzpatrick, for example.[12] Having a better job would not be good enough; laborers also demanded that their customs be treated with integrity and respect. Rank-and-file workers realized that the 1917 revolution significantly changed their lives by providing them with a powerful legitimating tool. That tool was not fail-safe, but they did consistently pick it up to skillfully blend the cultural models before them, to accept the advantages that revolution brought them, to resist its most bothersome impositions, to wield it as the justification for their actions.

It may be that workers' sense of revolutionary entitlement was particularly pronounced in St. Petersburg, where laborers regularly distinguished themselves by their support for opposition movements. St. Petersburg's workers, initiators of revolution, possessed a keen sense of their "proprietorial" right to the 1917 revolution, of their right to "reprimand" the regime.[13] But if St. Petersburg was distinguished by its frequent support for the opposition, it was no less noted for its reputation as Russia's "most cultured city."[14] Indeed, there is some evidence that anti-alcohol efforts of the late 1920s were relatively energetic in Leningrad. Certainly Larin lamented a more dire predicament in Moscow. The city soviet there, Larin stormed, took an "erroneous position" in resisting efforts to prohibit alcohol trade on holidays. "[In Moscow] 'the right to drunkenness,'" he bitterly intoned, "apparently is interpreted as one of the essential rights of the Soviet proletariat."[15] Of course, we have seen that many laborers in Leningrad also held that attitude, but it is nonetheless possible that the promotion of sobriety was relatively vigorous in that city. If the anti-alcohol movement confronted grave difficulties in Leningrad, a city with a proud cultural history and rich in its cultural institutions, a city whose proletariat was particularly self-conscious and of a "higher level" than workers living elsewhere in the Soviet state, it likely confronted such difficulties everywhere.[16]

The state's "Great Retreat" in alcohol policy thus anticipated the other retreats still to come. Forced to back down only partly because of its dependence on revenue from the drink trade, the state was also compelled to abdicate certain aspects of its cultural prescription because of workers' implacable opposition to them. Of course, because of the state's administrative power, in certain respects it prevailed and workers retreated or compromised, but the tenacity and success with which rank-and-file workers advocated their position helped to produce the remarkable blend of cultural tradition and innovation characteristic of early Soviet Russia.

CHRONOLOGY

1894		Disruptive public drunkenness punishable by up to seven days arrest and twenty-five-ruble fine.
1898		Government liquor monopoly established in St. Petersburg.
1906		Disruptive public drunkenness punishable by up to three days arrest and ten-ruble fine.
1914	July	Tsar bans sale of vodka during mobilization (except in first-class restaurants).
	August	Tsar extends ban on vodka sale until conclusion of war.
	December	St. Petersburg governor extends ban on vodka to beer and wine.
1917	March	Provisional Government prohibits sale of drink with more than 1.5 percent alcohol by volume; wines containing up to 12 percent alcohol content permitted; violations punishable by up to one year imprisonment and two-thousand-ruble fine.
	November	Military-Revolutionary Committee bans production of alcohol.
1918	May	All-Union Executive Committee (VTsIK) makes distillation of moonshine punishable by no less than ten years in prison at forced labor.
	October	Liquor stocks nationalized.
1919	December	Sovnarkom prohibits distillation or sale of beverages containing over 1.5 percent alcohol by

volume; sale of wines containing up to 12 percent alcohol content permitted; violations punishable by no less than five years in prison at forced labor; public drunkenness punishable by one year in prison.

1921	August	Sale of wine up to 14 percent alcohol content legalized.
	December	Sale of wine up to 20 percent alcohol content legalized; sale of wine for use in dining halls, restaurants, etc., legalized.
1922	February	Sale of beer legalized.
	June	Production of moonshine for personal use legalized.
1923		Production of moonshine criminalized.
	January	Sale of liqueurs up to 20 percent alcohol content legalized.
1924	December	Sale of liqueurs and vodka up to 30 percent alcohol content legalized.
1925	October	Sale of full-strength (40%) vodka resumes.
1926		Public drunkenness punished by up to three-ruble fine.
	March	Sale of all alcoholic beverages allowed in restaurants, dining halls, and buffets, subject to approval.
	September	Sovnarkom calls for stronger cultural measures against alcoholism, approves compulsory treatment for "socially dangerous alcoholics."
1927	January	Production of moonshine for personal use allowed.
	March	Sovnarkom prohibits sale of spirits to minors, to intoxicated individuals, and in cultural establishments; permits local government to prohibit sale of spirits during holidays and "nonwork time"; allows limitations of sale in factory districts. Applies to spirits only.
	May	VTsIK and Sovnarkom call on local soviets to create anti-alcohol commissions (future cells of the OBSA).

1928	January	Preparation of moonshine for personal use prohibited.
	February	OBSA established in Moscow.
	August	Leningrad Soviet prohibits sale of spirits on holidays.
	November	All-Union Soviet of Anti-Alcohol Societies (VSPO) established.
1929	January	Sovnarkom prohibits new places of vodka sale in industrial districts; prohibits sale of all alcoholic beverages on holidays, on paydays, and in cultural establishments; prohibits sale of alcoholic drinks to minors and intoxicated individuals; prohibits alcohol ads; permits local soviets to prohibit the sale of alcoholic beverages.
	May	Sale of alcoholic beverages prohibited on revolutionary holidays; sale on paydays in factory districts prohibited (up to two days per month).
1930		Larin and Deichman removed from the OBSA board; VSPO liquidated; OBSA instructed to concentrate on enlightenment work.

NOTES

INTRODUCTION

1. Katerina Clark, *Petersburg: Crucible of Cultural Revolution* (Cambridge, Mass., 1995). Also see Dorothy Atkinson, *The End of the Russian Land Commune, 1905–1930* (Stanford, Calif., 1983); Maria Carlson, *"No Religion Higher than Truth": A History of the Theosophical Movement in Russia, 1875–1922* (Princeton, N.J., 1993); Choitali Chatterjee, "Celebrating Women: International Women's Day in Russia and the Soviet Union, 1909–1939," Ph.D. diss., Indiana University, 1995; Heather J. Coleman, "The Most Dangerous Sect: Baptists in Tsarist and Soviet Russia, 1905–1929," Ph.D. diss., University of Illinois, 1998; Orlando Figes: *A People's Tragedy: A History of the Russian Revolution* (New York, 1997); Catriona Kelly and David Shepherd, eds., *Constructing Russian Culture in the Age of Revolution, 1881–1940* (Oxford, 1998); Richard Stites, *Russian Popular Culture: Entertainment and Society since 1900* (Cambridge, England, 1992); Richard Stites, *The Women's Liberation Movement in Russia: Feminism, Nihilism, and Bolshevism, 1860–1930* (Princeton, N.J., 1978); Mark D. Steinberg, "Workers on the Cross: Religious Imagination in the Writings of Russian Workers, 1910–1924," *Russian Review* 53 (April 1994): 213–39; Thomas Reed Trice, "The 'Body Politic': Russian Funerals and the Politics of Representation, 1841–1921," Ph.D. diss., University of Illinois, Urbana, 1998. Similar research is in progress.

2. Clark, *Petersburg,* 242.

3. Nicholas S. Timasheff, *The Great Retreat: The Growth and Decline of Communism in Russia* (New York, 1946).

4. Barbara Alpern Engel, *Between the Fields and the City: Women, Work, and Family in Russia, 1861–1914* (Cambridge, England, 1996); Anne E. Gorsuch, "'A Woman Is Not a Man': The Culture of Gender and Generation in Soviet Russia, 1921–1928," *Slavic Review* 55 (fall 1996): 636–60; Diane P. Koenker, "Men against Women on the Shop Floor in Early Soviet Russia: Gender and Class in the Socialist Workplace," *American Historical Review* 100 (December 1995): 1438–64; Joan Neuberger, *Hooliganism: Crime, Culture, and Power in St. Petersburg, 1900–1914* (Berkeley, Calif., 1993); and Charters Wynn, *Workers, Strikes and Pogroms: The Donbass-Dnepr Bend in*

Late Imperial Russia, 1870–1905 (Princeton, N.J., 1992).

5. Brian Harrison, *Drink and the Victorians: The Temperance Question in England, 1815–1872* (Pittsburgh, 1972), 366; Gareth Stedman Jones, *Languages of Class: Studies in English Working Class History, 1832–1982* (Cambridge, England, 1987), 209, 215, 228; W. Scott Haine, *The World of the Paris Café: Sociability among the French Working Class, 1789–1914* (Baltimore, 1996); Beverly Ann Tlusty, "The Devil's Altar: The Tavern and Society in Early Modern Augsburg," Ph.D. diss., University of Maryland, 1994; James S. Roberts, *Drink, Temperance and the Working Class in Nineteenth-Century Germany* (Boston, 1984); and Lynn Abrams, *Workers' Culture in Imperial Germany: Leisure and Recreation in the Rhineland and Westphalia* (New York, 1992).

6. Jean-Charles Sournia, *A History of Alcoholism* (Oxford, 1990), 154, 150; Patricia E. Prestwich, *Drink and the Politics of Social Reform: Antialcoholism in France since 1870* (Palo Alto, Calif., 1988), 4; Patricia E. Prestwich, "The Regulation of Drinking: New Work in the Social History of Alcohol," *Contemporary Drug Problems* 21 (fall 1994): 367; Dwight B. Heath, "Drinking and Drunkenness in Transcultural Perspective," *Transcultural Psychiatric Research* 1 (1986): 9.

7. David Christian, *Living Water: Vodka and Russian Society on the Eve of Emancipation* (Oxford, 1990), chap. 3; N. S. Polishchuk, "Obychai fabrichno-zavodskikh rabochikh Evropeiskoi Rossii, sviazannye s proizvodstvom i proizvodstvennymi otnosheniiami (konets XIX–nachalo XX v.)," *Étnografich-eskoe obozrenie* 1 (1994): 73–90. Kathy S. Transchel's recent dissertation tends to follow paths laid out by Christian and others. "Under the Influence: Drinking, Temperance, and Cultural Revolution in Russia, 1900–1932," University of North Carolina, Chapel Hill, 1996. W. Arthur McKee analyzes political and professional discourse about alcohol in "Taming the Green Serpent: Alcoholism, Autocracy, and Russian Society, 1890–1917," Ph.D. diss., University of California, Berkeley, 1997. To a greater or lesser extent, the perception that drinking in Russia was a problem underlies the following works: Vladimir G. Treml, *Alcohol in the USSR: A Statistical Study* (Durham, N.C., 1982); Boris M. Segal, *Russian Drinking: Use and Abuse of Alcohol in Pre-Revolutionary Russia* (New Brunswick, N.J., 1987); Boris M. Segal, *The Drunken Society: Alcohol Abuse and Alcoholism in the Soviet Union: A Comparative Study* (New York, 1990); Patricia Herlihy, "'Joy of the Rus'': Rites and Rituals of Russian Drinking," *Russian Review* 50 (April 1991): 131–47; George Snow, "Socialism, Alcoholism and the Russian Working Class before 1917," in Susanna Barrows and Robin Room, eds., *Drinking: Behavior and Belief in Modern History* (Berkeley, Calif., 1991), 243–64.

8. The city under investigation was named St. Petersburg until 1914, Petrograd from 1914 to 1924, Leningrad from 1924 to 1991, and St. Petersburg from 1991 to the present. In general, I adopt the name St. Petersburg, reserving Petrograd or Leningrad to refer specifically to the periods in which the city bore those names.

9. Andrey Biely, *St. Petersburg*, trans. John Cournos (New York, 1987), xxii, 75. On the Petersburg "myth," see Clark, *Petersburg*.

CHAPTER 1: ALCOHOL AND THE STATE

1. Robert Johnson, *Peasant and Proletarian: The Working Class of Moscow in the Late Nineteenth Century* (New Brunswick, N.J., 1979), chap. 3; Engel, *Between the Fields,* 134–35.

2. Laura Engelstein, *The Keys to Happiness: Sex and the Search for Modernity in Fin-de-Siècle Russia* (Ithaca, N.Y., 1992), 128, 160–62, 276, 298, 360, 369. On prostitution in prerevolutionary Russia, see Laurie Bernstein, *Sonya's Daughters: Prostitutes and Their Regulation in Imperial Russia* (Berkeley, Calif., 1995). On youthful "deviance" consult Neuberger, *Hooliganism.*

3. P. S. Alekseev, *Chem pomoch' velikomu goriu? Kak ostanovit' p'ianstvo?* (Moscow, 1906), 25–26; *Kak u nas chestvuiut imeninnika i ponimaiut usopshago* (St. Petersburg, 1907), 30; *O tainoi prodazhe vina* (St. Petersburg, n.d.), 4.

4. R. E. F. Smith and David Christian, *Bread and Salt: A Social and Economic History of Food and Drink in Russia* (Cambridge, England, 1984), 302.

5. *Gazeta kopeika,* 16 March 1913, 3; and I. Romashkov, *Kak smotrit sam narod na p'ianstvo* (Moscow, 1908), 3.

6. Prestwich, *Drink,* 284; Thomas Brennan, "Towards the Cultural History of Alcohol in France," *Journal of Social History* 23 (fall 1989): 82.

7. B. F. Didrikhson, *Alkogolizm i proizvoditel'nost' truda* (Leningrad, 1931), 10.

8. Prestwich, *Drink,* 284.

9. Kh. I. Indel'chik, M. N. Aruin, and A. I. Nesterenko, "I Vserossiiskii s"ezd po bor'be s p'ianstvom," *Sovetskoe zdravookhranenie* 2 (1972): 61.

10. *Trudy pervago vserossiiskago s"ezda po bor'be s p'ianstvom. S. Peterburg, 28 dekabria 1909 g.–6 ianvaria 1910 g.,* 3 vols. (St. Petersburg, 1910), 1:3–31 (henceforth *TPVS*). McKee, "Taming the Green Serpent," 392. Of these delegates, twenty-four hailed from St. Petersburg. *Russkii pechatnik* 15 (18 February 1910): 3.

11. Elaboration of this debate is provided in Kimberly Page Herrlinger, "Class, Piety, and Politics: Workers, Orthodoxy, and the Problem of Religious Identity in Russia, 1881–1914," Ph.D. diss., University of California, Berkeley, 1996, 471–72.

12. *TPVS,* 1:171; *Trezvye vskhody* 1 (1910): 137.

13. *TPVS,* 1:112, 129.

14. *TPVS,* 1:116–17.

15. *TPVS,* 1:151–52, 156–57; D. N. Borodin, *Itogi rabot pervago vserossiiskago s"ezda po bor'be s p'ianstvom* (St. Petersburg, 1910), 166; *Pechatnoe delo* 15 (12 January 1910): 10; *Fabrichnaia zhizn'* 1 (12 February 1910): 3.

16. GARF, f. 102, 4th deloproizvodstvo, 1909, d. 194, l. 30. Also reported in *Edinstvo* 14 (16 February 1910): 9; *Russkii vrach* 4 (23 January 1910): 130; *Vozrozhdenie* 1 (1910): 90; and *TPVS,* 1:96.

17. *TPVS,* 1:172.

18. Nikolai A. Liubimov, "Dnevnik uchastnika pervago Vserossiiskago s"ezda po bor'be s narodnym p'ianstvom. S.-Peterburg. 28 dekabria 1909 g.–6

ianvaria 1910 g.," a supplement to *V bor'be za trezvost'* 2 (February 1911), 61; *TPVS*, 1:190–91; GARF, f. 102, 4th deloproizvodstvo, 1909, d. 194, l. 23.

19. *Edinstvo* 12 (21 December 1909): 2.

20. *Ibid.*, 9 (18 October 1909): 5.

21. *TPVS*, 1:175–76.

22. *Vozrozhdenie* 2 (10 February 1910): 48; TsGA SPb, f. 6276, op. 269, d. 8, l. 250; *Russkii pechatnik* 15 (18 February 1910), 4.

23. Quoted in *Russkii pechatnik* 15 (18 February 1910): 4.

24. *TPVS*, 1:146–47; Borodin, *Itogi,* 144; *Pechatnoe delo* 15 (12 January 1910) 9.

25. *Nasha zaria* 1 (January 1910): 74.

26. *TPVS*, 1:169; *Pechatnoe delo* 16 (4 February 1910): 11; Geoffrey Swain, *Russian Social Democracy and the Legal Labour Movement, 1906–1914* (London, 1983), 90.

27. On arrests, see *Pechatnoe delo* 16 (4 February 1910): 11–12; *Russkii pechatnik* 15 (18 February 1910): 7; *Trezvye vskhody* 1 (1910): 156–58; and McKee, "Taming the Green Serpent," 395.

28. J[ohn] F. Hutchinson, "Medicine, Morality, and Social Policy in Imperial Russia: The Early Years of the Alcohol Commission," *Social History* 7 (November 1974): 215–16; McKee, "Taming the Green Serpent," 119–24.

29. *Nasha zaria* 1 (January 1910): 69.

30. *Russkii vrach* 3 (16 January 1910): 97.

31. T. S. Prot'ko, *V bor'be za trezvost': Stranitsy istorii* (Minsk, 1988), 81; RGIA, f. 1284, op. 188, d. 79, ll. 9–10.

32. Sale of spirits continued in first-class restaurants, which were inaccessible to the working class. See Prot'ko, *V bor'be,* 46–47; William E. Johnson, *The Liquor Problem in Russia* (Westerville, Ohio, 1915) 194–95.

33. A. L. Mendel'son, *Itogi prinuditel'noi trezvosti i novye formy p'ianstva* (Petrograd, 1916), 39; and Johnson, *The Liquor Problem,* 202–3.

34. A. Subbotin, *Pochemu sovetskaia vlast' razreshila prodazhu vodki* (Moscow, 1927), 9; A. L. Mendel'son, *Nervno-psikhicheskaia gigiena i profilaktika. Iz lektsii, chitannykh v gosudarstvennom institute dlia usovershenstvovaniia vrachei v Leningrade v 1921–1926 g.g.* (Leningrad, 1927), 138; Ernst Gordon, *Russian Prohibition* (Westerville, Ohio, 1916), 25; *Vestnik trezvosti* 242 (February 1915): 3.

35. Mendel'son, *Itogi,* 6, 9–11.

36. Dr. Mikhailov, *Vodku pit'—vse gubit'* (Moscow, 1927), 28.

37. V. I. Binshtok and L. S. Kaminskii, *Narodnoe pitanie i narodnoe zdravie* (Leningrad, 1929), 51.

38. *Zhurnal nevropatologii i psikhiatrii imeni S. S. Korsakova* 4 (1914): 559; *Russkii vrach* 7 (1915): 154–55; B. Evgeniev, *Zelenyi zmii: P'ianstvo i alkogolizm* (Petrograd, 1923), 13–14.

39. Mendel'son, *Itogi,* 40 (80 cases); *Zhurnal nevropatologii i psikhiatrii imeni S. S. Korsakova* 4 (1914): 553–66 (55 cases); *Russkii vrach* 7 (14 February 1915): 154 (1,292 cases).

40. *Nashe delo* 1 (1915): 90; David Christian, "Prohibition in Russia,

1914–1925," *Australian Slavonic and East European Studies* 9 (1995): 105–10.

41. *Vestnik trezvosti* 269–71 (May–July 1917): 10–11; J. Y. Simpson, *Some Notes on the State Sale Monopoly and Subsequent Prohibition of Vodka in Russia* (London, 1918), 42–43.

42. *Dekrety Sovetskoi vlasti,* vol. 7 (Moscow, 1974), 35, 37; A. G. Park-homenko, "Gosudarstvenno-pravovye meropriiatiia po bor'be s p'ianstvom v pervye gody Sovetskoi vlasti," *Sovetskoe gosudarstvo i pravo* 4 (1984): 113; and Prot'ko, *V bor'be,* 101–2, 106. Impressions that consumption began to rise during the course of prohibition are found in Mikhailov, *Vodku pit',* 28; and B. S. Kovgankin, *Alkogol', alkogolizm i bor'ba s nim: Konspekt dlia vystuplenii vrachei, sester, agitatorov i propagandistov* (Moscow, 1927), 25.

43. TsGA SPb, f. 9672, op. 1, d. 382, l. 4. On the alcohol raids, see Ia. Kann, "Bor'ba rabochikh Petrograda s p'ianymi pogromami (noiabr'–dekabr' 1917 g.)," *Istoriia SSSR* 3 (May–June 1962): 133–36; and *Narodnaia bor'ba za trezvost' v Russkoi istorii: Materialy seminara, provedennogo obshchestvami bor'by za trezvost' BAN SSSR, LGU, LOII AN SSSR* (Leningrad, 1989), 32–36.

44. *Administrativnyi vestnik* 9 (September 1927): 29

45. Soviet alcohol policy is summarized in A. I. Elistratov, *Administrativnoe pravo* (Moscow, 1929), 333–43; Helena Stone, "The Soviet Government and Moonshine, 1917–1929," *Cahiers du Monde Russe et Soviétique* 27 (1986): 359–79; and Neil Weissman, "Prohibition and Alcohol Control in the USSR: The 1920s Campaign against Illegal Spirits," *Soviet Studies* 38 (July 1986): 349–68.

46. TsGA SPb, f. 6255, op. 17, d. 2, l. 24. Also see L. Zheleznov, *Budem zhit' radostno bez sorokagradusnoi: Kak vesti antialkogol'nuiu rabotu* (Leningrad, 1929), 21; Ia. I. Lifshits, *Bor'ba s p'ianstvom* (Kharkov, 1929), 7, 21; V. M. Bekhterev, *Alkogolizm i bor'ba s nim* (Leningrad, 1927), 6; Mendel'son, *Nervno-psikhicheskaia,* 138; and V. N. Tolmachev, ed., *Khuliganstvo i khuligany: Sbornik* (Moscow, 1929), 137.

47. *God bor'by s alkogolizmom v Leningrade: (Materialy dlia dokladchikov)* (Moscow, 1929), 4.

48. The study of alcohol use is in D. Voronov, *Alkogol' v sovremennom bytu* (Leningrad, 1930), 52. Larin's comments and the congress resolutions may be found in *Bor'ba s alkogolizmom v SSSR: Pervyi plenum vsesoiuznogo soveta protivoalkogol'nykh obshchestv v SSSR, 30 maia–1 iunia 1929 g.* (Moscow, 1929), 18, 23, 89. Similar observations are found in *Leningradskii metallist* 1 (5 January 1925): 16; *Krasnaia gazeta,* 22 December 1925, 7; Bekhterev, *Alkogolizm,* 6; *Administrativnyi vestnik* 9 (September 1927): 30; 3 (March 1929): 18.

49. Iu. Larin, *Alkogolizm i sotsializm* (Moscow, 1929), 48–49; and É. I. Deichman, *Alkogolizm i bor'ba s nim* (Moscow, 1929), 88.

50. *Élektrosila,* 28 April 1928, 2.

51. In the early 1920s, the state did undertake campaigns against the production and distribution of moonshine in the countryside. These efforts have been treated in Stone, "The Soviet Government"; and Weissman, "Prohibition."

52. This argument is concisely presented in Subbotin, *Pochemu,* 10–12, 16–19. In the second half of the 1920s, the state derived approximately 10

percent of its income from liquor sales. Didrikhson, *Alkogolizm,* 21–22; Deichman, *Alkogolizm,* 143; and Elistratov, *Administrativnoe pravo,* 337.

53. Prot'ko, *V bor'be,* 107–8. Also see N. B. Lebina, "Tenevye storony zhizni sovetskogo goroda 20–30-kh godov," *Voprosy istorii* 2 (1994): 41; Transchel, "Under the Influence," 261.

54. I. V. Stalin, *Sochineniia,* vol. 10 (Moscow, 1946), 232. Also see Deichman, *Alkogolizm,* 139; *Pravda,* 21 February 1926, 5; 26 November 1927, 6. Sergei Shakhmaev and Igor' Kurukin claim that the only clear evidence of Lenin's views points to the contrary. *Kabak na Rusi: Pervaia pravdivaia istoriia rossiiskogo p'ianstva* (New York, 1996).

55. E. Iaroslavskii, "O bor'be s p'ianstvom," in A. Slepkov, ed., *Byt i molodezh': Sbornik statei* (Moscow, 1926), 18.

56. Elistratov, *Administrativnoe pravo,* 340. The code defined "socially dangerous alcoholics" as individuals who "systematically" disturbed public peace, whose "chronic drunkenness" led to destitution, or who suffered from "psychological disorder."

57. Ibid., 341; *Administrativnyi vestnik* 4 (April 1927): 64.

58. *Pravda,* 18 August 1928, 6.

59. *Bor'ba s alkogolizmom v SSSR,* 79; *Trezvost' i kul'tura* 1 (July 1928): 12; T. P. Korzhikhina, "Bor'ba s alkogolizmom v 1920-e-nachale 1930-kh godov," *Voprosy istorii* 9 (1985): 25. The history of the OBSA and the anti-alcohol movement of the 1920s unfortunately must be written without the society's records, which archivists report lost.

60. Deichman, *Alkogolizm,* 144–47. Also see *Trezvost' i kul'tura* 4–5 (March 1929): 4; Larin, *Alkogolizm,* 175–93.

61. The plan is reproduced in Deichman, *Alkogolizm,* 175–93.

62. The law is published in *Sobranie uzakonenii i rasporiazhenii rabochego i krest'ianskogo pravitel'stva.* Moscow, (n.d.) no. 20, article 224; *Administrativnyi vestnik* 3 (March 1929): 68.

63. *Bor'ba s alkogolizmom v SSSR,* 90–92. E. I. Lotova and Kh. I. Indel'chik, "Obshchestvennye organizatsii v bor'be s alkogolizmom v SSSR v 20-kh godakh," *Sovetskoe zdravookhranenie* 8 (1986): 29.

64. *Bor'ba s alkogolizmom v SSSR,* 45; Larin, *Novye zakony protiv alkogolizma i protivoalkogol'noe dvizhenie* (Moscow, 1929), 10; G. A. Bordiugov, "Problemy bor'by s sotsial'nymi anomaliiami v pervom piatiletnem plane," in Iurii S. Borisov, ed., *Istoricheskii opyt planirovaniia kul'turnogo stroitel'stva v SSSR: Sbornik statei* (Moscow, 1988), 144.

65. Prot'ko, *V bor'be,* 113, 127; Stephen White, *Russia Goes Dry: Alcohol, State and Society* (Cambridge, England, 1996), 25–27.

66. Cited in Deichman, *Alkogolizm,* 140.

67. Prot'ko, *V bor'be,* 124–25. On the relationship between Larin and Bukharin, see Anna Larina, *This I Cannot Forget: The Memoirs of Nikolai Bukharin's Widow* (New York, 1993), 37, 220.

68. Lotova and Indel'chik, "Obshchestvennye organizatsii," 30.

69. V. I. Kas'ianenko, "Razrabotka KPSS kontseptsii sotsialisticheskogo

obraza zhizni," *Voprosy istorii KPSS* 2 (1983): 36; White, *Russia Goes Dry,* 25.

70. Susan Gross Solomon, "David and Goliath in Soviet Public Health: The Rivalry of Social Hygienists and Psychiatrists for Authority over the Bytovoi Alcoholic," *Soviet Studies* 41 (April 1989): 254–75; E. I. Lotova and Kh. I. Indel'chik, "Alkogolizm kak sotsial'no-gigienicheskaia problema," *Sovetskoe zdravookhranenie* 3 (1986): 15; Prot'ko, *V bor'be,* 127; Bordiugov, "Problemy bor'by," 146.

CHAPTER 2: THE MEANINGS OF DRINK

1. Diane Koenker, "Urbanization and Deurbanization in the Russian Revolution and Civil War," *Journal of Modern History* 57 (September 1985): 424.

2. The population of St. Petersburg had grown to about 1 million in 1923 and about 1.5 million by 1926. V. B. Zhiromskaia, *Sovetskii gorod v 1921–1925 gg.: Problemy sotsial'noi struktury* (Moscow, 1988), 46, 77. Important works on Russia in the 1920s include Alan M. Ball, *Russia's Last Capitalists: The Nepmen, 1921–1929* (Berkeley, Calif., 1987); William J. Chase, *Workers, Society, and the Soviet State: Labor and Life in Moscow, 1918–1929* (Urbana, Ill., 1990); Sheila Fitzpatrick, Alexander Rabinowitch, and Richard Stites, eds., *Russia in the Era of NEP: Explorations in Soviet Society and Culture* (Bloomington, Ind., 1991); Diane P. Koenker, William G. Rosenberg, and Ronald Grigor Suny, eds., *Party, State, and Society in the Russian Civil War: Explorations in Social History* (Bloomington, Ind., 1989).

3. William H. Sewell, Jr., *Work and Revolution in France: The Language of Labor from the Old Regime to 1848* (Cambridge, England, 1980); Gareth Stedman Jones, "Working-Class Culture and Working-Class Politics in London, 1870–1900: Notes on the Remaking of a Working Class," in Stedman Jones, *Languages of Class,* 179–238; and Anna Clark, *The Struggle for the Breeches: Gender and the Making of the British Working Class* (Berkeley, Calif., 1995).

4. On migration, see Johnson, *Peasant and Proletarian;* Engel, *Between the Fields;* and Jeffrey Burds, *Peasant Dreams and Market Politics: Labor Migration and the Russian Village, 1861–1905* (Pittsburg, 1998). Working-class politics is the focus of Victoria Bonnell, *Roots of Rebellion: Workers' Politics and Organizations in St. Petersburg and Moscow, 1900–1914* (Berkeley, Calif., 1983); Laura Engelstein, *Moscow, 1905: Working-Class Organization and Political Conflict* (Stanford, Calif., 1982); Diane P. Koenker, *Moscow Workers and the 1917 Revolution* (Princeton, N.J., 1981); Robert B. McKean, *St. Petersburg between the Revolutions: Workers and Revolutionaries, June 1907–February 1917* (New Haven, Conn., 1990); and Steve A. Smith, *Red Petrograd: Revolution in the Factories, 1917–1918* (Cambridge, England, 1985).

5. Lewis H. Siegelbaum and Ronald Grigor Suny, "'Class Backwards'? In Search of the Soviet Working Class," in Lewis H. Sieglebaum and Ronald Grigor Suny, eds., *Making Workers Soviet: Power, Class, and Identity* (Ithaca, N.Y., 1994), 1–26; Steve A. Smith, "Writing the History of the Russian Revolution after the Fall of Communism," *Europe-Asia Studies* 46 (1994): 570.

6. Louis Chevalier, *Laboring Classes and Dangerous Classes in Paris during*

the First Half of the Nineteenth Century (Princeton, N.J., 1981), 56. Daniel R. Brower, in "The Penny Press and Its Readers," also comments on the value of such stories in Stephen P. Frank and Mark D. Steinberg, eds., *Cultures in Flux: Lower-Class Values, Practices, and Resistance in Late Imperial Russia* (Princeton, N.J., 1994), 152–53.

7. *Rabotnitsa i krest'ianka* 11 (June 1929): 24; D. Ia. Kurdachev, *Otvetstvennost'* (Perm, 1974), 11.

8. B[oris] I[vanovich] Ivanov, *Po stupeniam bor'by: Zapiski starogo bol'shevika* (Moscow, 1934), 69; B[oris] I[vanovich] Ivanov *Zapiski proshlogo: Povest' iz vospominanii detstva i iunoshestva rabochego-sotsialista* (Moscow, 1919): 60; Petr Sergeev, *Za kompaniiu! (Byl)* (St. Petersburg, n.d.), 6; A. Nalepko, *Butylka pogubila: Rasskaz* (St. Petersburg, 1909), 12; S. Semenov, *Bud' trezv! (Pis'mo k bratu)* (Moscow, 1911), 15; Aleksandr Nesterenko, S. M. Samet, F. V. Il'inskii, and M. N. Garkavi, *B'em trevogy (Antialkogol'naia zhivaia gazeta)* (Moscow, 1927), 14; Ia. Aleksandrov and P. Stel'makh, *Pochemu my p'em* (Leningrad, 1929), 28; N. P. Tiapugin, *Narodnye zabliuzhdeniia i nauchnaia pravda ob alkogole* (Moscow, 1929), 48.

9. A. M. Korovin, *Sakhar i bor'ba s alkogolizmom* (Moscow, 1904), 5; Tiapugin, *Narodnye zabliuzhdeniia,* 48; *Vestnik popechitel'stv o narodnoi trezvosti* 18 (8 May 1904): 456; *Obshchestvennyi vrach* 6 (August 1915): 331–32; *Gigiena i épidemiologiia* 1 (January 1927): 27.

10. N. Nikoforov, *Protiv starogo byta: Iz blok-nota partrabotnika* (Leningrad, n.d.), 36; *Rabochii bumazhnik* 10 (31 May 1925), cover.

11. *Slovar' russkogo iazyka* (Moscow, 1984); D. A. Drummond and G. Perkins, comps., *Dictionary of Russian Obscenities* (Oakland, Calif., 1987). *The Lubok: Russian Folk Pictures: 17th to 19th Century* (Leningrad, 1984), plates 54–55. Further equation between women and hens is found in Simion D. Dreiden, comp., *Za vashe zdorov'e: Antialkogol'naia khrestomatiia* (Leningrad, 1929), 169; Mir'ianin, *V p'ianom ugare* (St. Petersburg, 1910), 5. The associations described here are widespread in popular culture. The print, for example, was based on German models.

12. Grigorii Grigorevskii, *Pochemu on ne pil?* (St. Petersburg, n.d.), 1. Similar evidence is contained in Nalepko, *Butylka,* 12; *Rabochii bumazhnik* 20 (25 October 1926): 14; Nikoforov, *Protiv starogo byta,* 36; and Aleksandrov and Stel'makh, *Pochemu,* 20. *Baba* is a pejorative term for peasant woman. *Krest'ianin* and *krest'ianka,* which also refer to male and female peasants, do not carry the negative connotations associated with *baba* and *muzhik.*

13. G. Petrov, *Doloi p'ianstvo: Sbornik statei* (Moscow, 1903), 38; and A. Rozhdestvenskii, comp., *Zhertvy p'ianstva: Sbornik razskazov i statei dlia chteniia narodu o vrede p'ianstva* (St. Petersburg, 1909), 93. Connections between drinking and adulthood are also provided by *Istoriia Leningradskogo soiuza rabochikh poligraficheskogo proizvodstva,* vol. 1, *1904–1907 gg.* (Leningrad, 1925), 38; N. A. Kuznetsov, *Masterovshchina: Iz moei zhizni* (Leningrad, 1927), 52; I. N. Piotrovskii, *Rasskaz starogo mastera* (Novosibirsk, 1957), 18; Aleksandrov and Stel'makh, *Pochemu,* 28; Voronov, *Alkogol',* 14; and M. G. Frenkel', *Vodka—nash vrag* (Moscow, n.d.), 45.

14. *Sud idet* 16 (August 1929): 982; Kanatchikov quoted in Reginald E. Zelnik, trans. and ed., *A Radical Worker in Tsarist Russia: The Autobiography of Semen Ivanovich Kanatchikov* (Stanford, Calif., 1986), 73.

15. *TPVS*, 2:845, 3:1376–77; A. Lositskii and I. Chernyshev, *Alkogolizm peterburgskikh rabochikh* (St. Petersburg, 1913), 5, 8, 56; A. Mendel'son, *Lechenie alkogolizma v ambulatoriiakh S.-Peterburgskago gorodskogo popechitel'stva o narodnoi trezvosti, 1903–1909 gg.* (St. Petersburg, 1910), 47; *Leningradskii meditsinskii zhurnal* 7 (August–September 1928): 7; *Trezvost' i kul'tura* 6 (March 1929): 4; Zheleznov, *Budem zhit'*, 6; Deichman, *Alkogolizm*, 129; *Protiv alkogolizma: Sbornik materialov* (Leningrad, 1929), 78; and B. B. Kogan and M. S. Lebedinskii, *Byt rabochei molodezhi* (Moscow, 1929), 79.

16. Evidence that male children were encouraged to drink is found, for example, in D. G. Bulgakovskii, *Na pomoshch': Sbornik statei o vrednom vliianii spirtnykh napitkov na zdorov'e, material'noe blagosostoianie i nravstvennost' dlia naroda* (St. Petersburg, 1901), 50–51; B. I. Gladkov, *Spirtnye napitki—iad dlia dush i tela* (St. Petersburg, 1911), 5; *Metallist*, 21 March 1926, 26; *Sotsial'naia gigiena* 7 (1926): 21; I. M. Varushkin, *Alkogol': Kak ustroit' semeinyi antialkogol'nyi vecher: Sbornik* (n.p. 1928), 31; Dreiden, *Za vashe zdorov'e*, 167; Nikoforov, *Protiv starogo byta*, 36–37.

17. P. K. Ignatov, *Zhizn' prostogo cheloveka* (Moscow, 1965), 114; and a story in *Rabochii bumazhnik* 10 (31 May 1925): cover. Similar examples are contained in *Kul'turnaia revoliutsiia* 3 (10 February 1929): 31–32; and B. S. Kovgankin, *Komsomol na bor'bu s narkotizmom: Kak molodezhi pobedit' bolezni byta. P'ianstvo i kurenie tabaka* (Leningrad, 1929), 29.

18. Grigorevskii, *Pochemu*, 1.

19. D. G. Bulgakovskii, *Kak ia perestal pit'* (St. Petersburg, 1906), 7; *Vestnik trezvosti* 180 (December 1909): 25; *Rabochii klub* 3–4 (March–April 1924): 34; I. D. Strashun and A. S. Berliand, eds., *Sanitarnoe prosveshchenie v rabochem klube* (Moscow, 1925), 1:146; *Pravda*, 16 May 1926, 6; *Élektrosila*, 24 May 1928, 4; *Rabotnitsa i krest'ianka* 11 (June 1929): 24; *Sovetskie organy protiv alkogolizma: Stenogrammy dokladov Tsentrosoiuza SSSR, VSNKh SSSR, NKZdravov RSFSR i USSR na zasedanii protivoalkogol'nykh obshchestv SSSR* (Moscow, 1929), 16–17; Lositskii and Chernyshev, *Alkogolizm*, 10–11; Nikoforov, *Protiv starogo byta*, 35.

20. *Trezvost' i kul'tura* 24 (December 1929): 5. Workers' tolerance for high levels of alcohol consumption is indicated in *Leningradskii meditsinskii zhurnal* 7 (August–September 1928): 76; *TPVS*, 2:847; and *Krasnyi putilovets*, 17 December 1928, 2.

21. *Kul'turnaia revoliutsiia* 3 (10 February 1929): 31–32.

22. On the labor aristocracy in Britain, see Eric Hobsbawm, *Workers: Worlds of Labor* (New York, 1984).

23. These descriptions of "advanced" workers are taken from Tim McDaniel, *Autocracy, Capitalism, and Revolution in Russia* (Berkeley, Calif., 1988), 200-201; Eugene Anthony Swift, "Theater for the People: The Politics of Popular Culture in Urban Russia, 1861–1917," Ph.D. diss., University of California, Berkeley, 1992, 301; and Wynn, *Workers*, 85.

24. From the memoir of N. Koshchakov, in TsGA SPb, f. 4591, op. 52, d. 14, ll. 9, 11.

25. Wynn, *Workers*, esp. 222–26, 265–66.

26. Sander L. Gilman, *Picturing Health and Illness: Images of Identity and Difference* (Baltimore, 1995), 60; Sander L. Gilman, *Freud, Race, and Gender* (Princeton, N.J., 1993), 39; Engelstein, *The Keys to Happiness*, 320; George L. Mosse, *The Image of Man: The Creation of Modern Masculinity* (Oxford, 1996), 6, 56–57, 63–64, 68–70.

27. Igal Halfin, "The Rape of the Intelligentsia: A Proletarian Foundational Myth," *Russian Review* 56 (January 1997): 90–91.

28. Barrows and Room, *Drinking*, 7; Heath, "Drinking," 125; Dmitria Gefou-Madianou, ed., *Alcohol, Gender and Culture* (New York, 1992), 162.

29. *Pishchevik* 96 (30 November 1928): 4. Statistical data are provided by *TPVS*, 2:847; Lositskii and Chernyshev, *Alkogolizm*, 10, 57; M. Kurman, "Obsledovanie alkogolizma v Leningrade i Leningradskoi oblasti," *Biulleten' Leningradskago oblastnogo otdela statistiki* 21 (1929): 199; and *Leningradskii meditsinskii zhurnal* 7 (August–September 1928): 72.

30. Toasts appear in Sergeev, *Za kompaniiu*, 6–7; and *Trezvaia zhizn'* (May 1905): 67.

31. Ivanov, *Zapiski proshlogo*, 64; and D. G. Bulgakovskii, *Zhizn' Kass'iana: Chtenie s svetovymi kartinami* (St. Petersburg, 1910), 12.

32. *TPVS*, 3:1371; Mendel'son, *Lechenie alkogolizma*, 44; *Leningradskii meditsinskii zhurnal* 7 (August–September 1928): 75–76, 78. Also see Larin, *Alkogolizm*, 31; *Kul'turnaia revoliutsiia* 3 (10 February 1929): 31–32; Didrikhson, *Alkogolizm*, 36; *Zdravookhranenie* 7–8 (July–August 1929): 153.

33. *Trezvaia zhizn'* (May 1905): 67; A[leksandr] Buntilov, *Za pechatnym stankom* (Moscow, 1931), 7; *Leningradskii metallist* 27 (28 September 1928): 20; and Aleksandrov and Stel'makh, *Pochemu*, 30–31.

34. Sergeev, *Za kompaniiu*, 3.

35. Mikhailov, *Vodku pit'*, 11, 57.

36. *Rabochii bumazhnik* 10 (31 May 1925), cover. Similar evidence is contained in *Petrogradskaia pravda*, 30 January 1923, 4; *Pishchevik* 96 (30 November 1928): 4.

37. *Putilovtsy v 1905 godu* (Leningrad, 1931), 12; *Trezvaia zhizn'* (May 1905): 67–68.

38. Christian, *Living Water*, 75, 90–91, 83. The lack of communal controls on urban drinking in Russia is also mentioned in Herlihy, "'Joy of the Rus',"' 46; and Segal, *Russian Drinking*, 78, 82, 143.

39. *Vestnik popechitel'stv o narodnoi trezvosti* 24 (19 June 1904): 561; *Trezvaia zhizn'* (August 1907): 50, 52, 62.

40. *Pishchevik* 1 (1 January 1924): 2; *Leningradskii metallist* 26 (21 September 1928): 7; *Élektrosila*, 31 March 1928, 3; 28 April 1928, 2; A. Mil'chakov, *Komsomol v bor'be za kul'turnyi byt* (Leningrad, 1927), 57; A. S. Sholomovich, *40%*, *Sorok gradusov i rabochie* (Moscow, 1926), 6; *Pravda*, 5 February 1929, 1; *Pechatnyi dvor*, 8 January 1929, 4; Mikhailov, *Vodku pit'*, 12.

41. For example, I. Zhiga, *Novye rabochie* (Moscow, 1928), 111; Mil'chakov, *Komsomol*, 26; and Zheleznov, *Budem zhit'*, 9.

42. N. Amosov, *O p'ianykh prazdnikakh* (Moscow, n.d.), 23; *Élektrosila*, 31 March 1928, 3; *Pravda*, 2 June 1929, 4; A. G. Kagan, *Molodezh' posle gudka* (Moscow, 1930), 121; Zheleznov, *Budem zhit'*, 32; *Leningradskii metallist* 26 (21 September 1928): 7; M. Rafail, *Za novogo cheloveka* (Leningrad, 1928), 19–20; N. A. Semashko, *Kul'turnaia revoliutsiia i ozdorovlenie byta* (Moscow, 1929), 5, 32; Kovgankin, *Komsomol*, 26; Kagan, *Kak u nas*, 6.

43. Iaroslavskii, "O bor'be s p'ianstvom," 21 (emphasis in the original).

44. Excellent studies on celebrations in this period are Chatterjee, "Celebrating Women"; James von Geldern, *Bolshevik Festivals, 1917–1920* (Berkeley, Calif., 1993); and Hubertus F. Jahn, *Patriotic Culture in Russia during World War I* (Ithaca, N.Y., 1995).

45. *Vestnik profsoiuzov* 10–11 (October–November 1925): 14; *Petrogradskaia pravda*, 19 April 1922, 3; *Rabotnitsa* 4 (April 1923): 7.

46. *Perestanem pit' vino i ugoshchat' im* (St. Petersburg, 1902), 1.

47. Semenov, *Bud' trezv!* 25. *Russkii vrach* 4 (21 January 1915): 90 reported that the celebration of a wedding was one of the most frequent reasons for the use of alcohol substitutes during prohibition.

48. *Istoriia Leningradskogo soiuza*, 39.

49. Kuznetsov, *Masterovshchina*, 66–67; *Pechatnyi dvor*, 6 November 1928, 4.

50. Thanks to Thomas R. Trice for pointing this out to me. His dissertation is entitled "The 'Body Politic.'"

51. *Kak u nas*, 5. Drinking on name days in the Soviet period is also mentioned in *Élektrosila*, 17 June 1929, 4; *Krasnyi treugol'nik*, 28 March 1929, 4; and *Kozhevenik*, 15 January 1929, 2.

52. I. D. Strashun, *Na bor'bu za novyi trezvyi byt* (Moscow, 1927), 41.

53. TsGA SPb, f. 9672, op. 1, d. 469, l. 3. Similar routines are described in l. 25; Sergeev, *Za kompaniiu*, 5; and *Élektrosila*, 28 April 1928, 2. For statistical evidence, see *TPVS*, 2:814; *Sotsial'naia gigiena* 1 (1927): 28; Kurman, "Obsledovanie," 199; and *Leningradskii meditsinskii zhurnal* 7 (August–September 1928): 76.

54. *TPVS*, 3:1412.

55. *Sud idet* 12 (June 1929): 635.

56. *Leningradskii rabochii* 6 (31 March 1927): 11; see also *Rabochii bumazhnik* 18 (30 September 1927): 14.

57. *Leningradskii metallist* 26 (21 September 1928): 7; Larin, *Alkogolizm*, 26.

58. *Leningradskii rabochii*, 21 July 1924, 2; V. Sergeevich, *Zavod—kuznitsa revoliutsii* (Moscow, 1929), 44–45. Numerous sources mention crowded taverns and elevated drinking on weekends.

59. *Vestnik trezvosti* 158 (February 1908): 25.

60. TsGA SPb, f. 9672, op. 1, d. 557, l. 17. Similar evidence may be found in many sources, including Zelnik, *A Radical Worker*, 11; *Trezvye vskhody* 7–8 (1911): 73; *Leningradskii rabochii* 16 (5 November 1924): 3; *Pechatnyi stanok*, 11 February 1925, 1; Zhiga, *Novye rabochie*, 102; and A. Berezin, Z. Bobrov, E.

Guseva, L. Kondrat'eva, K. Levashov, V. Miasiashev, and V. Shiperovich, *Rabochaia molodezh' kak ona est': Opyt pedagogicheskogo izucheniia molodezhi odnogo zavoda* (Leningrad, 1930), 39.

61. *Nashe delo* 1 (1915): 92.

62. N. L. Brodskii, S. N. Dziubinskii, L. S. Mirskii, and V. P. Tsvetaev, comps., *Metallist: Istoriia, byt, bor'ba* (Moscow, 1925), 192–93. Also consult Ivanov, *Po stupeniam bor'by*, 6–7; *Pechatnik* 22 (12 August 1929): 10; A. Voinova, *Poluchka: Komediia v 2-kh deistviiakh i 3-kh kartinakh (iz sovremennogo rabochego byta)* (n.p., 1929), 35–36.

63. *Vestnik popechitel'stv o narodnoi trezvosti* 31 (7 August 1904): 698.

64. *Leningradskii rabochii* 12 (25 September 1926): 12; *Leningradskaia pravda*, 15 May 1926, 4; 11 August, 1926, 4.

65. TsGA SPb, f. 4591, op. 11, d. 1936, ll. 7–8; compilations from TsGA SPb, f. 6276, op. 119, d. 13, l. 312. Similar reports on labor discipline are contained in TsGA SPb, f. 4591, op. 11, d. 1936, ll. 7–8, 31; f. 4709, op. 10, d. 344, ll. 6–7; f. 6276, op. 114, d. 4, l. 228; op. 119, d. 4, l. 228.

66. TsGA SPb, f. 4591, op. 10, d. 215, l. 28; *Leningradskaia pravda*, 11 May 1926, 4.

67. *Gazeta kopeika*, 10 April 1914, 3; 11 April 1914, 3; and *Vestnik trezvosti* 232 (April 1914): 23. Sale of alcohol was again banned on Easter 1929 with doubtful success. *Voprosy zdravookhraneniia* 14 (August 1929): 39–40.

68. TsGA SPb, f. 4591, op. 11, d. 1936, ll. 83–84; f. 6276, op. 119, d. 13, ll. 58, 53; d. 4, l. 223; *Krasnaia gazeta*, 22 July 1927, 5; and *Pechatnyi stanok*, 21 August, 1928, 2.

69. Zheleznov, *Budem zhit'*, 8. Also see *Leningradskii rabochii* 7 (23 June 1924): 2; *Trezvost' i kul'tura* 11 (June 1929): 8; *Krasnaia gazeta*, 15 June 1927, 5.

70. *Pravda*, 10 November 1925, 7. The article's claim that this celebration had been superceded by celebrations of the October Revolution holiday the very next year is suspicious.

71. *Za novyi byt* 1 (January 1926): 17.

72. Zheleznov, *Budem zhit'*, 10; *Petrogradskaia pravda*, 30 December 1923, 7; Aleksandrov and Stel'makh, *Pochemu*, 16–17; TsGAIPD SPb, f. K-784, op. 1, d. 129, ll. 4, 99.

73. *Trezvost' i kul'tura* 8 (April 1920): 3.

74. *Rabotnitsa i krest'ianka* 11 (June 1929): 24.

75. In 1929 the Leningrad paper-making trust proved a shining example. *Rabochii bumazhnik* 7 (10 April 1929), unpaginated.

76. *Trezvost' i kul'tura* 7 (April 1929): 2; *Krasnyi putilovets*, 30 April 1929, 8.

77. TsGA SPb, f. 4709, op. 8, d. 68, l. 36 (my emphasis). Other resolutions appear in ll. 18, 21, 23, 25, 27, 28, 30, 31, 35, 36. The celebratory substitution was also promoted in *Leningradskii metallist* 10 (11 April 1928): 2.

78. TsGA RSFSR, f. 406, op. 7, d. 392, l. 38; *Élektrosila*, 29 April 1929, 3.

79. *Iskry*, May 1926, 1.

80. Tiapugin, *Narodnye zabliuzhdeniia*, 98. Similar passages are found in *Stroitel'* 9 (September 1923): 16; *Protiv alkogolizma*, 93; D. G. Ravich, *Vodopoi—*

mogil'shchik (Moscow, 1926), 34; Deichman, *Alkogolizm,* 223.

81. Larin, *Alkogolizm,* 140.

82. *Élektrosila,* 29 April 1929, 3; *Krasnyi putilovets,* 18 April 1928, 3.

83. *Zorkii glaz,* 22 December 1924, 1.

84. TsGA SPb, f. 6261, op. 33, d. 40, l. 104.

85. Ivanov, *Po stupeniam bor'by,* 88–89; Ivanov, *Zapiski proshlogo,* 50. Other mentions of May Day celebrations appear in *Novaia rabochaia gazeta,* 1 December 1913, 4; *Zorkii glaz,* 8 June 1927, 2; and *Iskry,* 1 May 1929, 4.

86. Rafail, *Za novogo cheloveka,* 8.

87. B. F. Didrikhson, *P'ianku–'k stenke'* (Leningrad, 1929), 13–14.

88. *Leningradskii rabochii* 17 (30 September 1927): 11. Indications of drinking on other Soviet holidays, including Industrialization Day, and at the opening of workers' clubs, are noted in A. L. Mendel'son, *Na p'ianom fronte* (Leningrad, 1925), 39; *Krasnaia gazeta,* 21 October 1925, 6; 16 March 1926, 3; 6 April 1926, 5; Rafail, *Za novogo cheloveka,* 10; *Iskry,* 1 May 1929, 4; *Skorokhodovskii rabochii,* 24 August, 1929, 4; and *Krasnyi treugol'nik,* 22 August 1929, 4.

89. Sergeev, *Za kompaniiu,* 6.

CHAPTER 3: MALE SOCIABILITY IN THE WORKPLACE

1. The adjective *prival'nyi* refers to docking fees collected from ships at rest stops in their journeys; the implication is that workers who "docked" at a particular mill owed a fee for the privilege. Other common designations for this custom included *vspriski* [sprinkling], *magarych* [wetting a bargain], and *kabluk* [heel]. Polishchuk, "Obychai," 79–80.

2. M[ikhail] P[etrovich] Nikolaev, "Za rabochee delo," *Zvezda* 5 (May 1957): 108.

3. *Edinstvo* 11 (1 December 1909): 14.

4. Quoted in *Listok rabochikh po obrabotke dereva* 6 (November 1907): 13. Similar criticisms appear in P. Timofeev, *Chem zhivet zavodskii rabochii* (St. Petersburg, 1906): 34; and *Chelnok* 1 (25 October 1907): 9.

5. I. V. Popov, *Vospominaniia* (Moscow 1971), 42.

6. Cited in P[avel] P[etrovich] Zinov'ev, *Na rubezhe dvukh épokh* (Moscow, 1932), 22–23. For similar schemes, see *Rabochii po metallu* 17 (12 July 1907): 12; and *Nash put'* 5 (12 August 1910): 11.

7. Examples of *prival'naia* expenditures are cited in the following: *Chelnok* 1 (25 October 1907): 9; *Edinstvo* 10 (22 October 1909): 14; *Gazeta kopeika,* 10 July 1909, 3; *Metallist* 2 (13 October 1911): 12; *Nadezhda* 1 (31 July 1908): 13; Nikolaev, "Za rabochee delo," 108; *Pechatnoe delo* 18 (17 March 1910): 14; *Rabochii po metallu* 17 (12 July 1907): 12; TsGA SPb, f. 6261, op. 33, d. 38, l. 13; Timofeev, *Chem zhivet,* 34.

8. *Gazeta kopeika,* 10 July 1909, 3. According to É. É. Kruze, in 1909 the average annual wage for St. Petersburg workers was 342 rubles, an average of 6 rubles, 57 kopeks per week. *Peterburgskie rabochii v 1912–1914 godakh* (Moscow, 1961), 105.

9. Stedman Jones, *Languages of Class*, 199; H. Medick, "Plebeian Culture in the Transition to Capitalism," in Raphael Samuel and Gareth Stedman Jones, eds., *Culture, Ideology and Politics: Essays for Eric Hobsbawm* (London, 1982), 91–92.

10. *Gazeta kopeika*, 1 November 1909, 5; Popov, *Vospominaniia*, 42; Kuznetsov, *Masterovshchina*, 52–53; *Istoriia Leningradskogo soiuza*, 38; GARF, f. 6864, op. 1, d. 60, l. 2; V. A. Zlotin, *Krasnoputilovskii Komsomol, 1917–1931: Sbornik statei i materialov k 14 letiiu organizatsii VLKSM zavoda "Krasnyi Putilovets"* (Leningrad, 1931), 6.

11. *Nash put'* 5 (12 August 1910): 12. Also see Timofeev, *Chem zhivet*, 33; M. Mitel'man, B. Glebov, and A. Ul'ianovskii, *Istoriia Putilovskogo zavoda, 1801–1917* (Moscow, 1961), 64. Alternatively, people were given a nickname signifying inclusion in a group after they had provided new acquaintances with drink. See Ivanov, *Zapiski proshlogo*, 60. Transchel hypothesizes that "Taras" was derived from *tarasun'*, a weak vodka made from previously distilled grain. "Under the Influence," 47.

12. *Metallist* 2 (13 October 1911): 13.

13. *Nadezhda* 1 (31 July 1908): 13.

14. *Gazeta kopeika*, 10 July 1909, 3; 21 October 1909, 4.

15. Cited in Zinov'ev, *Na rubezhe*, 17–18.

16. Zelnik, *A Radical Worker*, 56–57.

17. *Nadezhda* 1 (31 July 1908): 11. Also see *Edinstvo* 3 (19 March 1909): 13.

18. *Pechatnoe delo* 7 (29 May 1909): 15; P. Timofeev, "Ocherki zavodskoi zhizni," *Russkoe bogatstvo* 10 (October 1905): 75. For an exceptional report of violence against a foreman who refused to treat, see *Gazeta kopeika*, 11 September 1910, 3; 12 September 1910, 4.

19. *Metallist* 4 (10 November 1911): 10.

20. *Pechatnoe delo* 4 (21 March 1912): 2–5.

21. *Metallist* 24 (14 December 1912): 13. Also see *Metallist* 22 (26 October 1912): 13.

22. TsGA SPb, f. 9672, op. 1, d. 554, l. 21. *Prival'naia* in the 1920s is mentioned in *Krasnaia gazeta*, 21 February 1925, 7; 10 December 1926, 5; *Leningradskii rabochii* 6 (31 March 1927): 11; *Krasnyi putilovets*, 15 February 1928, 6; *Metallist* 8 (28 February 1929): 28; and Zheleznov, *Budem zhit'*, 55, 58.

23. The quotations are from *Krasnyi putilovets*, 17 December 1928, 2; and *Leningradskii rabochii*, 11 August 1924, 3. Some of the many examples of similar complaints are printed in the following issues of *Élektrosila* and *Krasnovyborzhets*. *Élektrosila*, 24 November 1928, 4; 20 January 1929, 6; 12 August 1929, 4; 9 September 1929, 4; *Krasnovyborzhets*, 1 March 1928, 4; 17 November 1928, 3; 5 April 1929, 1; 18 May 1929, 2; 3 June 1929, 3; 19 July 1929, 3.

24. TsGA SPb, f. 1360, op. 2, d. 480; d. 514; f. 4709, op. 9, d. 355.

25. *Skorokhodovskii rabochii*, 16 October 1929, 4.

26. From *Leningradskaia pravda*, 20 April 1929, 3; and *Krasnaia zaria*, 14 September 1929, 4.

27. Evidence of lunchtime drinking is abundant. Examples include

Leningradskii metallist 3 (15 April 1924): 9; *Leningradskaia pravda,* 20 October 1926, 5; *Pechatnyi stanok,* 16 June 1928, 1; *Krasnaia zaria,* 25 August 1928, 4; 9 March 1929, 2; *Skorokhodovskii rabochii,* 17 August 1929, 4. Closing trade at lunch is mentioned in *Iskry,* 10 September 1928, 3; *Krasnaia zaria,* 26 January 1929, 5; and *Skorokodovskii rabochii,* 17 August 1929, 4.

28. *Leningradskii metallist* 4 (20 February 1925): 21–22; *Pishchevik* 80 (5 October 1928): 4.

29. *Krasnaia zaria,* 17 December 1928, 2.

30. On secluded corners, see *Pechatnik* 26 (12 September 1928), 25; *Leningradskii rabochii,* 1 June 1925, 3. Drinking in restrooms is indicated by *Zorkii glaz,* 28 February 1927, 1; *Krasnaia zaria,* 23 February 1928, 2; *Leningradskii metallist* 17 (21 June 1928), 15. The restroom was also a place of relaxation for women. *Rabotnitsa i krest'ianka* 22 (June 1929): 17; Koenker, "Men against Women," 1444.

31. Chase, *Workers,* 137–41, 145–47; Douglas R. Weiner, "'Razmychka?' Urban Unemployment and Peasant In-Migration as Sources of Social Conflict," in Fitzpatrick, Rabinowitch, and Stites, *Russia in the Era,* 145–46.

32. Transchel, "Under the Influence," 198–99.

33. Ivanov, *Po stupeniam bor'by,* 69.

34. Chase, *Workers,* 152; John B. Hatch, "Labor Conflict in Moscow, 1921–1925," in Fitzpatrick, Rabinowitch, and Stites, *Russia in the Era,* 61.

35. *Leningradskii rabochii* 10 (15 April 1927): 27.

36. *Élektrosila,* 13 April 1928, 3; 28 April 1928, 3; *Iskry,* 6 June 1928, 3.

37. *Krasnaia zaria,* 26 January 1929, 5. Pooling resources in the prerevolutionary era is mentioned in *Istoriia Leningradskogo soiuza,* 38.

38. Zheleznov, *Budem zhit',* 60–61.

39. The quotation is from *Vestnik trezvosti* 134 (February 1906): 38. Toasting to health is indicated in Ignatov, *Zhizn' prostogo cheloveka,* 114; *Pechatnik* 1 (1 January 1925): 1; Nalepko, *Butylka,* 2; *Rabotnitsa i krest'ianka* 14 (July 1929): 8.

40. On France and Germany, see Brennan, "Towards the Cultural History," 79–80; Prestwich, *Drink,* 200; and Roberts, *Drink,* 107.

41. *Sud idet* 9 (May 1929): 491; *Krasnyi treugol'nik,* 8 April 1929, 2; Rafail, *Za novogo cheloveka,* 10. The link between sobriety and standing is also mentioned in Zelnik, *A Radical Worker,* 62; *Iskry,* 19 October 1929, 3; and *Leningradskaia pravda,* 29 August 1929, 4.

42. I. V. Sazhin, *Chto nado znat' o spirtnykh napitkakh* (Leningrad, 1929), 23; *TPVS,* 2:815; *Leningradskii meditsinskii zhurnal* 7 (August–September 1928): 76–79.

43. On France and Germany, see Susanna Barrows, *Distorting Mirrors: Visions of the Crowd in Late Nineteenth Century France* (New Haven, Conn., 1981), 61; Haine, *The World,* 101; Prestwich, *Drink,* 91; and Roberts, *Drink,* 17.

44. I. V. Sazhin, *Alkogol' kak pishchevoe veshchestvo* (St. Petersburg, 1910), 3–4; *Voprosy narkologii* 2 (1928): 14.

45. The quotations are from Mendel'son, *Nervno-psikhicheskaia,* 206; and *Kul'tura i byt* 6 (May 1930): 18. Also see *Sovetskie organy,* 46; N. P. Tiapugin,

Chto dolzhna znat' molodezh' ob alkogole (n.p., 1929), 16; Kovgankin, *Komsomol,* 9; L. A. Gabinov, *Pochemu v Sovetskom Soiuze razreshena prodazha spirtnykh napitkov* (Kharkov, 1927), 14.

46. Tiapugin, *Narodnye zabliuzhdeniia,* 51–53; Varushkin, *Alkogol',* 57; Gabinov, *Pochemu,* 13.

47. TsGA SPb, f. 9672, op. 1, d. 587, ll. 25–26; f. 6261, op. 33, d. 38, l. 13. For a similar report, see *Krasnaia zaria,* 21 June 1928, 5.

48. See, for example, A. L. M—n, *O vrede p'ianstva* (St. Petersburg, 1903), 6–7; *Prizadumaites'!* (St. Petersburg, 1911), 7.

49. Tiapugin, *Narodnye zabliuzhdeniia,* 46, 55–56. See also Strashun, *Na bor'bu,* 28; and Mikhailov, *Vodku pit',* 6; Navich, *Pit' ili ne pit'? (Otchego p'et rabochii narod?)* (St. Petersburg, n.d.), 23–24.

50. Quoted in Didrikhson, *P'ianku,* 5.

51. *Vestnik trezvosti* 134 (February 1906): 39.

52. V. Ia. Kanel', *Alkogolizm i bor'ba s nim* (Moscow, 1914), 362–63; *Vestnik trezvosti* 134 (February 1906): 38. For evidence of this belief in the West, see Prestwich, *Drink,* 91; Roberts, *Drink,* 129; Abrams, *Workers' Culture,* 64–65.

53. Quoted in Didrikhson, *P'ianku,* 5. The drunken reputation of cabbies and *dvorniki* is noted in TsGA SPb, f. 3215, op. 1, d. 307, l. 88; Navich, *Pit',* 26; and L. S. Minor, *Chisla i nabliudeniia iz oblasti alkogolizma* (Moscow, 1910), 18.

54. Abrams, *Workers' Culture,* 74–75.

55. For printers' complaints, see *Pechatnoe delo* 10 (30 August 1909): 16; 11 (30 September 1909): 14; 25 (5 October 1910): 15. Demands at Aivaz are reported in *Metallist* 8 (18 September 1913): 15.

56. *Leningradskii rabochii,* 30 July 1925, 3; *Skorokhodovskii rabochii,* 4 December 1929, 4. Abrams argues that alternative thirst-quenchers offered in cafeterias were important to reducing alcohol use in German factories. *Workers' Culture,* 74–75.

57. TsGA SPb, f. 9672, op. 1, d. 554, l. 21; Aleksei Buzinov, *Za Nevskoi zastavoi: Zapiski rabochego* (Moscow, 1930), 22. A high drinking rate among foundry workers and blacksmiths is also mentioned in Didrikhson, *P'ianku,* 5; *Vestnik trezvosti* 134 (February 1906): 38; Kanel', *Alkogolizm,* 362; *Élektrosila,* 28 April 1928, 2; *Skorokhodovskoe ékho,* 24 July 1929, 3; and TsGA SPb, f. 9672, op. 1. d. 587, l. 25. Statistical studies reinforce this picture. See, for example, *Biudzhety Leningradskikh rabochikh i sluzhashchikh 1922–1926 gg.* (Leningrad, 1927).

58. Ivanov, *Po stupeniam bor'by,* 29, 34, 42, 82. Similar observations about bakeries are contained in TsGA SPb, f. 6261, op. 33, d. 41, l. 45; d. 36, ll. 73–74; and *Pishchevik* 80 (5 October 1928): 4.

59. *Krasnaia gazeta,* 21 September 1926, 5.

60. *Istoriia Leningradskogo soiuza,* 39, 278. The drunken compositor is mentioned in Zinov'ev, *Na rubezhe,* 10; TsGA SPb, f. 3215, op. 1, d. 307, l. 88; f. 6261, op. 33, d. 38, l. 13; and Mark D. Steinberg, *Moral Communities: The Culture of Class Relations in the Russian Printing Industry, 1867–1907* (Berkeley, Calif., 1992), 74, 81.

61. *Pechatnoe delo* 14 (16 December 1909): 9. Also see *Istoriia Leningradskogo*

soiuza, 30; Diane P. Koenker, "Class and Consciousness in Socialist Society: Workers in the Printing Trades during NEP," in Fitzpatrick, *Russia in the Era,* 39.

62. *Pechatnoe delo* 8 (27 June 1909): 3–5.

63. TsGIA SPb, f. 569, op. 11, d. 843, l. 142; d. 865, l. 164; d. 916, l. 79; d. 1253, l. 20; op. 12, d. 4, l. 64; TsGAIPD SPb, f. 4000, op. 3, d. 337, l. 18.

64. TsGA SPb, f. 6276, op. 269, d. 8, ll. 19–20.

65. Rikhard Frelikh, *Alkogolizm i proletariat* (Moscow, 1906), 11; Minor, *Chisla i nabliudeniia,* 18; *Gazeta kopeika,* 11 January 1909, 3; and *Novaia rabochaia gazeta,* 23 August 1913, 4.

66. Rafail, *Za novogo cheloveka,* 20.

67. *Sud idet* 12 (June 1929): 633–37.

68. *Krasnyi putilovets,* 1 June–15 August 1928. Similar vows were published elsewhere. A pledge that seems particularly sincere (in view of its unpolished and repetitious nature) appears in *Rabotnitsa i krest'ianka* 11 (June 1929): 24.

69. *Krasnyi putilovets,* 11 July, 14 July, 15 August 1928.

70. *Pishchevik* 4 (15 January 1929): 4.

71. *Sud idet* 21 (November 1928): 1177–80.

72. TsGA SPb, f. 6255, op. 17, d. 175, ll. 8–9. *Trezvost' i kul'tura* 12 (June 1929): 18 also noted that the courts "are not always successful."

73. *Petrogradskaia pravda,* 30 June 1923, 4; TsGAIPD SPb, f. K-630, op. 1, d. 412, l. 119; Aleksandrov and Stel'makh, *Pochemu,* 45.

74. *Rabotnitsa i krest'ianka* 22 (November 1929): 16; *Golos kozhevnika* 41 (5–7 November 1928): 5; Semashko, *Kul'turnaia revoliutsiia,* 79.

75. Didrikhson, *P'ianku,* 17; TsGAIPD SPb, f. 76, op. 1, d. 209, l. 9; Mil'chakov, *Komsomol,* 65; *Leningradskii meditsinskii zhurnal* 7 (August–September 1928): 148–49; *Krasnaia gazeta,* 16 March, 1926, 3; *Sud idet* 8 (April 1929): 437.

76. TsGIAPD SPb, f. K-156, op. 1-a, d. 18, l. 173. Also see Kovgankin, *Komsomol,* 32; *Protiv alkogolizma,* 3; Deichman, *Alkogolizm,* 127; Larin, *Alkogolizm,* 115; *Krasnyi putilovets,* 19 January 1929, 3.

77. *Kul'tura i byt* 1 (April 1930): 16. On the OBSA, see Korzhikhina, "Bor'ba s alkogolizmom," 20–32.

78. *Bor'ba s alkogolizmom v SSSR,* 47.

79. *Krasnyi treugol'nik,* 21 March 1929, 2; 31 December 1929, 4.

80. TsGA SPb, f. 6276, op. 119. l. 131; *Rabotnitsa i krest'ianka* 22 (November 1929), 16. The inactivity of OBSA cells was also frequently mentioned elsewhere, including *Krasnyi putilovets,* 15 August 1928, 3; 5 August 1928, 3; *Skorokhodovskii rabochii,* 21 September 1929, 4; *Zorkii glaz,* 8 March 1929, 1; Simion D. Dreiden, *Antialkogol'naia rabota v klube: Posobie dlia klubnykh i antialkogol'nykh rabotnikov* (Leningrad, 1930), 80; TsGAIPD SPb, f. 2, op. 1, d. 1676, l. 11; f. 76, op. 1, d. 209, l. 137; f. 1012, op. 1, d. 685, ll. 69–70; d. 735, l. 4. The work of individual OBSA cells is positively assessed in *Pravda,* 18 August 1928, 5; Aleksandrov and Stel'makh, *Pochemu,* 47; Zheleznov, *Budem zhit',* 19; and TsGAIPD SPb, f. K-154, op. 1, d. 9, ll. 25–26.

81. TsGAIPD SPb, f. 1012, op. 1, 685, l. 69; d. 735, l. 5. Also see

Aleksandrov and Stel'makh, *Pochemu*, 47; *Bor'ba s alkogolizmom v SSSR*, 47.

82. TsGAIPD SPb, f. 3, op. 1, d. 1873, l. 56; f. 1012, op. 1, d. 735, l. 6.

83. *Voprosy zdravookhraneniia* 12 (July 1929): 59.

84. Although Swift has argued that "many of Russia's [prerevolutionary] industrialists viewed their workers' drinking customs with concern," he had progressive industrialists in mind. "Theater," 159–60, 168, 181, 184. Here I focus on the response of the worker's immediate superior, who often simply ignored drunkenness.

85. GARF, f. 6864, op. 1, d. 60, ll. 2–3. The responsibility of apprentices is also discussed in Buntilov, *Za pechatnym stankom*, 7; *Istoriia Leningradskogo soiuza*, 39; Ivanov, *Po stupeniam bor'by*, 38–39; Nikolaev, "Za rabochee delo," 106; Piotro-vskii, *Rasskaz*, 14–15; Zinov'ev, *Na rubezhe*, 3; *Naborshchik i pechatnyi mir* 126 (October 1906): 900; TsGA SPb, f. 6261, op. 33, d. 38, l. 13; f. 9672, op. 1, d. 501.

86. *Rabochaia mysl'* 8 (February 1900): 3. TsGA SPb, f. 9672, op. 1, d. 627, l. 9, contains similar evidence.

87. TsGA SPb, f. 9672, op. 1, d. 587, l. 25. Similar observations are made in TsGA SPb, f. 9672, op. 1, d. 58, l. 25; *Pechatnoe delo* 16 (4 February 1910): 14–15; 18 (17 March 1910): 14; Popov, *Vospominaniia*, 43; and GARF, f. 6864, op. 1, d. 60, l. 3.

88. Four of six metalworking plants questioned in 1929 about insobriety at the workplace provided no figures. TsGA SPb, f. 6276, op. 119, d. 13, ll. 53, 56.

89. *Pechatnik* 19 (5 July 1928): 8; TsGA SPb, f. 6276, op. 119, d. 13, l. 73.

90. Aleksandrov and Stel'makh, *Pochemu*, 40. Other evidence that supervisors basically ignored drunkenness is contained in *Krasnaia gazeta*, 22 October 1925, 7; *Élektrosila*, 1 February 1928, 4; *Krasnaia zaria*, 25 August 1928, 4; 26 January 1929, 5; *Krasnyi putilovets*, 31 January 1929, 2; TsGAIPD SPb, f. 1012, op. 1, d. 794, l. 38.

91. TsGA SPb, f. 6276, op. 119, d. 4, l. 49.

92. Compiled from TsGA SPb, f. 4591, op. 11, d. 1936, l. 36; op. 12, d. 2269, l. 7; f. 6276, op. 119, d. 13, ll. 71, 100–101.

93. No dismissals for drinking were indicated in 1924, 1925, and 1927. Compiled from TsGA SPb, f. 1360, op. 2, d. 481, 514.

94. TsGA SPb, f. 6276, op. 119, d. 4, l. 33.

95. *Kabel'shchik*, 25 September 1928, 3.

96. Rafail, *Za novogo cheloveka*, 6–7.

97. TsGA SPb, f. 4591, op. 12, d. 1061, l. 4; f. 4709, op. 9, d. 355, ll. 262, 279; f. 6276, op. 119, d. 4, l. 48; d. 13, ll. 132–33; and *Skorokhodovskoe ékho*, 24 November 1928, 2.

98. TsGA SPb, f. 1360, op. 1, d. 340, ll. 147, 199, 222. These cases are from 1926–1927. *Leningradskaia pravda*, 14 February 1929, 5.

99. *Leningradskii metallist* 17 (21 June 1928): 15. Other instances of workers being defended by foremen are enumerated in TsGA SPb, f. 4591, op. 8, d. 28, ll. 184–85; and *Élektrosila*, 21 March 1928, 4.

100. TsGA SPb, f. 4591, op. 12, d. 1061, ll. 5–6.

101. *Rabotnitsa i krest'ianka* 20 (October 1928): 14.

102. *Krasnaia zaria*, 3 December 1929, 6. The ability of skilled hands to

evade punishment for insobriety is also noted in *Krasnaia zaria,* 3 December 1929, 6; *Krasnovyborzhets,* 19 June 1929, 2; *Kul'tura i byt* 6 (May 1930): 18; Ts-GAIPD SPb, f. 16, d. 7410, op. 16–17, l. 3; TsGA SPb, f. 6276, op. 119, d. 4; l. 33; and Transchel, "Under the Influence," 201, 212.

103. "My na vsekh pomakhivaem," quoted in *Iskry,* 15 March 1929, 4.

104. TsGA SPb, f. 6276, op. 119, d. 13, ll. 132–33, comments on the lenient approach toward the lack of discipline at Krasnyi Treugol'nik. The mill's paper, *Krasnyi Treugol'nik,* waged the most extensive anti-alcohol campaign in Leningrad.

CHAPTER 4: FUNCTIONS OF THE TAVERN

1. The generalizations concerning tavern design and services are based on compilations derived through systematic examination of bureaucratic materials connected with government oversight of prerevolutionary taverns. Ts-GIA SPb, f. 569 op. 11, 12. These records contain descriptions of taverns and their clientele, floor plans, documents granting tavern owners permission to offer music or billiards in their establishments, and the like. My conclusions about ownership patterns, the geographic location of drinking establishments, and the persistence of drinking establishments are based on a database compiled from the St. Petersburg city directory, *Ves' Peterburg.* Entries in the city directory typically included the establishment's address, the name of its owner, and in some cases, its name. Readers seeking fuller explanation of these sources and my methodology may consult my dissertation, "Daily Life in Revolutionary Russia: Working-Class Drinking and Taverns in St. Petersburg, 1900–1929," University of Illinois, 1993.

2. The most extensive study of Russian taverns is Ivan Pryzhov's nineteenth-century study, *Istoriia kabakov v Rossii v sviazi s istoriei russkago naroda* [Kazan', 1868]. Despite the title, Shakhmaev and Kurukin's *Kabak na Rusi* is less a history of the tavern as such than a general history of alcohol consumption, the system of sale, and anti-alcohol campaigns in Russia. David Christian pays particular attention to the tavern's economic role in nineteenth-century Russia in *Living Water;* also see his earlier study coauthored with Smith, *Bread and Salt.* Jon M. Kingsdale, "The 'Poor Man's Club': Social Functions of the Urban Working-Class Saloon," *American Quarterly* 25 (1973): 472–89.

3. Here I am discussing taverns [*traktiry*] only—not beer halls [*pivnye*], for which I have no systematic information regarding layout. On village saloons, consult Burds, *Peasant Dreams,* 175.

4. Kingsdale, "The 'Poor Man's Club,'" 476; and Harrison, *Drink,* 47.

5. Ivanov, *Po stupeniam bor'by,* 72; Ivanov, *Zapiski proshlogo,* 61.

6. Billiard playing in Western taverns is noted, but not emphasized, in Perry R. Duis, *The Saloon: Public Drinking in Chicago and Boston, 1880–1920* (Urbana, Ill., 1983), 72; Kingsdale, "The 'Poor Man's Club,'" 478; and Abrams, *Workers' Culture,* 66.

7. Revoking permission for billiards is found in TsGIA SPb, f. 569, op. 11, d. 865, l. 34; d. 861, ll. 76–77; op. 12, d. 4, l. 39. Permission for additional tables during prohibition is indicated by TsGIA SPb, f. 569, op. 11, d. 841, l. 44; d. 612, ll. 66–68; op. 12, d. 1201, l. 15.

8. For example, TsGIA SPb, f. 569, op. 12, d. 1142, l. 50; op. 11, d. 854, l. 12; d. 861, l. 58; d. 910, l. 61; op. 12, d. 69, l. 57; and *Gazeta kopeika,* 2 May 1914, 2.

9. F. Pastupaev, *Zhena rabochego i drugie razskazy* (Moscow, 1906), 12; Rozhdestvenskii, *Zhertvy p'ianstva,* 91; Sergeevich, *Zavod,* 45; *Edinstvo* 4 (23 April 1909): 21; TsGA SPb, f. 9672, op. 1, d. 631, l. 10; d. 628, l. 7.

10. Zinov'ev, *Na rubezhe,* 21; *Pit' do dnia—ne vidat' dobra: Sbornik statei protiv p'ianstva* (St. Petersburg, 1902), 285.

11. TsGIA SPb, f. 569, op. 11, d. 900, l. 35.

12. Haine, *The World,* 27, 45, 130–34.

13. Verbal and pictorial evidence alike support this conclusion: Mitel'-man, Glebov, and Ul'ianovskii, *Istoriia* (1961), 67, 72; Zinov'ev, *Na rubezhe,* 20; Bulgakovskii, *Na pomoshch',* 135; TsGIA SPb, f. 569, op. 12, d. 1512, l. 9. Also see post-revolutionary evidence in *Krasnaia gazeta,* 17 August 1923, 5; 25 October 1923, 5; 3 June 1924, 5.

14. TsGIA SPb, f. 569, op. 12, d. 694, ll. 3, 5–6; d. 69, ll. 141–42.

15. Ibid., op. 11, d. 864, ll. 193, 196–97.

16. Zinov'ev, *Na rubezhe,* 17.

17. Kuznetsov, *Masterovshchina,* 45. Similar evidence is found in *Naborshchik* 47 (21 September 1903): 703; *Tonul da vyplyl, ili pokhozdeniia muzhichka v Pitere* (St. Petersburg, 1900), 36; TsGAIPD SPb, f. 4000, op. 3, d. 337, l. 18; TsGA SPb, f. 6261, op. 33, d. 33, l. 83.

18. V. V. Berenshtam, *Za pravo! Iz nabliudenii advokata* (St. Petersburg, 1905), 1.

19. Written and pictorial evidence, mostly from the 1920s, supports this conclusion. Examples include Ivanov, *Zapiski proshlogo,* 59; *Petrogradskaia pravda,* 20 October 1923, 4; *Shveinik* 18 (15 September 1926): 284; *Krasnaia zaria,* 31 March 1928, 6; *Leningradskii metallist* 5 (20 May 1924): 1; *Leningradskii rabochii,* 10 September 1926, 11; Ia. I. Lifshits, *Alkogol' i trud* (Kharkov, 1929), 37; *Krasnaia gazeta,* 17 August 1923, 5; 3 June 1924, 5. For France, see Thomas Brennan, *Public Drinking and Popular Culture in Eighteenth-Century Paris* (Princeton, N.J., 1988), 41, 241; Haine, *The World,* 161–62.

20. *Tonul da vyplyl,* 36. Further evidence of individuals approaching other drinkers is abundant. Examples include Zinov'ev, *Na rubezhe,* 17; I. Zhiga, *Dumy rabochikh, zaboty, dela (Zapiski rabkora)* (Moscow, n.d.), 53; *Pechatnik* 14 (15 December 1923): 15; *Sud idet* 16 (August 1925): 952; *Krasnaia gazeta,* 29 August 1924, 5; Nesterenko et al., *B'em trevogy,* 14.

21. *Vestnik trezvosti* 226 (October 1913): 17.

22. Skorobogatov, "Ot rabochei zastavy," 138; D. G. Bulgakovskii, *Ocherk deiatel'nosti popechitel'stv o narodnoi trezvosti za vse vremia ikh sushchestvovaniia (1895–1909 g.) v dvukh chastiakh* (St. Petersburg, 1910), 177; Ivanov, *Zapiski proshlogo,* 59, 61; and Ivanov, *Po stupeniam bor'by,* 72. Of the taverns I examined

in detail, 85 percent had an organ at some point in the tavern's history. A gramophone was present in 15 percent of the taverns; 23 percent had an orchestrion, 26 percent a balalaika orchestra, 13 percent a string orchestra.

23. Skorobogatov, "Ot rabochei zastavy," 138, 143; Mitel'man, Glebov, and Ul'ianovskii, *Istoriia* (1961), 77; V. N. Kirshin, *Orden na znameni: Kratkii ocherk istorii Leningradskogo ordena otechestvennoi voiny i stepeni zavoda poligraficheskikh mashin* (Moscow, 1965), 8, 28; Kuznetsov, *Masterovshchina,* 71. Small collections of drinking songs are published in M. D. Chulkov, *Sochinenie,* vol. 1, *Sobranie raznykh pesen* (St. Petersburg, 1913), 761–63; and *Sbornik okolo 500 noveishikh pesen, romansov i kupletov* (St. Petersburg, 1903), 8.

24. Abrams, *Workers' Culture,* 65, 80; Brennan, *Public Drinking,* 147.

25. *Naborshchik* 47 (21 September 1903): 703; Sergeevich, *Zavod,* 45; Dreiden, *Za vashe zdorov'e,* 206.

26. TsGAIPD SPb, f. 4000, op. 3, d. 337, ll. 17–18.

27. For example, Mitel'man, Glebov, and Ul'ianovskii, *Istoriia* (1961), 66; TsGIA SPb, f. 569, op. 11, d. 681, l. 2; d. 684, l. 193; d. 865, l. 34; op. 12, d. 27, l. 43; d. 74, l. 42; d. 1300, l. 14; *Gazeta kopeika,* 30 June 1909, 3; 27 July 1912, 3.

28. TsGIA SPb, f. 569, op. 11, d. 864, ll. 193, 196–97.

29. Female servants are discussed in TsGIA SPb, f. 569, op. 12, d. 129, ll. 6, 11, 21, 51. Stipulations on male musicians may be found in TsGIA SPb, f. 569, op. 11, d. 864, l. 192; d. 875, ll. 69, 72; d. 877, ll. 68, 79; op. 12, d. 27, l. 174.

30. Haine, *The World,* 199–206; Beverly Ann Tlusty, "Gender and Alcohol Use in Early Modern Augsburg," *Social History* 27 (November 1994): 242, 248.

31. GARF, f. 6861, op. 1, d. 82, l. 22. G. Grigorov and S. Shkotov, *Staryi i novyi byt* (Moscow, 1927), 136, may also be consulted.

32. TsGIA SPb, f. 569, op. 11, d. 900, l. 37.

33. Ibid., l. 19; op. 12, d. 134, ll. 43–44. For comparative perspective, consult Brennan, *Public Drinking,* 301.

34. This role is depicted in descriptions of an inn without the sale of drink. *Krasnaia gazeta,* 2 September 1923, 5.

35. *Leningradskaia pravda,* 23 October 1926, 4.

36. David Gilmore, *Manhood in the Making: Cultural Concepts of Masculinity* (New Haven, Conn., 1990), 1, 11, 220; Lyndal Roper, *Oedipus and the Devil: Witchcraft, Sexuality and Religion in Early Modern Europe* (London, 1994), 109, 117; John Tosh, "What Should Historians Do with Masculinity?" *History Workshop Journal* 38 (autumn 1994): 181.

37. *Vestnik trezvosti,* 161–62 (May–June 1908): 31–34; Buzinov, *Za Nevskoi zastavoi,* 24; *Gazeta kopeika,* 28 August 1913, 3; *Edinstvo* 2 (5 March 1909): 13; *Zhizn' pekarei* 1 (10 March 1914): 8; *Élektrosila,* 31 March 1928, 3; and Varushkin, *Alkogol',* 83.

38. *Leningradskii rabochii,* 28 September 1925, 6.

39. Anne Bobroff, "The Bolsheviks and Working Women, 1905–20," *Soviet Studies* 4 (October 1974): 554; Steinberg, *Moral Communities,* 78, 242; and Koenker, "Men against Women," 1448, 1450–51.

40. TsGIA SPb, f. 569, op. 11, d. 1254, l. 6; op. 12, d. 77, l. 20; d. 421, ll. 1–3.

41. Craig MacAndrew and Robert B. Edgerton, *Drunken Comportment: A Social Explanation* (Chicago, 1969), 24–25, 35–42, 76, 83, 88, 165; D[wight] B. Heath, "Alcohol and Aggression: A 'Missing Link' in Worldwide Perspective," in Edward Gottheil, Keith A. Druley, Thomas E. Skolada, and Howard M. Waxman, eds., *Alcohol, Drug Abuse and Aggression* (Springfield, Ill., 1983)," 92, 95. Also see, for example, W. Madsen and C. Madsen, "The Cultural Structure of Mexican Drinking Behavior," *Quarterly Journal of Studies on Alcohol* 30 (1969), 708, 713; Michael Stewart, "'I Can't Drink Beer, I've Just Drunk Water': Alcohol, Bodily Substance and Commesality amoung Hungarian Rom," in Gefou-Madianou, *Alcohol,* 146; W. Scott Haine, "A Spectrum of Cultural Constructs: The Interrelationship between Social, Legal, and Medical Constructs of Intemperate Behavior in Parisian Drinking, 1860–1914," *Contemporary Drug Problems* 21 (Winter 1994): 550–51.

42. See, for example, Zlotin, *Krasnoputilovskii Komsomol,* 6; *Gazeta kopeika,* 7 December 1911, 4; 25 August 1913, 4; 17 June 1913, 3; 2 December 1913, 3.

43. A. M. Buiko, *Put' rabochego: Vospominaniia putilovtsa* (Leningrad, 1964), 20–21. For fistfight rules, in addition to Buiko, see P. P. Aleksandrov, *Za Narvskoi zastavoi: Vospominaniia starogo rabochego* (Leningrad, 1963), 12; Mitel'man, Glebov, and Ul'ianovskii, *Istoriia* (1961), 68; *Putilovtsy v 1905 godu,* 11; *Krasnaia gazeta,* 8 February 1923, 7; and Wynn, *Workers,* 91–92. On the history of fistfights in Russia, see A. A. Lebedev, "K istorii kulachnykh boev na Rusi," *Russkaia starina* 7 (July 1913): 103–23; 8 (August 1913): 322–40; and B. V. Gorbunov, "Narodnye vidy sportivnoi bor'by kak élement traditsionnoi kul'tury russkikh (XIX–nachalo XX v.)," *Sovetskaia étnografiia* 4 (1989): 90–101.

44. Brennan, *Public Drinking,* 45 (quotation), 60–61, 71–74.

45. On conspiracy, see I. Ia. Papernikov, *Ocherk po istorii Leningradskogo soiuza kozhevnikov: K 25-letniiu iubileiu soiuza, 1905–1930 gg.* (Leningrad, 1930), 99; TsGA SPb, f. 6255, op. 17, d. 2, l. 165; f. 9672, op. 1, d. 631, l. 10; *Rabochaia gazeta,* 43 (1906), 1–2. Illegal literature is mentioned in TsGA SPb, f. 9672, op. 1, d. 628, l. 73; TsGIA SPb, f. 569, op. 12, d. 53, ll. 8–9.

46. TsGA SPb, f. 6276, op. 269, d. 35, ll. 113–14.

47. Ibid., f. 4774, op. 17, d. 1, l. 59.

48. A. Shotman, *Zapiski starogo bol'shevika* (Leningrad, 1963), 83; TsGA SPb, f. 4591, op. 52, d. 17, l. 5; f. 6255, op. 17, d. 1, ll. 9–10, 32, 40, 94; f. 6261, op. 33, d. 41, l. 44; f. 9672, op. 1, d. 553, l. 25; d. 556, l. 31. M. Mitel'man, B. Glebov, and A. Ul'ianovskii, *Istoriia Putilovskogo zavoda* (Moscow, 1939), 180–82; Mitel'man, Glebov, and Ul'ianovskii, *Istoriia* (1961), 169–72.

49. TsGA SPb, f. 9672, op. 1, d. 556, ll. 21–22. The people who gathered reportedly drank tea.

50. E. P. Onufriev, *Za Nevskoi zastavoi: Vospominaniia starogo bol'shevika* (Moscow, 1968), 41. GARF, f. 6869, op. 1, d. 41, l. 33; *Istoriia Leningradskoi gosudarstvennoi ordena Lenina i ordena Trudovogo Krasnogo Znameni obuvnoi fabriki "Skorokhod" imeni Ia. Kalinina* (Leningrad, 1969), 48.

51. The link between taverns and politics in the West is prominently discussed in Kingsdale, "The 'Poor Man's Club'," 482–84; David W. Conroy, *In*

Public Houses: Drink and the Revolution of Authority in Colonial Massachusetts (Chapel Hill, N.C., 1995), esp. chap. 4 and 254–55; Prestwich, *Drink,* 88–90; Haine, *The World,* esp. chap. 8; James S. Roberts, "The Tavern and Politics in the German Labor Movement, c. 1870–1914," in Barrows and Room, *Drinking,* 101–3; Abrams, *Workers' Culture,* 81–82; and Eve Rosenhaft, *Beating the Fascists? The German Communists and Political Violence, 1929–1933* (Cambridge, England, 1983), 19–20.

52. Mitel'man, Glebov, and Ul'ianovskii, *Istoriia* (1961), 239–40.

53. From the memoirs of N. A. Zaitsev. TsGA SPb, f. 9672, op. 1, d. 484, l. 2. A second account is provided in TsGA SPb, f. 4591, op. 52, d. 17, l. 33.

54. *Russkoe znamia,* 2 February 1906, 2.

55. *Peterburgskaia gazeta,* 1 February 1906, 4. These events are also described in TsGA SPb, f. 9672, op. 1, d. 501, ll. 9–10. Reports on the Tver' incident appeared in several daily newspapers: *Peterburgskaia gazeta,* 29 January 1906, 4; 30 January 1906, 3; 1 February 1906; 4; *Russkoe znamia,* 31 January 1906, 1–2; 1 February 1906, 2–3; 2 February 1906, 2–3.

56. Sergeevich, *Zavod,* 45.

57. TsGA SPb, f. 9672, op. 1, d. 457, ll. 14–15. Also see Buzinov, *Za Nevskoi zastavoi,* 86–87; and N. P. Paialin, *Zavod imeni Lenina, 1857–1918* (Moscow, 1933), 174.

58. *Rabochii po metallu* 17 (27 June 1907): 11; 18 (26 July 1907): 14; 23 (25 October 1907): 12.

59. One observer notes that the boycott "was forgotten," whereas another reports that it was lifted. TsGA SPb, f. 9672, op. 1, d. 457, ll. 14–15; Paialin, *Zavod,* 241. *Rabochii po metallu* and Buzinov report only on the continuation of the boycott. Buzinov, *Za Nevskoi zastavoi,* 127.

60. Mitel'man, Glebov, and Ul'ianovskii, *Istoriia* (1961), 665.

61. Stedman Jones, *Languages of Class,* 220, 236–37; Conroy, *In Public Houses,* 158, 255; and Haine, *The World,* 48, 211, 222–23.

62. Roberts, "The Tavern and Politics," in Barrows and Room, *Drinking,* 101–3; Abrams, *Workers' Culture,* 65, 81–82.

63. Rosenhaft, *Beating the Fascists,* 19–20, 111–27; Anthony McElligott, "Street Politics in Hamburg, 1932–33," *History Workshop* 16 (autumn 1983): 84–87.

64. On German actions, see Alf Ludtke, "Organizational Order or Eigensinn? Workers' Privacy and Workers' Politics in Imperial Germany," in Sean Wilentz, ed., *Rites of Power: Symbolism, Ritual, and Politics since the Middle Ages* (Philadelphia, 1985), 304; E. L. Turk, "The Great Berlin Beer Boycott of 1894," *Central European History* 15 (1982): 377–97; and Roberts, *Drink,* 104, 109.

65. McKee, "Taming the Green Serpent," chap. 8.

66. Because prohibition had been implemented, alcohol boycotts were not characteristic of the demonstrations in 1917. Buzinov, *Za Nevskoi zastavoi,* 4, 74; Mitel'man, Glebov, and Ul'ianovskii, *Istoriia* (1939), 264–65; *Rabochii golos,* 26 November 1905, 12. Also see *Istoriia Leningradskogo soiuza,* 279.

67. Buzinov, *Za Nevskoi zastavoi,* 36, 73–74; *Rabochii golos,* 26 November 1905, 12; Mitel'man, Glebov, and Ul'ianovskii, *Istoriia* (1939), 264–65; and TsGA

SPb, f. 9672, op. 1, d. 503, l. 7.

68. RGIA, f. 575, op. 3, d. 3943, ll. 107–8; d. 3944, ll. 67–68.

69. *Gazeta kopeika,* 8 July 1914, 3; 9 July 1914, 3; 10 July 1914, 2; 11 July 1914, 2.

70. M. I. Fridman, *Vinnaia monopoliia,* vol. 2, *Vinnaia monopoliia v Rossii* (St. Petersburg, 1916): 467; Deichman, *Alkogolizm,* 77.

71. Sergeevich, *Zavod,* 45; *Edinstvo* 2 (5 March 1909): 13; TsGIA SPb, f. 569, op. 11, d. 877, l. 23; *Putilovtsy v 1905 godu,* 11; *Leningradskaia pravda,* 24 July 1929, 4. Similar links are made in *Edinstvo* 4 (23 April 1909): 21; *Naborshchik* 47 (21 September 1903): 703; *Metallist* 22 (26 October 1912): 11; Zinov'ev, *Na rubezhe,* 13; TsGIA SPb, f. 569, op. 11, d. 900, l. 35; op. 12, d. 169, l. 11; d. 133, l. 36.

72. Mitel'man, Glebov, and Ul'ianovskii, *Istoriia* (1961), 66; TsGAIPD SPb, f. 4000, op. 3, d. 337, ll. 2, 18; TsGA SPb, f. 9672, op. 1, d. 631, ll. 9–10.

73. McKean, *St. Petersburg,* 18.

74. Perhaps the lack of taverns named after Pskov or Vitebsk is at least partly due to the tendency of persons from those regions to labor in unskilled jobs. Evel G. Economakis, "Patterns of Migration and Settlement in Prerevolutionary St. Petersburg: Peasants from Iaroslavl and Tver Provinces," *Russian Review* 56 (January 1997): 13–14.

75. Potentially genuine claims of ignorance are found in TsGIA SPb, f. 569, op. 12, d. 1294, ll. 2–3; d. 1734, ll. 4–5. Claims that do not seem reliable are in TsGIA SPb, f. 569, op. 12, d. 1512, ll. 1, 9; d. 1521, ll. 1–2.

76. *Krasnaia gazeta,* 2 September 1923, 5.

77. *Vestnik profsoiuzov* 8 (August 1924): 95. *Krasnaia gazeta* regularly carried such reports on dining halls; see 27 September 1923, 3; 28 September 1923, 3; 23 October 1923, 4; 25 October 1923, 5; 4 January 1924, 5; 5 March 1924, 7; 15 April 1924, 6; 3 June 1924, 5; 16 September 1925, 7; 6 January 1926, 6; 14 January 1926, 7; 4 February 1926, 5; 2 March 1926, 5.

78. TsGAIPD SPb, f. K-156, op. 1-a, d. 6, l. 21; *Krasnaia gazeta,* 28 October 1925, 5.

79. *Krasnaia gazeta,* 10 October 1925, 6; 12 December 1925, 7.

80. Ibid., 18 October 1925, 5. On the lack of spontaneity in club life, also see *Krasnaia gazeta,* 10 October 1926, 5; and *Pravda,* 23 July 1924, 5.

81. *Krasnaia gazeta,* 12 December 1925, 7. A few examples of drinking in clubs include *Krasnaia gazeta,* 10 October 1925, 6; 15 December 1926, 5; 21 April 1927, 5; *Iskry,* 1 May 1928, 3; TsGAIPD SPb, f. 2, op. 1, d. 1676, l. 21; f. 3, op. 1, d. 134, l. 152; f. 366, op. 1, d. 90, l. 96.

82. According to the Adminotdel, 3,386 businesses and government outlets sold alcohol in St. Petersburg in 1914, whereas in 1928 there were 1,100 such establishments. (These figures include establishments that sold alcohol for takeout.) Didrikhson, *Alkogolizm,* 61; or *God bor'by s alkogolizmom,* 9.

83. *Pravda,* 2 August 1928, 5; *Trezvost' i kul'tura* 1 (January 1929), cover; *Bor'ba s alkogolizmom v SSSR,* 46.

84. Aleksandrov and Stel'makh, *Pochemu,* 51; *Leningradskaia pravda,* 23 October 1926, 4; and *Krasnyi treugol'nik,* 17 December 1928, 4. Similar incidents

are reported in *Krasnovyborzhets,* 17 November 1928, 3; *Bor'ba s alkogolizmom v SSSR,* 46; *Pravda,* 25 August 1928, 7.

85. *Leningradskaia pravda,* 24 July 1929, 4; 17 October 1926, 4; and *Leningradskii rabochii,* 2 November 1925, 2. Gorshok was over three kilometers from the Putilov factory. Other indications that workers from several mills shared social space is provided by *Krasnaia gazeta,* 6 April 1927, 7; and Aleksandrov and Stel'makh, *Pochemu,* 51.

86. Lositskii and Chernyshev, *Alkogolizm,* 10; *Leningradskii meditsinskii zhurnal* 7 (August–September 1928): 72. Also see Kogan and Lebedinskii, *Byt rabochei,* 79, and *Zdravookhranenie* 7–8 (July–August 1929): 152.

87. Aleksandrov and Stel'makh, *Pochemu,* 42, 49, 50; Nesterenko et al., *B'em trevogy,* 9; and *Leningradskii metallist* 17 (21 June 1928): 7.

88. *Krasnaia gazeta,* 13 July 1923, 5.

89. Ibid., 2 March 1923, 5; 10 October 1926, 5; Dreiden, *Za vashe zdorov'e,* 205.

90. In the 1920s, names of proprietors were no longer published in the city directory.

91. The presence of billiards is indicated by *Krasnaia gazeta,* 17 May 1923, 6; 2 September 1923, 5; 23 November 1923, 5; 4 January 1924, 5 (the most recent reference to be found).

92. *Stroitel'* 6 (June 1925): 41–44. See also *Krasnaia gazeta,* 29 August, 1924, 5; and *Stroitel'* 7 (July 1925): 42.

93. Il'ia Rubanovskii, *Za knigu ili v pivnuiu?* (Leningrad, 1928), 15; *Krasnaia gazeta,* 13 July 1923, 5.

94. *Krasnaia gazeta,* 27 October 1923, 3. The attraction and presence of music is also noted elsewhere, including Dreiden, *Antialkogol'naia rabota,* 129; *Kul'turnaia revoliutsiia* 3 (10 February 1929): 31–32; and *Krasnaia gazeta,* 2 March 1923, 5; 17 May 1923, 6; 29 July 1925, 4; 10 December 1926, 5.

95. *Leningradskaia pravda,* 7 September 1926, 3. Similar observations may be found in *Leningradskaia pravda,* 17 October 1926, 4; *Leningradskii metallist* 17 (20 November 1924): 13; *Vestnik profsoiuzov* 8 (August 1924): 95; *Leningradskii rabochii,* 26 May 1924, 3; 9 June 1924, 3; 23 June 1924, 3; and *Krasnovyborzhets,* 17 November 1928, 3; *Krasnaia gazeta,* 1 August 1923, 6; 24 October 1923, 5.

96. Dreiden, *Za vashe zdorov'e,* 206; *Krasnaia gazeta,* 2 October 1924, 7. Also see *Pravda,* 6 May 1928, 3; Grigorov and Shkotov, *Staryi i novyi byt,* 136; *Leningradskii rabochii,* 26 May 1924, 3; and *Krasnaia gazeta,* 17 May 1923, 6; 2 September 1923, 5; 2 October 1924, 7; 5 October 1924, 6; 19 November 1924, 7; 12 February 1926, 5.

97. *Krasnaia gazeta,* 21 September 1924, 7.

98. Christine D. Worobec, *Peasant Russia: Family and Community in the Post-Emancipation Period* (Princeton, N.J., 1991), 175.

99. The legal codes that I consulted do not specify what beverages could be sold in "beer halls," but literary evidence confirms that it was illegal to drink spirits in these institutions. The evidence for this is most explicit in *Vestnik profsoiuzov* 10–11 (October–November 1925): 26; *Golos kozhevnika* 29 (29 July 1926): 8; *Leningradskaia pravda,* 31 January 1926, 4; 6 August 1926, 5; and

Sovetskie organy, 16.

100. See, for example, *Petrogradskaia pravda,* 5 January 1924, 3; *Leningrad-skaia pravda,* 6 August 1926, 5; Didrikhson, *P'ianku,* 16; Zhiga, *Dumy,* 219; *Krasnaia gazeta,* 23 May 1923, 7; 2 August 1924, 5; 2 October 1924, 7; 12 February 1926, 5; 21 April 1927, 5.

101. Restrictions on consumption are mentioned in *Krasnaia gazeta,* 28 September 1923, 3; 31 March 1926, 3; *Pravda,* 23 July 1924, 5; *Vestnik profsoiuzov* 8 (August 1924): 96; Strashun, *Na bor'bu,* 4; and TsGA SPb, f. 4709, op. 9, d. 94, l. 13. Failed enforcement is evident in *Leningradskii rabochii,* 9 June 1924, 3; 23 June 1924, 3; and *Rabochii klub* 3–4 (March–April 1924): 58–60.

102. Quotations are from TsGA SPb, f. 9672, op. 1, d. 469, l. 27; Lositskii and Chernyshev, *Alkogolizm,* 40; and *Vestnik trezvosti* 226 (October 1913): 17. See also Kanel', *Alkogolizm,* 384.

CHAPTER 5: WOMEN, CHILDREN, AND SOBRIETY

1. For example, D. G. Bulgakovskii, *Gorkaia pravda o p'ianstve* (St. Petersburg, 1909), 10; Varushkin, *Alkogol',* 31; Dreiden, *Antialkogol'naia rabota,* 86; R. Vlassek, I. D. Strashun, E. I. Deichman, and L. G. Politov, *Alkogolizm kak nauchnaia i bytovaia problema* (Moscow, 1928), 184; *Rabotnitsa* 4 (February 1929): 18. A statistical study also showed that young boys were treated by their elders. Didrikhson, *P'ianku,* 10. The practice of quieting babies with alcohol was also part of Irish culture. James R. Barrett, "Why Paddy Drank: The Social Importance of Whiskey in Pre-Famine Ireland," *Journal of Popular Culture* 11 (summer 1977): 160.

2. Bulgakovskii, *Gorkaia pravda,* 10; N. G., *Pagubnyi obychai* (St. Petersburg, 1908): 6–7; Lifshits, *Doloi kurenie,* 4; and Vlassek et al., *Alkogolizm,* 184.

3. Sources that speak of treating children to drink usually employ masculine terms in reference to the child. Sources centering on the child as entertainment employ the more ambiguous *deti* [children]. Examples of sources are enumerated in notes 1 and 2 of this chapter.

4. Cited in *Sud idet* 16 (August 1929): 979–82. A similar show trial is described in Dreiden, *Antialkogol'naia rabota,* 48.

5. N. G., *Pagubnyi obychai,* 4; *Vestnik trezvosti* 180 (December 1909): 23. Herlihy also notes the custom of treating youngsters as a preventive measure. See "'Joy of the Rus',"' 140.

6. V. Ketlinskaia and V. Stepkov, *Zhizn' bez kontrolia (Polovaia zhizn' i semia rabochei molodezhi)* (Leningrad, 1929), 24–25; TsGAIPD SPb, f. 4000, op. 18, d. 287, l. 13; and Kagan, *Molodezh',* 49.

7. Kagan, *Molodezh',* 61.

8. *Gul vereten* 1 (November 1928): 3.

9. *Leningradskii rabochii* 6 (31 March 1927): 11. For more on youth cultures in the 1920s, see Anne Elizabeth Gorsuch, "Enthusiasts, Bohemians, and Delinquents: Soviet Youth Cultures, 1921–1928," Ph.D. diss., University of Michigan, 1992.

10. Kagan, *Molodezh'*, 10, 46.

11. Dwight B. Heath, "Cross-Cultural Perspectives on Women and Alcohol," in Edith S. Lisansky Gomberg and Ted D. Nirenberg, eds., *Women and Substance Abuse* (Norwood, N.J., 1993), 106–9, 111.

12. *Trezvost' i kul'tura* 13–14 (July 1929): 14; *Metallist*, 14 March 1926, 25; the quotation is in *Rabotnitsa i krest'ianka* 22 (November 1929): 17. Some other women in the shop were reportedly "afraid" to betray the "drunkards."

13. Examples include RGIA, f. 575, op. 3, d. 4013, l. 204; *TPVS*, 3:1350; *Vestnik trezvosti* 176 (August 1909): 27; *Trudy vserossiiskago s"ezda prakticheskikh deiatelei po bor'be s alkogolizmom, sostoiavshagosia v Moskve s 6–12 avgusta 1912 g.* (Petrograd, 1914–15), 2:20 (henceforth *TVSPD*); *Voprosy alkogolizma* 1 (1913): 47–48, 60; TsGA SPb, f. 4301, op. 1, d. 3414, ll. 103–7, 112; *Materialy po statistike Petrograda* (Petrograd, 1921), 62–63; *Krasnaia gazeta*, 22 January 1927, 3; 18 April 1927, 3; *Leningradskii meditsinskii zhurnal* 7 (August–September 1928): 62–63; *Trezvost' i kul'tura* 13–14 (July 1929): 2; Deichman, *Alkogolizm*, 109; *God bor'by s alkogolizmom*, 7.

14. Kagan, *Molodezh'*, 46; *Zdravookhranenie* 7–8 (July–August 1929): 87. Men provided similar information about the drinking habits of their mothers and wives. *Leningradskii meditsinskii zhurnal* 7 (August–September 1928): 74; and *Voprosy alkogolizma* 1 (1913): 60. A higher female alcohol use is indicated in Kurman, "Obsledovanie," 192 (62% drink); and *Protiv alkogolizma*, 71 (50% drink). Kogan, *Byt rabochei*, 75, shows that 21 percent of female respondents drank.

15. TsGA SPb, f. 9672, op. 1, d. 632, ll. 6–7.

16. Ibid., l. 8.

17. Anne Louise Bobroff, "Working Women, Bonding Patterns, and the Politics of Daily Life: Russia at the End of the Old Regime," Ph.D. diss., University of Michigan, 1982, 199–207. Also see Cathy A. Frierson, ed. and trans., *Aleksandr Nikolaevich Engelgardt's Letters from the Country, 1872–1887* (New York, 1993), 188–89; Linda J. Ivanits, *Russian Folk Belief* (New York, 1989), 9–10; and G. A. Nosova, "Mapping of Russian Shrovetide Ritual (from Materials of the Nineteenth and Early Twentieth Centuries)," *Soviet Anthropology and Archeology* 14 (summer–fall 1975): 61.

18. TsGA SPb, f. 9672, op. 1, d. 632, l. 8.

19. *Krasnaia gazeta*, 9 June 1922, 4; 31 May 1923, 5.

20. *Leningradskaia pravda*, 6 March 1929, 4; *Zorkii glaz*, 8 March 1929, 1; *Kommunistka* 6 (June 1928): 40; Larin, *Alkogolizm*, 134. During a 1927 meeting at Krasnyi Treugol'nik, activists admonished that it was inappropriate to observe Women's Day with drink: TsGAIPD SPb, f. 3, op. 1, d. 1570, l. 15.

21. *Krasnyi treugol'nik*, 8 April 1929, 4 (my emphasis).

22. Zhiga, *Dumy*, 66–67. Domestic celebration is also discussed in TsGAIPD SPb, f. 3, op. 1, d. 1570, ll. 13–16.

23. Scattered additional drinking occasions for women are noted in *Za novyi byt* 17–18 (September 1927): 20; Zheleznov, *Budem zhit'*, 63; *Zdravookhranenie* 7–8 (July–August 1929), 88; and Deichman, *Alkogolizm*, 164, 166–67.

24. *Trezvye vskhody* 10–12 (1911): 110; D. G. Bulgakovskii, *Do chego dovodit' p'ianstvo: Kartiny iz zhizni* (St. Petersburg, 1900), unpaginated. Also see Tiapugin, *Narodnye zabliuzhdeniia*, 57.

25. *Rabotnitsa i krest'ianka* 3 (February 1929): 20.

26. *P'ianstvo—velikoe zlo: Sbornik statei o vrede p'ianstve* (St. Petersburg, 1902), 95; *Velikoe gore zemli russkoi—p'ianstvo* (St. Petersburg, [1907]), 5.

27. S. Zhivotskii, *Gorod zagubil: Razskaz* (St. Petersburg, n.d.), 3–4, 19, 22–24.

28. Kagan, *Molodezh'*, 49–50; *Rabochii klub* 4 (April 1928): 9–10; and Ts-GAIPD SPb, f. 4000, op. 18, d. 287, l. 15. The validity of perceived links between drink and sex is difficult to ascertain: according to a 1929 study, 60 percent of the young women who engaged in premarital sex had begun their sexual activity while intoxicated. See Ketlinskaia and Stepkov, *Zhizn'*, 3, 36.

29. Kagan, *Molodezh'*, 52. Similar observations about female conduct at parties are found in *Krasnyi treugol'nik*, 2 April 1928, 3; and *Rabochii klub* 4 (April 1928): 9.

30. Ketlinskaia and Stepkov, *Zhizn'*, 36.

31. Engel, *Between the Fields*, 198. This problem applies to labor history more broadly. See, for example, Lenard R. Berlanstein, ed., *Rethinking Labor History: Essays on Discourse and Class Analysis* (Urbana, Ill., 1993), 208–9; and Ava Baron, *Work Engendered: Toward a New History of American Labor* (Ithaca, N.Y., 1991), 4.

32. Rose L. Glickman, *Russian Factory Women: Workplace and Society, 1880–1914* (Berkeley, 1984), 25, 104–5, 154–55; Beatrice Farnsworth and Lynne Viola, eds., *Russian Peasant Women* (New York, 1992), 140.

33. Gorsuch, "Enthusiasts," 191, 230.

34. Sergeev, *Za kompaniiu*, 6.

35. *Zhurnal Russkogo obshchestva okhraneniia narodnogo zdraviia* 6–7 (June–July 1900): 563; M—ov, *Pis'mo k rabochim* (St. Petersburg, 1907), 6; *TPVS*, 1:90–91; *TVSPD*, 1:177.

36. *Golos sakharinka* 9 (5 May 1929): 5.

37. *Shveinik* 18 (15 September 1926): 285; A. Voinova, *Na buksir: P'esa v 3-kh destviiakh i 4-kh kartinakh* (Leningrad, 1931), 20–23, 38, 40, 49; and *Metallistik*, 30 November 1928, 12–13, issued as a supplement to *Leningradskii metallist* 33 (30 November 1928).

38. See, for example, *Gazeta kopeika*, 25 September 1911, 2–3; 30 September 1911, 4; 27 April 1913, 3; 28 April 1913, 3, 5; 29 April 1913, 2–3; 30 August 1913, 2; 9 September 1913, 3.

39. Sources include Deichman, *Alkogolizm*, 165–66; Larin, *Alkogolizm*, 141; Tiapugin, *Narodnye zabliuzhdeniia*, 105; Zheleznov, *Budem zhit'*, 41–47; *Krasnyi putilovets*, 13 May 1929, 2; TsGAIPD SPb, f. 76, op. 1, d. 209, ll. 1, 12.

40. Sheila Fitzpatrick, ed., *Cultural Revolution in Russia, 1928–1931* (Bloomington, Ind., 1984).

41. *V borbe za trezvost'* 7–8 (July–August 1911): 55–61. Typical warnings concerning courtship and marriage appear in D. G. Bulgakovskii, *Zakryli: K krest'ianskim zhenam: Narodnoe chitenie s svetovymi kartinami* (St. Petersburg,

1911), 10–11; L. Bogdanovich, *Golubchik! Eshche riumochky!* (Moscow, 1915), 14–15; *Protiv alkogolizma*, 38; *Rabotnitsa i kresti'anka* (December 1927): 27; V. A. Tikhomirova, *Na bor'bu s p'ianstvom, khrestomatiia po voprosam alkogolizma i bor'bu s nim v shkole i cherez shkolu* (Leningrad, 1931), 135–38.

42. For example, *Zhurnal Russkogo obshchestva okhraneniia narodnogo zdraviia* 1 (October 1901): 635; A. M. Korovin, *Ob"iazannosti russkoi zhenshchiny v bor'be s alkogolizmom* (St. Petersburg, 1901), 4–8; *TPVS*, 1:200; *Trudy 1-go Vserossiiskago zhenskago s"ezda pri russkom zhenskom obshchestve v S.-Peterburge, 10–16 dekabria 1908 goda* (St. Petersburg, 1909), 358 (henceforth *TPVZhS*); *Rabotnitsa i krest'ianka* 24 (December 1927): 27; Larin, *Alkogolizm*, 135; *Leningradskaia pravda*, 6 March 1929, 4; *Zorkii glaz*, 8 March 1929, 1.

43. For example, E. A. Chebysheva-Dmitrieva, *Rol' zhenshchin v bor'be s alkogolizmom* (St. Petersburg, 1904), 8–15; *Rabotnitsa* 6 (March 1924): 6–7; *Rabotnitsa i krest'ianka* 24 (December 1927): 27; *Skorokhodskoe ékho*, 6 November 1929, 4.

44. "Educated" women, priests' wives, and teachers were summoned in *Zhurnal Russkogo obshchestva okhraneniia narodnogo zdraviia* 6–7 (June–July 1900): 562; Korovin, *Ob"iazannosti*, 3, 12; *Vestnik trezvosti* 105 (September 1903): 23–24; *Trezvye vskhody* 2 (1909): 80; *V bor'be za trezvost'* 8–9 (August–September 1912): 15. For Boduén-de-Kurtené's comments, consult *TPVZhS*, 753. Korovin's work was recommended in *Zhurnal Russkogo obshchestva okhraneniia narodnogo zdraviia* 1 (January 1913): 39.

45. N. N. Shipov, *Alkogolizm i revoliutsiia* (St. Petersburg, 1908), 76–77. Also see *TPVS*, 1:93.

46. Larin, *Alkogolizm*, 135–36.

47. *Shveinik* 18 (15 September 1926): 285. *Shveinik* explicitly solicited complaints from women and children in 19 (1 October 1928): 9.

48. TsGAIPD SPb, f. K-156, op. 1a, d. 18, ll. 116–18.

49. A. I. Bukharev, "Komsomol v bor'be za novyi byt (1926–1932 gg.)," in A. I. Bukharev, I. E. Krutsko, and O. V. Galkova, eds., *Bor'ba partii za sotsialisticheskii byt (1921–1937 gg.): Sbornik nauchnykh trudov* (Volgograd, 1985)," 82.

50. Larin, *Alkogolizm*, 11, 137 (emphasis in the original); and *Krasnyi putilovets*, 26 December 1929, 1.

51. TsGAIPD SPb, f. 4000, op. 18, d. 287, ll. 11–12, 15–16.

52. *Bor'ba s alkogolizmom v SSSR*, 10, 56–57.

53. *Zdravookhranenie* 7–8 (July–August 1929): 83. Scattered additional information shows similar or lower female involvement. *Zdravookhranenie* 1 (October 1928): 53; *Golos kozhevnika* 43 (19 November 1928): 6; *Skorokhodovskoe ékho*, 20 October 1928, 1; TsGAIPD SPb, f. 1012, op. 1, d. 735, ll. 4–6; *Bor'ba s alkogolizmom v SSSR*, 93. Pre-revolutionary organizations were less likely to have attracted working-class women, but 10 percent of the individuals listed as temperance society officeholders in St. Petersburg's 1914 city directory were women. Compiled from *Ves' Peterburg: Adresnaia i spravochnaia kniga* (Petrograd, 1914), 1068–70.

54. *Dobrovol'nye obshchestva v Petrograde-Leningrade v 1917–1937 gg.: Sbornik statei* (Leningrad, 1989), 29, 45; *Kommunistka* 3 (February 1929), 27–30; 6

(June 1928): 20; 3 (February 1929): 23–26; *Revoliutsiia i kul'tura* 3–4 (1928): 94–96. Only Leningrad's branches of the Friends of Radio and the sports society Dinamo embraced female consitutencies under 20 percent. *Dobrovol'nye obshchestva*, 117, 144; *Revoliutsiia i kul'tura* 3–4 (31 December 1927): 114–15.

55. *TPVS*, 1:276; *Rabotnitsa* 34 (September 1929): 19; *Bor'ba s alkogolizmom v SSSR*, 72–75; *V bor'be za trezvost'* 8–9 (August–September 1912): 10; *Rabotnitsa i krest'ianka* 15 (July 1928): 2; *Zorkii glaz*, 8 March 1929, 1. Abrams similarly argues that women "were not particularly active in the German temperance movement." *Workers' Culture*, 84.

56. For examples see Nikolaev, "Za rabochee delo," 112–13; *Gazeta kopeika*, 7 February 1909, 3; 16 December 1911, 4; *Leningradskaia pravda*, 3 November 1926, 4; 16 May 1929, 3; *Leningradskii metallist* 24 (31 August 1928): 18; *V bor'be za trezvost'* 2 (March–April 1914): 72; Mikhailov, *Vodku pit'*, 60; Larin, *Alkogolizm*, 133–34.

57. Examples of women who seem to have been beaten whether their husbands were drunk or sober are found in TsGA SPb, f. 3215, op. 1, d. 84, l. 216; and *Krasnyi putilovets*, 1 March 1928, 5. For general discussions of wife-beating in Russia, see Glickman, *Russian Factory Women*, 33–34; Worobec, *Peasant Russia*, 130, 188–96; Barbara Evans Clements, Barbara Alpern Engel, and Christine D. Worobec, eds., *Russia's Women: Accommodation, Resistance, Transformation* (Berkeley, Calif., 1991), 22, 150; Engel, *Between the Fields*, 23–30. Other scholars have noted that lower-class women tended to couple complaints of physical abuse with accusations of nonsupport. See Pamela Haag, "'The Ill-Use of a Wife': Patterns of Working-Class Violence in Domestic and Public New York City, 1860–1880," *Journal of Social History* 25 (April 1992): 450, 466–67; and Tlusty, "Gender and Alcohol," 246. A few Russian petitions are similar in this respect. TsGA SPb, f. 3215, op. 1, d. 84, ll. 112, 166.

58. McKee, "Taming the Green Serpent," 44.

59. TsGA SPb, f. 3215, op. 1, d. 84, l. 107 (my emphasis). The occupations of Fedotova and her husband are not stated in the petition; the couple lived on Vasil'evskii Island.

60. *Krasnaia zaria*, 26 January 1929, 5. Further evidence of men's attempts to evade their wives is contained in Buiko, *Put' rabochego*, 15; Mitel'man, Glebov, and Ul'ianovskii, *Istoriia* (1961), 64, 66; *Krasnaia gazeta*, 27 August 1926, 5; and *Iskry*, 10 October 1928, 3.

61. *Pechatnik* 36 (25 December 1928): 29. Also see Mitel'man, Glebov, and Ul'ianovskii, *Istoriia* (1961), 64; Nalepko, *Butylka*, 5; *Rabotnitsa i krest'ianka* 13 (June 1929): 7.

62. *Krasnaia gazeta*, 11 January 1926, 6; *Iskry*, 10 October 1928, 3; *Pechatnyi dvor*, 6 November 1928, 4; *Krasnaia zaria*, 26 January, 1929, 5.

63. *Krasnyi treugol'nik*, 8 April 1929, 2.

64. For example, Nikolaev, "Za rabochee delo," 112; Mitel'man, Glebov, and Ul'ianovskii, *Istoriia* (1961), 64; Popov, *Vospominaniia*, 14; *Krasnaia gazeta*, 10 December 1926, 5; *Krasnaia zaria*, 26 January 1929, 5; Dreiden, *Za vashe zdorov'e*, 206; Zhiga, *Dumy*, 219–20.

65. K. Fomushkin, *Schastlivyi den' Dudkina* (n.p., 1906), 54; *Krasnyi derevoobdelochnik* 15 (1 August 1928), 11.

66. Nikolaev, "Za rabochee delo," 112; and *Krasnaia zaria,* 26 January 1929, 5. Similar incidents are described in TsGIA SPb, f. 569, op. 11, d. 854, l. 26; and *Rabochii bumazhnik* 13 (15 July 1926): 13.

67. *Rabotnitsa i krest'ianka* 21 (November 1926): 16–17. One of the most important budget studies from this period is *Biudzhety Leningradskikh rabochikh.*

68. *Pechatnik* 36 (25 December 1928): 29. Women's specific material concerns are also evident in *Vestnik trezvosti* 216 (December 1912): 10; *Krasnaia gazeta,* 20 July 1924, 7; 14 January 1926, 4; *Shveinik* 18 (15 September 1926): 285; *Rabotnitsa i krest'ianka* 3 (February 1928): 6; and *Krasnyi putilovets,* 18 April 1928, 5.

69. *Krasnovyborzhets,* 15 February 1929, 4.

70. *Krasnaia gazeta,* 17 February 1927, 5.

71. *Pechatnik* 14 (15 December 1923): 14; and *Golos kozhevnika* 20 (20 July 1926): 8, for example.

72. TsGA SPb, f. 9672, op. 1, d. 57, l. 9.

73. *Nash put'* 15 (30 March 1911): 13

74. Nalepko, *Butylka,* 5.

75. Nesterenko et al., *B'em trevogy,* 10.

76. *Rabochii bumazhnik* 13 (15 July 1926): 14. See also *Rabotnitsa i krest'ianka* 21 (November 1926): 16–17; 13 (June 1929): 6.

77. The quoted phrase is an ironic remark penned by Buzinov. See his *Za Nevskoi zastavoi,* 26.

78. *Za novyi byt* 1–2 (January 1929): 17–18.

79. TsGA SPb, f. 9672, op. 1, d. 627, l. 9. Further support for this contention is indicated by *Naborshchik* 47 (21 September 1903): 702–3; *Krasnaia gazeta,* 11 January 1925, 6; *Leningradskaia pravda,* 17 September 1926, 3; and *Iskry,* 10 October 1928, 3.

80. Commercial advertisements for these products typically ran several times a week in the popular *Gazeta kopeika.* For examples see 18 March 1909, 4; 13 June 1910, 2; 22 January 1912, 5; 11 February 1913, 3; and 18 February 1913, 3. Pre-revolutionary folk cures are discussed at greater length in Herlihy, "'Joy of the Rus',"" 140–41; and "Narodnyia sredstvia ot p'ianstva," *Deiatel'* 13 (1904): 488–93. Home and secret remedies dating from the 1920s are mentioned in *Krasnaia gazeta,* 25 January 1927, 6; Varushkin, *Alkogol',* 85–86; *Za novyi byt* 1–2 (January 1929): 17–18.

81. Buzinov, *Za Nevskoi zastavoi,* 36, 73–74. Buzinov also notes that one member of the workshop expressed his approval of the boycott.

82. Viktor Obninskii, *Polgoda russkoi revoliutsii: Sbornik materialov k istorii russkoi revoliutsii (oktiabr' 1905–aprel' 1906 gg.)* (Moscow, 1906), 13.

83. *Gazeta kopeika,* 7 July 1914, 3. Reporting on the same event, *Rech',* 7 July 1914, 2, failed to mention any connection with strike activity.

84. *Novoe vremia,* 10 July 1914, 4; John Newton, *Alcohol and the War: The Example of Russia* (London, n.d.), 3.

85. Diane P. Koenker and William G. Rosenberg, *Strikes and Revolution in Russia, 1917* (Princeton, N.J., 1989), 20, 314; Steve A. Smith, "Class and Gender: Women's Strikes in St. Petersburg, 1895–1917 and in Shanghai, 1895–1927," *Social History* 19 (May 1994): 143.

86. Events in 1905 are described in RGIA, f. 575, op. 3, d. 3944, ll. 67–68. Demonstrations in 1914 are described in *Rech'*, 8 July (21 August) 1914, 4; *Peterburgskaia gazeta*, 11 July 1914, 3; 12 July 1914, 3; *Novoe vremia*, 10 July 1914, 4; *Peterburgskii listok* 11 July 1914, 4; 12 July 1914, 4. For Smith, see "Class and Gender," 147.

87. In observing that the fall 1905 boycott was motivated by a desire to uphold the honor of strikers, Obninskii parrots Social Democratic language. Whether working women agreed with this goal is unclear. Obninskii, *Polgoda*, 13.

88. Temma Kaplan, "Female Consciousness and Collective Action: The Case of Barcelona, 1910–1928," *Signs* 7 (spring 1982): 565.

89. Ibid., 551.

90. James C. Scott, *Domination and the Arts of Resistance: Hidden Transcripts*, New Haven, Conn., 1990.

91. On women's protest, see Lynne Viola, "*Bab'i bunty* and Peasant Women's Protest during Collectivization," *Russian Review* 45 (January 1986): 23–42; Barbara Alpern Engel, "Women, Men, and the Languages of Peasant Resistance, 1870–1907," in Frank and Steinberg, *Cultures in Flux*, 34–53; and Smith, "Class and Gender."

92. Kaplan, "Female Consciousness," 564–65.

93. Laura Lee Downs, "Women's Strikes and the Politics of Popular Egalitarianism in France, 1916–18," in Berlanstein, *Rethinking Labor History*, 114–48; Sara E. Melzer and Leslie W. Rabine, eds., *Rebel Daughters: Women and the French Revolution* (New York, 1992), esp. the introduction and the contributions by Joan B. Landes and by Darline Gay Levy and Harriet B. Applewhite.

94. Kaplan, "Female Consciousness," 551.

95. Chatterjee, "Celebrating Women," 123. Chatterjee's work devotes a chapter to the February revolution.

96. The hooligans studied by Neuberger may be an exception. See *Hooligans*.

97. Gorsuch, "Enthusiasts," 2.

98. Downs, "Women's Strikes," in Berlanstein, *Rethinking Labor History*, 114; Scott, *Domination*, 227.

CHAPTER 6: WORKER CULTURE AND REVOLUTIONARY LEGITIMACY

1. Examples of historians' comments include Moshe Lewin, *Russian Peasants and Soviet Power: A Study of Collectivization* (London, 1968,) 132–33; Theodore H. Von Laue, *Why Lenin? Why Stalin? Why Gorbachev? The Rise and Fall of the Soviet System* (New York, 1993), 62–64, 84; and William G. Rosenberg,

introduction to Fitzpatrick, Rabinowitch, and Stites, *Russia in the Era,* 7.

2. *Rabochaia gazeta,* 15 December 1913, 4; *Edinstvo* 3 (19 March 1909): 15; *Metallist* 7 (30 December 1911): 12; 22 (26 October 1912): 11; 6 (10 August 1913): 17; 10 (25 October 1913): 14.

3. *Edinstvo* 2 (5 March 1909): 13; 6 (15 June 1909): 16; *Nash put'* 18 (17 June 1911): 15; *Kuznets* 3–4 (20 December 1907): 17; and *Zhizn' pekarei* 2 (10 May 1914): 4.

4. *Edinstvo* 6 (15 June 1909): 16.

5. *Metallist* 6 (10 August 1913): 9.

6. Quoted in *Metallist* 7 (24 August 1913): 14. Also see, for example, *Kuznets* 5–6 (19 January 1908): 27; *Metallist* 22 (26 October 1912): 11; and *Nash put'* 18 (17 June 1911): 15.

7. Navich, *Pit',* 43.

8. *Golos derevoobdelochnika* 1 (28 June 1909): 7.

9. *Pechatnoe delo* 1 (19 January 1912): 10. Specific complaints about failed strikes are also contained in *Metallist* 6 (10 August 1913): 18; and *Novoe pechatnoe delo* 4 (11 April 1913): 13.

10. *Fabrichnaia zhizn'* 4–5 (19 December 1910): 5.

11. *Trezvost' i berezhlivost'* 10 (October 1902): 5. Similar sentiment was expressed in *Trud tabachnika,* 17 May 1907, 11.

12. Tiushin's memoirs are held in TsGA SPb, f. 6255, op. 17, d. 2, l. 76. See also Buiko, *Put' rabochego,* 28; and *Listok soiuza rabochikh portnykh, portnikh, i skorniakov,* 24 March 1907, 7.

13. G. M. Sharshavin, *Ia—partii riadovoi* (Vologda, 1962), 11.

14. Frank and Steinberg, *Cultures in Flux,* 10.

15. The same observation is made by Koenker in "Class and Consciousness," in Fitzpatrick, Rabinowitch, and Stites, *Russia in the Era,* 45.

16. *Rabochii bumazhnik* 21 (7 November 1928): 18; *Pechatnyi dvor,* 8 January 1929, 4.

17. Kagan, *Molodezh',* 176–80; Amosov, *O p'ianykh,* 22–23. The need to spend leisure time sensibly is also discussed in Semashko, *Kul'turnaia revoliutsiia,* 32; *Krasnyi derevoobdelochnik* 12 (15 June 1928): 1; Iaroslavskii, "O bor'be s p'ianstvom," 21; and *Pishchevik* 1 (1 January 1924): 2.

18. K. Mironov, *Iz vospominanii rabochago* (Moscow, 1906), 23–24.

19. Bulgakovskii, *Zhizn' Kass'iana,* 25. Also see Ia. I. Lifshits, *Doloi kurenie i p'ianstvo* (n.p., 1928), 8; Sazhin, *Chto nado znat',* 33; and Iuli Martov, *Zapiski Sotsial-Demokrata* (Cambridge, England, 1975), 286–87.

20. *TPVS,* 2:822.

21. TsGA SPb, f. 9672, op. 1, d. 587, l. 25. *Rabochee ekho,* 3 December 1910, 12; and Popov, *Vospominaniia,* 43, may also be consulted.

22. TsGA SPB, f. 6255, op. 17, d. 2, l. 162.

23. Skorobogatov, "Ot rabochei zastavy," 147. It should be noted that images of "alcoholic" revolutionaries also haunted the minds of the dominant classes. Shipov, *Alkogolizm,* 10–11, 31–34; *Trezvaia zhizn'* (December 1905): 72; (January 1907): 75–94; *Novaia rabochaia gazeta,* 18 January 1914, 2; *Vestnik*

trezvosti 153 (September 1907): 27; and TsGA SPb, f. 6261, op. 22, d. 38, l. 13ob. For similar associations in France, see Susanna Barrows, "After the Commune: Alcoholism, Temperance, and Literature in the Early Third Republic," in John M. Merriman, ed., *Consciousness and Class Experience in Nineteenth Century Europe* (New York, 1979), 208–9.

24. *Krasnyi treugol'nik*, 21 May 1928, 1. *Krasnyi derevoobdelochnik* 12 (15 June 1928): 1 contains a similar statement.

25. *Iunyi kozhevnik* (April–May 1924): 15–18. *Golos kozhevnika* 1 (7 January 1929): 11; *Krasnyi putilovets*, 30 September 1929, 2.

26. Zheleznov, *Budem zhit'*, 74; *Bor'ba s alkogolizmom v SSSR*, 46–47.

27. *Novyi luch*, 6 December 1917, 3; *V dni Velikoi Proletarskoi revoliutsii: Épizody bor'by v Petrograde v 1917 godu* (Moscow, 1937), 218; *Zhenshchiny goroda Lenina* (Leningrad, 1963), 161; *Bastiony revoliutsii*, vol. 2, *Bor'ba za uprochenie Sovetskoi vlasti i gody grazhdanskoi voiny* (Leningrad, 1959), 426; *Znamia truda: Kratkii ocherk istorii Leningradskogo armaturnogo zavoda "Znamia truda"* (Leningrad, 1960), 78–79; I. I. Gaza, ed., *Putilovets na putiakh k Oktiabriu: Iz istorii "Krasnogo Putilovtsa"* (Leningrad, 1933), 148. Not all Red Guardists conform to the image of committed revolutionary: for contemporary accounts showing members participating in the pogroms, see *Novyi luch*, 6 December 1917, 3; 7 December 1917, 2; and *Fakel*, 25 November 1917, 2.

28. *Golos kozhevnika* 22 (10 November 1925): 15 (emphasis mine); *Krasnyi putilovets*, 17 December 1928, 2; *Rabochii bumazhnik* 22 (November 1929): 2 (emphasis mine); *Krasnovyborzhets*, 1 September 1928, 4; Kovgankin, *Komsomol*, 26; *Leningradskii metallist* 6 (6 June 1924): 12. Less typically, activists characterized drinking as an "abnormality," a "diseased phenomenon" that left workers vulnerable to their "class enemies." TsGAIPD SPb, f. 4000, op. 18, d. 287, l. 10; f. 1012, op. 1, d. 794, l. 38; *Krasnaia gazeta*, 22 October 1925, 7.

29. Kovgankin, *Alkogol'*, 17 (emphasis mine). Gorsuch makes a similar point in "Enthusiasts," 122.

30. Stephen Kotkin, "Coercion and Identity: Workers' Lives in Stalin's Showcase City," in Siegelbaum and Suny, *Making Workers*, 295.

31. *Leningradskii rabochii* 1 (4 January 1926): 3.

32. *Trezvost' i kul'tura* 1 (July 1928): 11; *Rabochii bumazhnik* 4 (28 February 1925): 14; and *Krasnyi treugol'nik*, 21 December 1929, 4. Similar incidents are described in *Krasnaia gazeta*, 24 January 1926, 6; 7 June 1927, 5; *Iskry*, 28 February 1929, 4; *Kozhevnik*, 6 November 1929, 6.

33. *Leningradskaia pravda*, 30 May 1926, 5.

34. *Pechatnyi stanok*, 1 January 1924, 1.

35. *Krasnovyborzhets*, 4 January 1929, 4 and *Krasnyi putilovets*, 15 August 1928, 3.

36. *Élektrosila*, 28 October 1929, 2 (emphasis in the original). *Kozhevenik*, 28 July 1928, 5. Other typical examples of indifference and defiance are contained in *Skorokhodovskii ékho*, 24 November 1928, 2; *Krasnovyborzhets*, 19 December 1928, 5; *Leningradskaia pravda*, 30 May 1929, 4; and *Skorokhodovskii rabochii*, 6 July 1929, 1; *Shilo*, 1 May 1929, 4; TsGA SPb, f. 4591, op. 1, d. 1936, l.

32; f. 4709, op. 8, d. 67, l. 6; f. 6276, op. 119, d. 13, ll. 15, 122.

37. *Kabel'shchik*, 25 September 1928, 3.

38. *Krasnyi putilovets*, 14 November 1929, 4 (emphasis mine). Also see Zhiga, *Novye rabochie*, 29.

39. *Vestnik profsoiuzov* 10–11 (October–November 1925): 15. Article 47 enumerated the conditions under which employers might terminate workers. Occasional drunkenness was not sufficient grounds for legal dismissal. The labor code is published as *Kodeks zakonov o trude RSFSR* (Moscow, 1927).

40. TsGA RSFSR, f. 406, op. 7, d. 392, l. 53.

41. *Golos kozhevnika* 1 (7 January 1929): 10.

42. Dreiden, *Antialkogol'naia rabota*, 70; Aleksandrov and Stel'makh, *Pochemu*, 23. Also see Rafail, *Za novogo cheloveka*, 8; Lifshits, *Alkogol'*, 3; *Kak u nas*, 8; Larin, *Alkogolizm*, 131.

43. E. P. Thompson, "Time, Work-Discipline, and Industrial Capitalism," *Past and Present* 38 (December 1967): 85.

44. David L. Hoffmann, *Peasant Metropolis: Social Identities in Moscow, 1929–1941* (Ithaca, N.Y., 1994), 205; Sheila Fitzpatrick, "Supplicants and Citizens: Public Letter-Writing in Soviet Russia in the 1930s," *Slavic Review* 55 (spring 1996): 94; Boris I. Kolonitskii, "Antibourgeois Propaganda and Anti-'Burzhui' Consciousness in 1917," *Russian Review* 53 (April 1994): 183–96, 190; Stephen Kotkin, *Magnetic Mountain: Stalinism as Civilization* (Berkeley, Calif., 1995), 220. Orlando Figes similarly argues that peasants reinterpreted language to suit their needs. "The Russian Revolution and Its Language in the Village," *Russian Review* 56 (1997): 334.

45. *Golos kozhevnika* 1 (7 January 1929): 10.

46. *Gul vereten* 1 (November 1928): 3.

47. *Pechatnyi stanok*, 24 December 1924, 1. Other references to alcohol's benefits to the state budget may be found in *Revoliutsiia i kul'tura* 13 (1928): 29; Rafail, *Za novogo cheloveka*, 8; *Voprosy narkologii* (1928): 7; *Pravda*, 18 October 1925, 2; TsGAIPD SPb, f. 18, op. 1, d. 241, l. 20. Similarly, laborers who arrived at work intoxicated on Industrialization Day subtly protested the state's expectation that they volunteer time to the factory. *Krasnyi treugol'nik*, 22 August 1929, 4; and *Skorokhodovskii rabochii*, 24 August 1929, 4. The meaning of parties celebrating the death of Lenin is less clear. For this, see *Krasnaia gazeta*, 16 March 1926, 3. Plausible deniability was not present in all cases. In 1925, a special issue of *Novaia vechernaia gazeta* reportedly celebrated the renewed sale of vodka. Its spoof on revolutionary language included Ivan Prutkov's announcement that he "eagerly drank a bottle" and challenged a comrade to follow this example. *Pravda*, 14 October 1925, 1.

48. *Krasnyi treugol'nik*, 10 March 1929, 4.

49. *Pechatnik* 11 (13 March 1926): 3.

50. Aleksandrov and Stel'makh, *Pochemu*, 55. Also see *Kul'turnaia revoliutsiia* 3 (10 February 1929): 31–32.

51. Quoted in Rafail, *Za novogo cheloveka*, 83–84. Dress as an indicator of class status is further discussed in Gorsuch, "Enthusiasts," 314–27; and in N.

A. Semashko, *Iskusstvo odevat'sia* (Leningrad, 1927), 17–20. Nondrinking is associated with the "petty bourgeoisie" in *Rabochii klub* 3–4 (March–April 1924): 3–4, 59; and Grigorov and Shkotov, *Staryi i novyi byt*, 138.

52. Zhiga, *Novye rabochie*, 52–53 (emphasis mine). Anti-Semitic proclivities among Russian workers have been analyzed in detail by Wynn in *Workers*.

53. Sarah Davies, *Popular Opinion in Stalin's Russia: Terror, Propaganda and Dissent, 1934–41* (Cambridge, England, 1997), 85–88, 126.

54. Fitzpatrick, "Supplicants and Citizens," 97.

55. *Pravda*, 22 November 1925, 1.

56. A. Z. Vakser and V. S. Izmozik, "Izmenenie obshchestvennogo oblika Sovetskogo rabochego 20–30-kh godov," *Voprosy istorii* 11 (November 1984): 100.

57. *Gazeta kopeika*, 30 September 1911, 4; *Pishchevik* (15 January 1929): 4; *Krasnyi putilovets*, 15 April 1929, 3; Mironov, *Iz vospominanii*, 16; *Metallist* (23 June 1926): 41; TsGA SPb, f. 9672, op. 1, d. 469, l. 5.

58. TsGA SPb, f. 9672, op. 1, d. 469, l. 5.

59. *Leningradskii metallist* 7 (20 June 1924): 8.

60. *Krasnaia gazeta*, 2 July 1924, 7. Komsomoltsy (like other workers) often considered drink a "personal," or a "small" matter undeserving of their attention. Mil'chakov, *Komsomol*, 16; TsGAIPD SPb, f. K-156, op. 1-a, d. 18, l. 3; *Pravda*, 18 October 1925, 2; 15 February 1928, 4.

61. TsGAIPD SPb, f. K-1889, op. 1, d. 34, l. 78.

62. Ibid., f. K-784, op. 1, d. 476, l. 57; *Bor'ba s alkogolizmom v SSSR*, 46–47; TsGAIPD SPb, f. K-156, op. 1-a, d. 18, l. 117; and *Tribuna khalturintsev*, 18 June 1929, 1.

63. TsGAIPD SPb, f. 1200, op. 1, d. 370, l. 67.

64. Steve Smith, "Russian Workers and the Politics of Social Identity," *Russian Review* 56 (January 1997): 4.

65. McDaniel has similarly suggested that "consciousness" was a fluid category. *Autocracy*, 185.

66. Wynn, *Workers*, 6.

67. Ivanov, *Po stupeniam bor'by*, 149–50.

68. Ivanov, *Zapiski proshlogo*, 77–78.

69. *O revoliutsionnom proshlom Peterburgskogo metallicheskogo zavoda* (Leningrad, 1926), 44; *Metallurgi s Matisova ostrova: Kratkii ocherk istorii Leningradskogo zavoda po obrabotke tsvetnykh metallov* (Leningrad, 1967), 51; *Rabochii golos*, 26 November 1905, 12; *Naborshchik i pechatnyi mir* 125 (September 1906): 862; *Golos pechatnika* 11 (4 November 1906): 13; GARF, f. 6876, op. 1, d. 59, l. 22.

70. *Rech'*, 12 July 1914, 5; and *Novoe vremia*, 10 July 1914, 3–4.

71. Neuberger, *Hooliganism*, esp. 262–66, 270–72.

72. Evidence for the link between drunkenness and hooliganism is abundant in contemporary sources. For examples, see Deichman, *Alkogolizm*, 117; and Kovgankin, *Komsomol*, 16.

73. In November 1905, Putilov workers renounced drink for three months. Mitel'man, Glebov, and Ul'ianovskii, *Istoriia* (1939), 264–65; and *Rabochii golos*, 26 November 1905, 12.

74. Scott, *Domination*, 92.

75. Jeffrey J. Rossman, "The Teikovo Cotton Workers' Strike of April 1932: Class, Gender, and Identity Politics in Stalin's Russia," *Russian Review* 56 (January 1997): 69.

76. *Leningradskii metallist* 1 (5 January 1925): 16.

77. *Verstatka*, 25 September 1924, 1.

CONCLUSION

1. Gabinov, *Pochemu*, 22.

2. Steinberg, "Workers on the Cross"; Bernice Glatzer Rosenthal, ed., *The Occult in Russian and Soviet Culture* (Ithaca, N.Y., 1997), 397–413.

3. For secondary works that explore certain leisure activities, see Jeffrey Brooks, *When Russia Learned to Read: Literacy and Popular Literature, 1861–1917* (Princeton, N.J., 1985); Charles E. Clark, "Doloi negramotnost': The Literacy Campaign in the RSFSR, 1923–1927," Ph.D. diss., University of Illinois, 1993; Robert Edelman, *Serious Fun: A History of Spectator Sports in the USSR* (New York, 1993); and Al'bin M. Konechnyi, "Shows for the People: Public Amusement Parks in Nineteenth-Century St. Petersburg," in Frank and Steinberg, *Cultures in Flux;* Swift, "Theater."

4. Koenker, "Men against Women"; Gorsuch, "'A Woman Is Not a Man,'"; Engel, *Between the Fields.*

5. On the gendered construction of revolution, see Chatterjee, "Celebrating Women," chap. 2.

6. F. V. Gladkov, *Cement: A Novel,* trans. A. S. Arthur and C. Ashleigh (New York, 1980), 4.

7. Joanna Bourke, *Dismembering the Male: Men's Bodies, Britain and the Great War* (London, 1996), esp. 133–35, 153–55, 252. Also see Tosh, "What Should Historians Do," 193, and Robert A. Nye, *Masculinity and Male Codes of Honor in Modern France* (Oxford, 1993), 125–31.

8. George L. Mosse has alternatively suggested that Social Democrats, both in the Soviet Union and elsewhere, attempted unsuccessfully to promote an alternate form of masculinity. *The Image*, 126–32.

9. Baron, *Work Engendered*, 51; Mark C. Carnes and Clyde Griffen, eds., *Meanings for Manhood: Constructions of Masculinity in Victorian America* (Chicago, 1990), 102; Francis G. Couvares, *The Remaking of Pittsburgh: Class and Culture in an Industrializing City, 1877–1919* (Albany, N.Y., 1984), 56.

10. On family policy, see Wendy Z. Goldman, *Women, The State, and Revolution: Soviet Family Polcy and Social Life, 1917–1936* (Cambridge, England, 1993).

11. The state's policies toward homosexuality may also have reflected these "masculinizing" trends. Homosexuality, decriminalized in 1922, was re-criminalized in 1933. Daniel Healy, "The Russian Revolution and the Decriminalization of Homosexuality," *Revolutionary Russia* 6 (June 1993): 33, 40.

12. Hoffmann, *Peasant Metropolis*, 4, 188; Figes, "The Russian Revolution"; Kotkin, *Magnetic Mountain;* Sheila Fitzpatrick, *The Russian Revolution,*

1917–1932 (Oxford, 1982).

13. Fitzpatrick, "Supplicants and Citizens," 88. Clayton Black, "Party Crisis and the Shop Floor: Krasnyi Putilovets and the Leningrad Opposition," *Europe-Asia Studies* 46 (1994): 107–26; Gorsuch, "Enthusiasts," 221, 224.

14. *Pravda*, 19 August 1928, 6. The notion that things should have been better in Leningrad is also present in Dreiden, *Antialkogol'naia rabota*, 9; Voronov, *Alkogol'*, 53.

15. Larin, *Novye zakony*, 16.

16. *Protiv alkogolizma*, 23.

SOURCES CITED

ARCHIVAL SOURCES

Gosudarstvennyi arkhiv Russkoi federatsii (GARF, formerly TsGAOR)
  f. 102. Departament politsii.
  f. 6861. Istprof pri TsK soiuza narpita.
  f. 6864. Istprof pri TsK soiuza pechatnikov.
  f. 6869. Istprof pri TsK shveinikov.
  f. 6876. Istprof pri TsK khimikov.
Rossiiskii gosudarstvennyi istoricheskii arkhiv (RGIA, formerly TsGIA)
  f. 575. Glavnoe upravlenie neokladnykh sborov, Ministerstvo finansov.
  f. 1284. Ministerstvo vnutrennikh del, Departament obshchikh del.
Tsentral'nyi gosudarstvennyi arkhiv istoriko-politicheskikh dokumentov
    Sankt-Peterburga (TsGAIPD SPb, formerly PAIIPLO)
  f. 2. Vyborgskii raionnyi komitet VKP(b) goroda Leningrada.
  f. 3. Moskovsko-Narvskii raionnyi komitet VKP(b).
  f. 16. Leningradskii gubernskii komitet VKP(b).
  f. 18. Pervichnaia partorganizatsiia zavoda "Krasnyi Vyborzhets."
  f. 76. Kollektiv RKV(b) Aleksandrovskogo zavoda.
  f. 1012. Kollektiv RKP(b) Putilovskogo zavoda.
  f. 1200. Kollektiv RVK(b) zavoda "Krasnyi Treugol'nik."
  f. 4000. Vospominaniia.
  f. K-154. KSM—zavod imeni Karla Marksa.
  f. K-156. KSM—zavod "Krasnyi Treugol'nik."
  f. K-630. Vyborgskii raikom RKSM.
  f. K-784. Moskovsko-Narvskii raikom RKSM.
  f. K-1889. KSM—Nevskii sudostroitel'nyi i mekhanicheskii zavod im. Lenina.
Tsentral'nyi gosudarstvennyi arkhiv RSFSR (TsGA RSFSR)
  f. 406. Narodnyi komissariat raboche-krest'ianskoi inspektsii.
Tsentral'nyi gosudarstvennyi arkhiv Sankt Peterburg (TsGA SPb, formerly Ts-
    GAORSSL)
  f. 1360. Leningradskii zavod "Krasnyi Treugol'nik."
  f. 3215. Otdel zdravookhraneniia Ispolnitel'nogo komiteta Leningradskogo

oblastnogo soveta rabochikh, krest'ianskikh i krasnoarmeiskikh deputatov.

f. 4301. Leningradskii gubernskii otdel zdravookhraneniia.

f. 4591. Leningradskii oblastnoi komitet profsoiuza rabochikh metallistov.

f. 4709. Leningradskii gubernskii otdel soiuza khimikov.

f. 4774. Leningradskii oblastnoi komitet profsoiuza rabochikh kozhevennoi promyshlennosti.

f. 6255. Leningradskii oblastnoi otdel profsoiuza rabochikh tekstil'noi promyshlennosti.

f. 6261. Petrogradskii gubernskii otdel professional'nogo soiuza rabochikh pishchevoi i vkusovoi promyshlennosti.

f. 6276. Leningradskii oblastnoi sovet professional'nykh soiuzov.

f. 9672. Kollektsiia dokumental'nykh materialov redaktsii po istorii fabrik i zavodov goroda Leningrada.

Tsentral'nyi gosudarstvennyi istoricheskii arkhiv Sankt-Peterburga (TsGIA SPb, formerly TsGIAL)

f. 569. Kantseliariia Peterburgskogo gradonachal'nika.

NEWSPAPERS AND JOURNALS

Some of these items were published for a limited readership, specified here following the range of dates.

Administrativnyi vestnik. Moscow, 1925–1929. Ministry of Internal Affairs.

Chelnok. St. Petersburg, 1907. Textile workers.

Edinstvo. St. Petersburg, 1909–1910. Metalworkers.

Élektrosila. Leningrad, 1927–1929. Élektrosila power plant.

Fabrichnaia zhizn'. St. Petersburg, 1910–1911. Textile workers.

Fakel. Petrograd, 1917. Social Democrats.

Gazeta kopeika. St. Petersburg, 1909–1916.

Gigiena i épidemiologiia. Moscow-Leningrad, 1922–1929. Physicians.

Golos derevoobdelochnika. St. Petersburg, 1908. Woodworkers.

Golos kozhevnika. Moscow, 1922–1929. Leather workers' union.

Golos pechatnika. St. Petersburg, 1906–1907. Printers.

Golos sakharinka. Moscow, 1923–1929. Sugar workers' union.

Gul vereten. Leningrad, 1926–1929. Ravenstvo spinning mill.

Iskry. Leningrad, 1925–1929. Sokolova print shop.

Iunyi kozhevnik. Supplement to *Golos kozhevnika.*

Kabel'shchik. Leningrad, 1927–1929. Sevkabel' mill.

Kommunistka. Communist Party, 1927–1929.

Kozhevenik. Leningrad, 1928–1929. Marxist and Radishchev leather mills.

Kozhevnik. Leningrad, 1929. Marxist leather mill.

Krasnaia gazeta. Leningrad, 1918–1929.

Krasnaia zaria. Leningrad, 1927–1929. Krasnaia Zaria telephone factory.

Krasnovyborzhets. Leningrad, 1928–1929. Krasnovyborzhets metalworks.

Krasnyi derevoobdelochnik. Moscow, 1927–1929. Woodworkers' union.

Krasnyi putilovets. Leningrad, 1926–1929. Putilov metalworks.

Krasnyi treugol'nik. Leningrad, 1928–1929. Krasnyi Treugol'nik rubber works.

Kul'tura i byt. Moscow,1930. VTsSPS and the Society for Healthy Lifestyle (byt).

Kul'turnaia revoliutsiia. Moscow, 1928–1929. All-Union Council of Trade Unions (VTsSPS).

Kuznets. St. Petersburg, 1907–1908. Metalworkers.

Leningradskaia pravda. Leningrad, 1925–1929. Leningrad Communist Party.

Leningradskii meditsinskii zhurnal. Leningrad, 1925–1928. Leningrad province Department of Public Health.

Leningradskii metallist. Leningrad, 1924–1929. Leningrad region metalworkers' union.

Leningradskii rabochii. Leningrad, 1924–1926, 1926–1928. Leningrad province trade union.

Listok rabochikh po obrabotke dereva. St. Petersburg, 1907. Woodworkers.

Listok soiuza rabochikh portnykh, portnikh, i skorniakov. St. Petersburg, 1907. Tailors and furriers.

Metallist. Moscow, 1918–1929. Metalworkers' union.

Metallist. St. Petersburg, 1911–1914. Metalworkers.

Metallistik. Leningrad, 1928. Supplement to *Leningradskii metallist.*

Naborshchik. St. Petersburg, 1902–1904. Compositors.

Naborshchik i pechatnyi mir. St. Petersburg, 1905–1917. Printers.

Nadezhda. St. Petersburg, 1908. Metalworkers.

Nasha zaria. St. Petersburg, 1910–1913.

Nashe delo. Petrograd, 1915.

Nash put'. St. Petersburg, 1910–1911. Metalworkers.

Novaia rabochaia gazeta. St. Petersburg, 1913–1914.

Novoe pechatnoe delo. St. Petersburg, 1911–1913. Printers.

Novoe vremia. St. Petersburg, January 1905, October 1905, July 1914.

Novyi luch. Petrograd, 1917. Social Democrats.

Obshchestvennyi vrach. Moscow, 1909, 1911–1916. Pirogov Society.

Pechatnik. Moscow, 1922–1929. Printers' union.

Pechatnoe delo. St. Petersburg, 1908–1912. Printers.

Pechatnyi dvor. Leningrad, 1924–1929. Pechatnyi Dvor print shop.

Pechatnyi stanok. Leningrad, 1924–1929. Military print shop.

Peterburgskaia gazeta. St. Petersburg, January 1906, July 1914.

Peterburgskii listok. St. Petersburg, January 1905, December 1905, July 1914.

Petrogradskaia pravda. Petrograd, 1918–1924. Petrograd Communist Party.

Pishchevik. Moscow, 1922–1929. Food workers' union.

Pravda. Moscow, 1923–1929. Social Democrats.

Rabochaia gazeta. St. Petersburg, 1906. Independent Social Workers' Party.

Rabochaia mysl'. St. Petersburg, 1900–1902.

Rabochee ékho. St. Petersburg, 1910–1911. Society of Woodworkers.

Rabochii bumazhnik. Moscow, 1924–1929. Paper makers' union.

Rabochii golos. St. Petersburg, 1905. Social Democrats.

Rabochii klub. Moscow, 1924, 1928. Proletkul't.

Rabochii po metallu. St. Petersburg, 1906–1907. Metalworkers.

Rabotnitsa. Moscow, 1923–1929. Women workers.

Rabotnitsa i krest'ianka. Leningrad, 1922–1929. Women.

Rech'. St. Petersburg, July 1914.

Revoliutsiia i kul'tura. Moscow, 1927–1928.

Russkii pechatnik. Moscow, 1909–1910. Printers.

Russkii vrach. St. Petersburg, 1902–1917. Physicians.

Russkoe znamia. St. Petersburg, January 1906.

Shilo. Leningrad, 1924–1929. Volodarskii print shop.

Shveinik. Moscow, 1923–1929. Garment workers' union.

Skorokhodovskii rabochii. Leningrad, 1929. Skorokhod shoe factory.

Skorokhodovskoe ékho. Leningrad, 1928–1929. Skorokhod shoe factory.

Sotsial'naia gigiena. Moscow, 1922, 1925–1929. Gosizdat.

Stroitel'. Moscow, 1917–1925. Construction workers' union.

Sud idet. Leningrad, 1925–1929. Leningrad region court.

Trezvaia zhizn'. St. Petersburg, 1905–1914. Aleksandr Nevskii Temperance Society.

Trezvost' i berezhlivost'. St. Petersburg, 1902–1904.

Trezvost' i kul'tura. Moscow, 1928–1929. VTsSPS.

Trezvye vskhody. St. Petersburg, 1908–1914.

Tribuna khalturintsev. Leningrad, 1928–1929. Khalturin textile factory.

Trud tabachnika. St. Petersburg, 1907. Tobacco workers.

V bor'be za trezvost'. Moscow, 1911–1914. Moscow Diocesan Society for the Struggle with Public Drunkenness.

Verstatka. Leningrad, 1924–1926. Guttenberg print shop.

Vestnik popechitel'stv o narodnoi trezvosti. St. Petersburg, 1903–1905.

Vestnik profsoiuzov. Leningrad, 1922–1926. Leningrad province trade union.

Vestnik trezvosti. St. Petersburg, 1900–1916.

Voprosy alkogolizma. St. Petersburg, 1913.

Voprosy narkologii. Moscow, 1926, 1928.

Voprosy zdravookhraneniia. Moscow, 1928–1929. Russian Commissariat of Public Health.

Vozrozhdenie. Moscow, 1908–1910.

Za novyi byt. Moscow, 1925–1929. Moscow Department of Public Health.

Zdravookhranenie. Leningrad, 1928–1929. Leningrad district Department of Public Health.

Zhizn' pekarei. St. Petersburg, 1913–1914. Bakers and confectioners.

Zhurnal nevropatologii i psikhiatrii imeni S. S. Korsakova. Moscow, 1901–1917. Society of Neuropathologists and Psychiatrists at Moscow University.

Zhurnal Russkogo obshchestva okhraneniia narodnogo zdraviia. St. Petersburg, 1900–1913. The Russian Society for the Protection of Public Health.

Zorkii glaz. Leningrad, 1924–1929. Zinov'ev print shop.

PUBLISHED PRIMARY SOURCES

Aleksandrov, Ia., and P. Stel'makh, *Pochemu my p'em.* Leningrad, 1929.

Aleksandrov, P. P. *Za Narvskoi zastavoi: Vospominaniia starogo rabochego.*

Leningrad, 1963.

Alekseev, P. S. *Chem pomoch' velikomu goriu? Kak ostanovit' p'ianstvo?* Moscow, 1906.

Amosov, N. *O p'ianykh prazdnikakh.* Moscow, n.d.

Bekhterev, V. M. *Alkogolizm i bor'ba s nim.* Leningrad, 1927.

Berenshtam, V. V. *Za pravo! Iz nabliudenii advokata.* St. Petersburg, 1905.

Berezin, A., Z. Bobrov, E. Guseva, L. Kondrat'eva, K. Levashov, V. Miasiashev, and V. Shiperovich. *Rabochaia molodezh' kak ona est': Opyt pedagogicheskogo izucheniia molodezhi odnogo zavoda.* Leningrad, 1930.

Biely, Andrey. *St. Petersburg.* Trans. John Cournos. New York, 1987.

Binshtok, V. I., and L. S. Kaminskii. *Narodnoe pitanie i narodnoe zdravie.* Leningrad, 1929.

Biudzhety Leningradskikh rabochikh i sluzhashchikh 1922–1926 gg. Leningrad, 1927.

Bogdanovich, L. *Golubchik! Eshche riumochku!* Moscow, 1915.

Bor'ba s alkogolizmom v SSSR: Pervyi plenum vsesoiuznogo soveta protivoalkogol'nykh obshchestv v SSSR, 20 maia–1 iuna 1929 g. Moscow, 1929.

Borodin, D. N. *Itogi rabot pervago vserossiiskago s"ezda po bor'be s p'ianstvom.* St. Petersburg, 1910.

Brodskii, N. L., S. N. Dziubinskii, L. S. Mirskii, and V. P. Tsvetaev, comps. *Metallist: Istoriia, byt, bor'ba.* Moscow, 1925.

Buiko, A. M. *Put' rabochego: Vospominaniia putilovtsa.* Leningrad, 1964.

Bulgakovskii, D. G. *Do chego dovodit' p'ianstvo: Kartiny iz zhizni.* St. Petersburg, 1900.

———. *Gorkaia pravda o p'ianstve.* St. Petersburg, 1909.

———. *Kak ia perestal pit'.* St. Petersburg, 1906.

———. *Na pomoshch': Sbornik statei o vrednom vliianii spirtnykh napitkov na zdorov'e, material'noe blagosostoianie i nravstvennost' dlia naroda.* St. Petersburg, 1901.

———. *Ocherk deiatel'nosti popechitel'stv o narodnoi trezvosti za vse vremia ikh sushchestvovaniia (1895–1909 g.) v dvukh chastiakh.* St. Petersburg, 1910.

———. *Zakryli: K krest'ianskim zhenam: Narodnoe chitenie s svetovymi kartinami.* St. Petersburg, 1911.

———. *Zhizn' Kass'iana: Chtenie s svetovymi kartinami.* St. Petersburg, 1910.

Buntilov, A[leksandr]. *Za pechatnym stankom.* Moscow, 1931.

Buzinov, Aleksei. *Za Nevskoi zastavoi: Zapiski rabochego.* Moscow, 1930.

Chebysheva-Dmitrieva, E. A. *Rol' zhenshchin v bor'be s alkogolizmom.* St. Petersburg, 1904.

Chulkov, M. D. *Sochinenie.* Vol. 1, *Sobranie raznykh pesen.* St. Petersburg, 1913.

Deichman, É. I. *Alkogolizm i bor'ba s nim.* Moscow, 1929.

Dekrety Sovetskoi vlasti. Vol. 7. Moscow, 1974.

Didrikhson, B. F. *Alkogolizm i proizvoditel'nost' truda.* Leningrad, 1931.

———. *P'ianku—'k stenke'.* Leningrad, 1929.

Dreiden, Simion D. *Antialkogol'naia rabota v klube: Posobie dlia klubnykh i antialkogol'nykh rabotnikov.* Leningrad, 1930.

———, comp. *Za vashe zdorov'e: Antialkogol'naia khrestomatiia.* Leningrad, 1929.

Elistratov, A. I. *Administrativnoe pravo.* Moscow, 1929.

Evgeniev, B. *Zelenyi zmii: P'ianstvo i alkogolizm.* Petrograd, 1923.

Fomushkin, K. *Schastlivyi den' Dudkina.* n.p., 1906.

Frelikh, Rikhard. *Alkogolizm i proletariat.* Moscow, 1906.

Frenkel', M. G. *Vodka—nash vrag.* Moscow, n.d.

Fridman, M. I. *Vinnaia monopoliia.* Vol. 2, *Vinnaia monopoliia v Rossii.* St. Petersburg, 1916.

Frierson, Cathy A., ed. and trans. *Aleksandr Nikolaevich Engelgardt's Letters from the Country, 1872–1887.* New York, 1993.

G., N. *Pagubnyi obychai.* St. Petersburg, 1908.

Gabinov, L. A. *Pochemu v Sovetskom Soiuze razreshena prodazha spirtnykh napitkov.* Kharkov, 1927.

Gladkov, B. I. *Spirtnye napitki—iad dlia dush i tela.* St. Petersburg, 1911.

Gladkov, F. V. *Cement: A Novel.* Trans. A. S. Arthur and C. Ashleigh. New York, 1980.

God bor'by s alkogolizmom v Leningrade: Materialy dlia dokladchikov. Moscow, 1929.

Gordon, Ernst. *Russian Prohibition.* Westerville, Ohio, 1916.

Grigorevskii, Grigorii. *Pochemu on ne pil?* St. Petersburg, n.d.

Grigorov, G., and S. Shkotov. *Staryi i novyi byt.* Moscow, 1927.

Iaroslavskii, E. "O bor'be s p'ianstvom." In A. Slepkov, ed., *Byt i molodezh': Sbornik statei,* 18–22. Moscow, 1926.

Ignatov, P. K. *Zhizn' prostogo cheloveka.* Moscow, 1965.

Istoriia Leningradskogo soiuza rabochikh poligraficheskogo proizvodstva. Vol. 1, *1904–1907 gg.* Leningrad, 1925.

Ivanov, B[oris] I[vanovich]. *Po stupeniam bor'by: Zapiski starogo bol'shevika.* Moscow, 1934.

———. *Zapiski proshlogo: Povest' iz vospominanii detstva i iunoshestva rabochego-sotsialista.* Moscow, 1919.

Johnson, William E. *The Liquor Problem in Russia.* Westerville, Ohio, 1915.

Kagan, A. G. *Molodezh' posle gudka.* Moscow, 1930.

Kak u nas chestvuiut imeninnika i ponimaiut usopshago. St. Petersburg, 1907.

Kanel', V. Ia. *Alkogolizm i bor'ba s nim.* Moscow, 1914.

Ketlinskaia, V., and V. Stepkov. *Zhizn' bez kontrolia (Polovaia zhizn' i semia rabochei molodezhi).* Leningrad, 1929.

Kodeks zakonov o trude RSFSR. Moscow, 1927.

Kogan, B. B., and M. S. Lebedinskii. *Byt rabochei molodezhi.* Moscow, 1929.

Korovin, A. M. *Ob"iazannosti russkoi zhenshchiny v bor'be s alkogolizmom.* St. Petersburg, 1901.

———. *Sakhar i bor'ba s alkogolizmom.* Moscow, 1904.

Kovgankin, B. S. *Alkogol', alkogolizm i bor'ba s nim: Konspekt dlia vystuplenii vrachei, sester, agitatorov i propagandistov.* Moscow, 1927.

———. *Komsomol na bor'bu s narkotizmom: Kak molodezhi pobedit' bolezni byta. P'ianstvo i kurenie tabaka.* Leningrad, 1929.

Kurdachev, D. Ia. *Otvetstvennost'.* Perm, 1974.

Kurman, M. "Obsledovanie alkogolizma v Leningrade i Leningradskoi oblasti."

Biulleten' Leningradskago oblastnogo otdela statistiki 21 (1929): 190–206.

Kuznetsov, N. A. *Masterovshchina: Iz moei zhizni.* Leningrad, 1927.

Larin, Iu. *Alkogolizm i sotsializm.* Moscow, 1929.

———. *Novye zakony protiv alkogolizma i protivoalkogol'noe dvizhenie.* Moscow, 1929.

Larina, Anna. *This I Cannot Forget: The Memoirs of Nikolai Bukharin's Widow.* New York, 1993.

Lebedev, A. A. "K istorii kulachnykh boev na Rusi." *Russkaia starina* 7 (July 1913): 103–23; 8 (August 1913): 322–40.

Lifshits, Ia. I. *Alkogol' i trud.* Kharkov, 1929.

———. *Bor'ba s p'ianstvom.* Kharkov, 1929.

———. *Doloi kurenie i p'ianstvo.* n.p., 1928.

Liubimov, Nikolai A. "Dnevnik uchastnika pervago Vserossiiskago s"ezda po bor'be s narodnym p'ianstvom. S.-Peterburg. 28 dekabria 1909 g.-6 ianvaria 1910 g." Supplement to *V bor'be za trezvost'* 2 (February 1911).

Lositskii, A., and I. Chernyshev. *Alkogolizm peterburgskikh rabochikh.* St. Petersburg, 1913.

M—n, A. L. *O vrede p'ianstva.* St. Petersburg, 1903.

M—ov. *Pis'mo k rabochim.* St. Petersburg, 1907.

Martov, Iulii. *Zapiski Sotsial-Demokrata.* Cambridge, England, 1975.

Materialy po statistike Petrograda. Vol. 5. Petrograd, 1921.

Mendel'son, A. L. *Itogi prinuditel'noi trezvosti i novye formy p'ianstva.* Petrograd, 1916.

———. *Lechenie alkogolizma v ambulatoriiakh S.-Peterburgskago gorodskogo popechitel'stva o narodnoi trezvosti, 1903–1909 gg.* St. Petersburg, 1910.

———. *Na p'ianom fronte.* Leningrad, 1925.

———. *Nervno-psikhicheskaia gigiena i profilaktika. Iz lektsii, chitannykh v gosudarstvennom institute dlia usovershenstvovaniia vrachei v Leningrade v 1921–1926 g.g.* Leningrad, 1927.

Mikhailov, Dr. *Vodku pit'—vse gubit'.* Moscow, 1927.

Mil'chakov, A. *Komsomol v bor'be za kul'turnyi byt.* Leningrad, 1927.

Minor, L. S. *Chisla i nabliudeniia iz oblasti alkogolizma.* Moscow, 1910.

Mirianin. *V p'ianom ugare.* St. Petersburg, 1910.

Mironov, K. *Iz vospominanii rabochago.* Moscow, 1906.

Nalepko, A. *Butylka pogubila: Rasskaz.* St. Petersburg, 1909.

"Narodnyia sredstvia ot p'ianstva." *Deiatel'* 13 (1904): 488–93.

Navich. *Pit' ili ne pit'? (Otchego p'et rabochii narod?).* St. Petersburg, n.d.

Nesterenko, Aleksandr, S. M. Samet, F. V. Il'inskii, and M. N. Garkavi. *B'em trevogy (Antialkogol'naia zhivaia gazeta).* Moscow, 1927.

Newton, John. *Alcohol and the War: The Example of Russia.* London, n.d.

Nikoforov, N. *Protiv starogo byta: Iz blok-nota partrabotnika.* Leningrad, n.d.

Nikolaev, M[ikhail] P[etrovich]. "Za rabochee delo." *Zvezda,* no. 5 (May 1957): 103–15.

Obninskii, Viktor. *Polgoda russkoi revoliutsii: Sbornik materialov k istorii russkoi revoliutsii (oktiabr' 1905–aprel' 1906 gg.).* Moscow, 1906.

Onufriev, E. P. *Za Nevskoi zastavoi: Vospominaniia starogo bol'shevika*. Moscow, 1968.

O revoliutsionnom proshlom peterburgskogo metallicheskogo zavoda. Leningrad, 1926.

O tainoi prodazhe vina. St. Petersburg, n.d.

Papernikov, I. Ia., *Ocherk po istorii Leningradskogo soiuza kozhevnikov: K 25-letniiu iubileiu soiuza, 1905–1930 gg*. Leningrad, 1930.

Pastupaev, F. *Zhena rabochego i drugie razskazy*. Moscow, 1906.

Perestanem pit' vino i ugoshchat' im. St. Petersburg, 1902.

Petrov, G. *Doloi p'ianstvo: Sbornik statei*. Moscow, 1903.

P'ianstvo—velikoe zlo: Sbornik statei o vrede p'ianstve. St. Petersburg, 1902.

Piotrovskii, I. N. *Rasskaz starogo mastera*. Novosibirsk, 1957.

Pit' do dnia—ne vidat' dobra: Sbornik statei protiv p'ianstva. St. Petersburg, 1902.

Popov, I. V. *Vospominaniia*. Moscow, 1971.

Prizadumaites'! St. Petersburg, 1911.

Protiv alkogolizma: Sbornik materialov. Leningrad, 1929.

Pryzhov, Ivan. *Istoriia kabakov v Rossii v sviazi s istoriei russkago naroda*. [Kazan', 1868].

Putilovtsy v 1905 godu. Leningrad, 1931.

Rafail, M. *Za novogo cheloveka*. Leningrad, 1928.

Ravich, D. G. *Vodopoi—mogil'shchik*. Moscow, 1926.

Romashkov, I. *Kak smotrit sam narod na p'ianstvo*. Moscow, 1908.

Rozhdestvenskii, A., comp. *Zhertvy p'ianstva: Sbornik razskazov i statei dlia chteniia narodu o vrede p'ianstva*. St. Petersburg, 1909.

Rubanovskii, Il'ia. *Za knigu ili v pivnuiu?* Leningrad, 1928.

Sazhin, I. V. *Alkogol' kak pishchevoe veshchestvo*. St. Petersburg, 1910.

———. *Chto nado znat' o spirtnykh napitkakh*. Leningrad, 1929.

Sbornik okolo 500 noveishikh pesen, romansov i kupletov. St. Petersburg, 1903.

Semashko, N. A. *Iskusstvo odevat'sia*. Leningrad, 1927.

———. *Kul'turnaia revoliutsiia i ozdorovlenie byta*. Moscow, 1929.

Semenov, S. *Bud' trezv! (Pis'mo k bratu)*. Moscow, 1911.

Sergeev, Petr. *Za kompaniiu! (Byl)*. St. Petersburg, n.d.

Sergeevich, V. *Zavod—kuznitsa revoliutsii*. Moscow, 1929.

Sharshavin, G. M. *Ia—partii riadovoi*. Vologda, 1962.

Shipov, N. N. *Alkogolizm i revoliutsiia*. St. Petersburg, 1908.

Sholomovich, A. S. *40%, Sorok gradusov i rabochie*. Moscow, 1926.

Shotman, A. *Zapiski starogo bol'shevika*. Leningrad, 1963.

Simpson, J. Y. *Some Notes on the State Sale Monopoly and Subsequent Prohibition of Vodka in Russia*. London, 1918.

Skorobogatov, K. V. "Ot rabochei zastavy: Iz vospominanii artista." *Zvezda* 1 (January 1967): 131–49.

Sobranie uzakonenii i rasporiazhenii rabochego i krest'ianskogo pravitel'stva. Moscow, n.d.

Sovetskie organy protiv alkogolizma: Stenogrammy dokladov Tsentrosoiuza SSSR, VSNKh SSSR, NKZdravov RSFSR i USSR na zasedanii protivoalkogol'nykh obshchestv SSSR. Moscow, 1929.

Stalin, I. V. *Sochineniia*. Vol. 10. Moscow, 1946.

Strashun, I. D. *Na bor'bu za novyi trezvyi byt*. Moscow, 1927.

Strashun, I. D., and A. S. Berliand, eds. *Sanitarnoe prosveshchenie v rabochem klube*. 2 vols. Moscow, 1925.

Subbotin, A. *Pochemu sovetskaia vlast' razreshila prodazhu vodki*. Moscow, 1927.

Tiapugin, N. P. *Chto dolzhna znat' molodezh ob alkogole*. n.p., 1929.

———. *Narodnye zabliuzhdeniia i nauchnaia pravda ob alkogole*. Moscow, 1929.

Timofeev, P. *Chem zhivet zavodskii rabochii*. St. Petersburg, 1906.

———. "Ocherki zavodskoi zhizni." *Russkoe bogatstvo* 10 (October 1905): 71–91.

Tolmachev, V. N., ed. *Khuliganstvo i khuligany: Sbornik*. Moscow, 1929.

Tonul da vyplyl, ili pokhozhdeniia muzhichka v Pitere. St. Petersburg, 1900.

Trudy 1-go Vserossiiskago zhenskago s"ezda pri russkom zhenskom obshchestve v S.-Peterburge, 10–16 dekabria 1908 goda. St. Petersburg, 1909.

Trudy pervago vserossiiskago s"ezda po bor'be s p'ianstvom. S. Peterburg, 28 dekabria 1909 g.–6 ianvaria 1910 g. 3 vols. St. Petersburg, 1910.

Trudy vserossiiskago s"ezda prakticheskikh deiatelei po bor'be s alkogolizmom, sostoiavshagosia v Moskve s 6–12 avgusta 1912 g. 3 vols. Petrograd, 1914–15. Vol. 1 issued as a supplement to *Trezvaia zhizn'*, 1914; vols. 2–3 issued as supplements to *Rodnaia zhizn'*, 1915.

Varushkin, I. M. *Alkogol': Kak ustroit' semeinyi antialkogol'nyi vecher: Sbornik*. n.p., 1928.

V dni Velikoi Proletarskoi revoliutsii: Épizody bor'by v Petrograde v 1917 godu. Moscow, 1937.

Velikoe gore zemli russkoi—p'ianstvo. St. Petersburg, [1907].

Ves' Peterburg: Adresnaia i spravochnaia kniga. St. Petersburg, 1900–1929. Alternate title: *Ves' Petrograd, Ves' Leningrad*.

Vlassek, R., I. D. Strashun, E. I. Deichman, and L. G. Politov. *Alkogolizm kak nauchnaia i bytovaia problema*. Moscow, 1928.

Voinova, A. *Na buksir: P'esa v 3-kh destviiakh i 4-kh kartinakh*. Leningrad, 1931.

———. *Poluchka: Komediia v 2-kh deistviiakh i 3-kh kartinakh (iz sovremennogo rabochego byta)*. n.p. 1929.

Voronov, D. *Alkogol' v sovremennom bytu*. Leningrad, 1930.

Zelnik, Reginald E., ed. and trans. *A Radical Worker in Tsarist Russia: The Autobiography of Semen Ivanovich Kanatchikov*. Stanford, Calif., 1986.

Zheleznov, L. *Budem zhit' radostno bez sorokagradusnoi: Kak vesti antialkogol'nuiu rabotu*. Leningrad, 1929.

Zhenshchiny goroda Lenina. Leningrad, 1963.

Zhiga, I. *Dumy rabochikh, zaboty, dela (Zapiski rabkora)*. Leningrad, n.d.

———. *Novye rabochie*. Moscow, 1928.

Zhivotskii, S. *Gorod zagubil: Razskaz*. St. Petersburg, n.d.

Zinov'ev, P[avel] P[etrovich]. *Na rubezhe dvukh épokh*. Moscow, 1932.

Zlotin, V. A. *Krasnoputilovskii Komsomol, 1917–1931: Sbornik statei i materialov k 14 letiiu organizatsii VLKSM zavoda "Krasnyi Putilovets."* Leningrad, 1931.

SECONDARY WORKS

Abrams, Lynn. *Workers' Culture in Imperial Germany: Leisure and Recreation in the Rhineland and Westphalia.* New York, 1992.

Atkinson, Dorothy. *The End of the Russian Land Commune, 1905–1930.* Stanford, Calif., 1983.

Ball, Alan M. *Russia's Last Capitalists: The Nepmen, 1921–1929.* Berkeley, Calif., 1987.

Baron, Ava. *Work Engendered: Toward a New History of American Labor.* Ithaca, N.Y., 1991.

Barrett, James R. "Why Paddy Drank: The Social Importance of Whiskey in Pre-Famine Ireland." *Journal of Popular Culture* 11 (summer 1977): 155–66.

Barrows, Susanna. "After the Commune: Alcoholism, Temperance, and Literature in the Early Third Republic." In John M. Merriman, ed., *Consciousness and Class Experience in Nineteenth Century Europe,* 205–215. New York, 1979.

———. *Distorting Mirrors: Visions of the Crowd in Late Nineteenth Century France.* New Haven, Conn., 1981.

Barrows, Susanna, and Robin Room, eds., *Drinking: Behavior and Belief in Modern History.* Berkeley, Calif., 1991.

Bastiony revoliutsii. Vol. 2, *Bor'ba za uprochenie Sovetskoi vlasti i gody grazhdanskoi voiny.* Leningrad, 1959.

Berlanstein, Lenard R., ed. *Rethinking Labor History: Essays on Discourse and Class Analysis.* Urbana, Ill., 1993.

Bernstein, Laurie. *Sonya's Daughters: Prostitutes and Their Regulation in Imperial Russia.* Berkeley, Calif., 1995.

Black, Clayton. "Party Crisis and the Shop Floor: Krasnyi Putilovets and the Leningrad Opposition." *Europe-Asia Studies* 46 (1994): 107–26.

Bobroff, Anne. "The Bolsheviks and Working Women, 1905–20." *Soviet Studies* 4 (October 1974): 540–67.

———. "Working Women, Bonding Patterns, and the Politics of Daily Life: Russia at the End of the Old Regime." Ph.D. diss., University of Michigan, 1982.

Bonnell, Victoria. *Roots of Rebellion: Workers' Politics and Organizations in St. Petersburg and Moscow, 1900–1914.* Berkeley, Calif., 1983.

Bordiugov, G. A. "Problemy bor'by s sotsial'nymi anomaliiami v pervom piatiletnem plane." In Iurii S. Borisov, ed. *Istoricheskii opyt planirovaniia kul'turnogo stroitel'stva v SSSR: Sbornik statei,* 134–51. Moscow, 1988.

Bourke, Joanna. *Dismembering the Male: Men's Bodies, Britain and the Great War.* London, 1996.

Brennan, Thomas. *Public Drinking and Popular Culture in Eighteenth-Century Paris.* Princeton, N.J., 1988.

———. "Towards the Cultural History of Alcohol in France." *Journal of Social History* 23 (fall 1989): 71–92.

Brooks, Jeffrey. *When Russia Learned to Read: Literacy and Popular Literature,*

1861–1917. Princeton, N.J., 1985.

Bukharev, A. I. "Komsomol v bor'be za novyi byt (1926–1932 gg.)." In A. I. Bukharev, I. E. Krutsko, and O. V. Galkova, eds., *Bor'ba partii za sotsialisticheskii byt (1921–1937 gg.): Sbornik nauchnykh trudov*, 74–102. Volgograd, 1985.

Burds, Jeffrey. *Peasant Dreams and Market Politics: Labor Migration and the Russian Village, 1861–1905.* Pittsburgh, 1998.

Carlson, Maria. *"No Religion Higher Than Truth": A History of the Theosophical Movement in Russia, 1875–1922.* Princeton, N.J., 1993.

Carnes, Mark C., and Clyde Griffen, eds. *Meanings for Manhood: Constructions of Masculinity in Victorian America.* Chicago, 1990.

Chase, William J. *Workers, Society and the Soviet State: Labor and Life in Moscow, 1918–1929.* Urbana, Ill., 1990.

Chatterjee, Choitali. "Celebrating Women: International Women's Day in Russia and the Soviet Union, 1909–1939." Ph.D. diss., Indiana University, 1995.

Chevalier, Louis. *Laboring Classes and Dangerous Classes in Paris during the First Half of the Nineteenth Century.* Princeton, N.J., 1981.

Christian, David. *Living Water: Vodka and Russian Society on the Eve of Emancipation.* Oxford, 1990.

———. "Prohibition in Russia, 1914–1925." *Australian Slavonic and East European Studies* 9 (1995): 89–118.

Clark, Anna. *The Struggle for the Breeches: Gender and the Making of the British Working Class.* Berkeley, Calif., 1995.

Clark, Charles E. "Doloi negramotnost': The Literacy Campaign in the RSFSR, 1923–1927." Ph.D. diss., University of Illinois, 1993.

Clark, Katerina. *Petersburg: Crucible of Cultural Revolution.* Cambridge, Mass., 1995.

Clements, Barbara Evans, Barbara Alpern Engel, and Christine D. Worobec, eds. *Russia's Women: Accommodation, Resistance, Transformation.* Berkeley, Calif., 1991.

Coleman, Heather, J. "The Most Dangerous Sect: Baptists in Tsarist and Soviet Russia, 1905–1929." Ph.D. diss., University of Illinois, 1998.

Conroy, David W. *In Public Houses: Drink and the Revolution of Authority in Colonial Massachusetts.* Chapel Hill, N.C., 1995.

Couvares, Francis G. *The Remaking of Pittsburgh: Class and Culture in an Industrializing City, 1877–1919.* Albany, N.Y., 1984.

Davies, Sarah. *Popular Opinion in Stalin's Russia: Terror, Propaganda and Dissent, 1934–1941.* Cambridge, England, 1997.

Dobrovol'nye obshchestva v Petrograde–Leningrade v 1917–1937 gg.: Sbornik statei. Leningrad, 1989.

Drummond, D. A., and G. Perkins, comps. *Dictionary of Russian Obscenities.* Oakland, Calif., 1987.

Duis, Perry R. *The Saloon: Public Drinking in Chicago and Boston, 1880–1920.* Urbana, Ill., 1983.

Economakis, Evel G. "Patterns of Migration and Settlement in Prerevolutionary St. Petersburg: Peasants from Iaroslavl and Tver Provinces." *Russian Review* 56 (January 1997): 8–24.

Edelman, Robert. *Serious Fun: A History of Spectator Sports in the USSR.* New York, 1993.

Engel, Barbara Alpern. *Between the Fields and the City: Women, Work, and Family in Russia, 1861–1914.* Cambridge, England, 1996.

Engelstein, Laura. *The Keys to Happiness: Sex and the Search for Modernity in Fin-de-Siècle Russia.* Ithaca, N.Y., 1992.

———. *Moscow, 1905: Working-Class Organization and Political Conflict.* Stanford, Calif., 1982.

Farnsworth, Beatrice, and Lynne Viola, eds. *Russian Peasant Women.* New York, 1992.

Figes, Orlando. *A People's Tragedy: A History of the Russian Revolution.* New York, 1997.

———. "The Russian Revolution and Its Language in the Village." *Russian Review* 56 (1997): 323–45.

Fitzpatrick, Sheila. *The Russian Revolution, 1917–1932.* Oxford, 1982.

———. "Supplicants and Citizens: Public Letter-Writing in Soviet Russia in the 1930s." *Slavic Review* 55 (spring 1996): 78–105.

———, ed. *Cultural Revolution in Russia, 1928–1931.* Bloomington, Ind., 1984.

Fitzpatrick, Sheila, Alexander Rabinowitch, and Richard Stites, eds. *Russia in the Era of NEP: Explorations in Soviet Society and Culture.* Bloomington, Ind., 1991.

Frank, Stephen P., and Mark D. Steinberg, eds. *Cultures in Flux: Lower-Class Values, Practices, and Resistance in Late Imperial Russia.* Princeton, N.J., 1994.

Gaza, I. I., ed. *Putilovets na putiakh k Oktiabriu: Iz istorii "Krasnogo Putilovtsa."* Leningrad, 1933.

Gefou-Madianou, Dimitra, ed. *Alcohol, Gender and Culture.* New York, 1992.

Gilman, Sander. *Freud, Race, and Gender.* Princeton, N.J., 1993.

———. *Picturing Health and Illness: Images of Identity and Difference.* Baltimore, 1995.

Gilmore, David, D. *Manhood in the Making: Cultural Concepts of Masculinity.* New Haven, Conn., 1990.

Glickman, Rose L. *Russian Factory Women: Workplace and Society, 1880–1914.* Berkeley, Calif., 1984.

Goldman, Wendy Z. *Women, the State and Revolution: Soviet Family Policy and Social Life, 1917–1936.* Cambridge, England, 1993.

Gorbunov, B. V. "Narodnye vidy sportivnoi bor'by kak élement traditsionnoi kul'tury russkikh (XIX–nachalo XX v.)." *Sovetskaia étnografiia* 4 (1989): 90–101.

Gorsuch, Anne Elizabeth. "Enthusiasts, Bohemians, and Delinquents: Soviet Youth Cultures, 1921–1928." Ph.D. diss., University of Michigan, 1992.

———. "'A Woman Is Not a Man': The Culture of Gender and Generation in

Soviet Russia, 1921–1928." *Slavic Review* 55 (fall 1996): 636–60.

Haag, Pamela. "'The Ill-Use of a Wife': Patterns of Working-Class Violence in Domestic and Public New York City, 1860–1880." *Journal of Social History* 25 (April 1992): 447–77.

Haine, W. Scott. "A Spectrum of Cultural Constructs: The Interrelationship between Social, Legal, and Medical Constructs of Intemperate Behavior in Parisian Drinking, 1860–1914." *Contemporary Drug Problems* 21 (winter 1994): 535–56.

———. *The World of the Paris Café: Sociability among the French Working Class, 1789–1914.* Baltimore, 1996.

Halfin, Igal. "The Rape of the Intelligentsia: A Proletarian Foundational Myth." *Russian Review* 56 (January 1997): 90–109.

Harrison, Brian. *Drink and the Victorians: The Temperance Question in England, 1815–1872.* Pittsburgh, 1972.

Healy, Daniel. "The Russian Revolution and the Decriminalization of Homosexuality." *Revolutionary Russia* 6 (June 1993): 26–54.

Heath, D[wight] B. "Alcohol and Aggression: A 'Missing Link' in Worldwide Perspective." In Edward Gottheil, Keith A. Druley, Thomas E. Skolada, Howard M. Waxman, eds., *Alcohol, Drug Abuse and Aggression,* 89–103. Springfield, Ill., 1983.

———. "Cross Cultural Perspectives on Women and Alcohol." In Edith S. Lisansky Gomberg and Ted D. Nirenberg, eds., *Women and Substance Abuse,* 100–117. Norwood, N.J., 1993.

———. "Drinking and Drunkenness in Transcultural Perspective." *Transcultural Psychiatric Research* 1 (196):7–42; 2 (1986): 103–25.

Herlihy, Patricia. "'Joy of the Rus'': Rites and Rituals of Russian Drinking." *Russian Review* 50 (April 1991): 131–47.

Herrlinger, Kimberly Page. "Class, Piety, and Politics: Workers, Orthodoxy, and the Problem of Religious Identity in Russia, 1881–1914." Ph.D. diss., University of California, Berkeley, 1996.

Hobsbawm, Eric. *Workers: Worlds of Labor.* New York, 1984.

Hoffmann, David L. *Peasant Metropolis: Social Identities in Moscow, 1929–1941.* Ithaca, N.Y., 1994.

Hutchinson, J[ohn] F. "Medicine, Morality, and Social Policy in Imperial Russia: The Early Years of the Alcohol Commission." *Social History* 7 (November 1974): 202–26.

Indel'chik, Kh. I., M. N. Aruin, and A. I. Nesterenko. "I Vserossiiskii s"ezd po bor'be s p'ianstvom." *Sovetskoe zdravookhranenie* 2 (1972): 61–65.

Istoriia Leningradskoi gosudarstvennoi ordena Lenina i ordena Trudovogo Krasnogo Znameni obuvnoi fabriki "Skorokhod" imeni Ia. Kalinina. Leningrad, 1969.

Ivanits, Linda J. *Russian Folk Belief.* New York, 1989.

Jahn, Hubertus F. *Patriotic Culture in Russia during World War I.* Ithaca, N.Y., 1995.

Johnson, Robert E. *Peasant and Proletarian: The Working Class of Moscow in the*

Late Nineteenth Century. New Brunswick, N.J., 1979.

Kann, P. Ia. "Bor'ba rabochikh Petrograda s p'ianymi pogromami (noiabr'–dekabr' 1917 g.)." *Istoriia SSSR* 3 (May–June 1962): 133–36.

Kaplan, Temma. "Female Consciousness and Collective Action: The Case of Barcelona, 1910–1918." *Signs* 7 (spring 1982): 545–66.

Kas'ianenko, V. I. "Razrabotka KPSS kontseptsii sotsialisticheskogo obraza zhizni." *Voprosy istorii KPSS* 2 (1983): 29–44.

Kelly, Catrina, and David Shepherd, eds. *Constructing Russian Culture in the Age of Revolution, 1881–1940.* Oxford, 1998.

Kingsdale, Jon M. "The 'Poor Man's Club': Social Functions of the Urban Working-Class Saloon." *American Quarterly* 25 (1973): 472–89.

Kirshin, V. N. *Orden na znameni: Kratkii ocherk istorii Lenigradskogo ordena otechestvennoi voiny i stepeni zavoda poligraficheskikh mashin.* Moscow, 1965.

Koenker, Diane P. "Men against Women on the Shop Floor in Early Soviet Russia: Gender and Class in the Socialist Workplace." *American Historical Review* 100 (December 1995): 1438–64.

———. *Moscow Workers and the 1917 Revolution.* Princeton, N.J., 1981.

———. "Urbanization and Deurbanization in the Russian Revolution and Civil War." *Journal of Modern History* 57 (September 1985): 424–50.

Koenker, Diane P., and William G. Rosenberg. *Strikes and Revolution in Russia, 1917.* Princeton, N.J., 1989.

Koenker, Diane P., William G. Rosenberg, and Ronald Grigor Suny, eds. *Party, State, and Society in the Russian Civil War: Explorations in Social History.* Bloomington, Ind., 1989.

Kolonitskii, Boris I. "Antibourgeois Propaganda and Anti-'Burzhui' Consciousness in 1917." *Russian Review* 53 (April 1994): 183–96.

Korzhikina, T. P. "Bor'ba s alkogolizmom v 1920-e-nachale 1930-kh godov." *Voprosy istorii* 9 (1985): 20–32.

Kotkin, Stephen. *Magnetic Mountain: Stalinism as Civilization.* Berkeley, Calif., 1995.

Kruze, É. É. *Peterburgskie rabochii v 1912–1914 godakh.* Moscow, 1961.

Lebina, N. B. "Tenevye storony zhizni sovetskogo goroda 20–30-kh godov." *Voprosy istorii* 2 (1994): 30–42.

Lewin, Moshe. *Russian Peasants and Soviet Power: A Study of Collectivization.* London, 1968.

Lotova, E. I., and Kh. I. Indel'chik. "Alkogolizm kak sotsial'no-gigienicheskaia problema." *Sovetskoe zdravookhranenie* 3 (1986): 12–17.

———. "Obshchestvennye organizatsii v bor'be s alkogolizmom v SSSR v 20-kh godakh." *Sovetskoe zdravookhranenie* 8 (1986): 26–31.

The Lubok: Russian Folk Pictures: 17th to 19th Century. Leningrad, 1984.

Ludtke, Alf. "Organizational Order or Eigensinn? Workers' Privacy and Workers' Politics in Imperial Germany." In Sean Wilentz, ed., *Rites of Power: Symbolism, Ritual, and Politics since the Middle Ages,* 303–33. Philadelphia, 1985.

MacAndrew, Craig, and Robert B. Edgerton. *Drunken Comportment: A Social Explanation*. Chicago, 1969.

Madsen, W., and C. Madsen, "The Cultural Structure of Mexican Drinking Behavior." *Quarterly Journal of Studies on Alcohol* 30 (1969): 701–18.

McDaniel, Tim. *Autocracy, Capitalism, and Revolution in Russia*. Berkeley, Calif., 1988.

McElligott, Anthony. "Street Politics in Hamburg, 1932–33." *History Workshop* 16 (autumn 1983): 83–90.

McKean, Robert B. *St. Petersburg between the Revolutions: Workers and Revolutionaries, June 1907–February 1917*. New Haven, Conn., 1990.

McKee, W. Arthur. "Taming the Green Serpent: Alcoholism, Autocracy, and Russian Society, 1890–1917." Ph.D. diss., University of California, Berkeley, 1997.

Medick, H. "Plebeian Culture in the Transition to Capitalism." In Raphael Samuel and Gareth Stedman Jones, eds., *Culture, Ideology and Politics: Essays for Eric Hobsbawm*, 84–108. London, 1982.

Melzer, Sara E., and Leslie W. Rabine, eds. *Rebel Daughters: Women and the French Revolution*. New York, 1992.

Metallurgi s Matisova ostrova: Kratkii ocherk istorii Leningraskogo zavoda po obrabotke tsvetnykh metallov. Leningrad, 1967.

Mitel'man, M., B. Glebov, and A. Ul'ianovskii. *Istoriia Putilovskogo zavoda*. Moscow, 1939.

———. *Istoriia Putilovskogo zavoda: 1801–1917*. Moscow, 1961.

Mosse, George L. *The Image of Man: The Creation of Modern Masculinity*. Oxford, 1996.

Narodnaia bor'ba za trezvost' v Russkoi istorii: Materialy seminara, provedennogo obshchestvami bor'by za trezvost' BAN SSSR, LGU, LOII AN SSSR. Leningrad, 1989.

Neuberger, Joan. *Hooliganism: Crime, Culture, and Power in St. Petersburg, 1900–1914*. Berkeley, Calif., 1993.

Nosova, G. A. "Mapping of Russian Shrovetide Ritual (from Materials of the Nineteenth and Early Twentieth Centuries)." *Soviet Anthropology and Archeology* 14 (summer–fall 1975): 50–70.

Nye, Robert A. *Masculinity and Male Codes of Honor in Modern France*. Oxford, 1993.

Paialin, N. P. *Zavod imeni Lenina, 1857–1918*. Moscow, 1933.

Parkhomenko, A. G. "Gosudarstvenno-pravovye meropriiatiia po bor'be s p'ianstvom v pervye gody Sovetskoi vlasti." *Sovetskoe gosudarstvo i pravo* 4 (1984): 112–16.

Polishchuk, N. S. "Obychai fabrichno-zavodskikh rabochikh Evropeiskoi Rossii, sviazannye s proizvodstvom i proizvodstvennymi otnosheniiami (konets XIX–nachalo XX v.)." *Étnograficheskoe obozrenie* 1 (1994): 73–90.

Prestwich, Patricia E. *Drink and the Politics of Social Reform: Antialcoholism in France since 1870*. Palo Alto, Calif., 1988.

————. "The Regulation of Drinking: New Work in the Social History of Alcohol." *Contemporary Drug Problems* 21 (fall 1994): 365–74.

Prot'ko, T. S. *V bor'be za trezvost': Stranitsy istorii.* Minsk, 1988.

Roberts, James S. *Drink, Temperance and the Working Class in Nineteenth-Century Germany.* Boston, 1984.

Roper, Lyndal. *Oedipus and the Devil: Witchcraft, Sexuality and Religion in Early Modern Europe.* London, 1994.

Rosenhaft, Eve. *Beating the Fascists? The German Communists and Political Violence, 1929–1933.* Cambridge, England, 1983.

Rosenthal, Bernice Glatzer, ed. *The Occult in Russian and Soviet Culture.* Ithaca, N.Y., 1997.

Rossman, Jeffrey J. "The Teikovo Cotton Workers' Strike of April 1932: Class, Gender, and Identity Politics in Stalin's Russia." *Russian Review* 56 (January 1997): 44–69.

Scott, James C. *Domination and the Arts of Resistance: Hidden Transcripts.* New Haven, Conn., 1990.

Segal, Boris M. *The Drunken Society: Alcohol Abuse and Alcoholism in the Soviet Union: A Comparative Study.* New York, 1990.

————. *Russian Drinking: Use and Abuse of Alcohol in Pre-Revolutionary Russia.* New Brunswick, N.J., 1987.

Sewell, William H., Jr., *Work and Revolution in France: The Language of Labor from the Old Regime to 1848.* Cambridge, England, 1980.

Shakhmaev, Sergei, and Igor' Kurukin. *Kabak na Rusi: Pervaia pravdivaia istoriia rossiiskogo p'ianstva.* New York, 1996.

Siegelbaum, Lewis H., and Ronald Grigor Suny, eds. *Making Workers Soviet: Power, Class, and Identity.* Ithaca, N.Y., 1994.

Slovar' russkogo iazyka. Moscow, 1984.

Smith, R. E. F., and David Christian. *Bread and Salt: A Social and Economic History of Food and Drink in Russia.* Cambridge, England, 1984.

Smith, Steve A. "Class and Gender: Women's Strikes in St. Petersburg, 1895–1917 and in Shanghai, 1895–1927." *Social History* 19 (May 1994): 141–68.

————. *Red Petrograd: Revolution in the Factories, 1917–1918.* Cambridge, England, 1985.

————. "Russian Workers and the Politics of Social Identity." *Russian Review* 56 (January 1997): 1–7.

————. "Writing the History of the Russian Revolution after the Fall of Communism." *Europe-Asia Studies* 46 (1994): 563–78.

Solomon, Susan Gross. "David and Goliath in Soviet Public Health: The Rivalry of Social Hygienists and Psychiatrists for Authority over the Bytovoi Alcoholic." *Soviet Studies* 41 (April 1989): 254–75.

Sournia, Jean-Charles. *A History of Alcoholism.* Oxford, 1990.

Stedman Jones, Gareth. *Languages of Class: Studies in English Working Class History, 1832–1982.* Cambridge, England, 1987.

Steinberg, Mark D. *Moral Communities: The Culture of Class Relations in the Russ-*

ian Printing Industry, 1867–1907. Berkeley, Calif., 1992.

———. "Workers on the Cross: Religious Imagination in the Writings of Russian Workers, 1910–1924." *Russian Review* 53 (April 1994): 213–39.

Stites, Richard. *Russian Popular Culture: Entertainment and Society since 1900.* Cambridge, England, 1992.

———. *The Women's Liberation Movement in Russia: Feminism, Nihilism, and Bolshevism, 1860–1930*. Princeton, N.J., 1978.

Stone, Helena. "The Soviet Government and Moonshine, 1917–1929." *Cahiers du Monde Russe et Soviétique* 27 (1986): 359–79.

Swain, Geoffrey. *Russian Social Democracy and the Legal Labour Movement, 1906–1914*. London, 1983.

Swift, Eugene Anthony. "Theater for the People: The Politics of Popular Culture in Urban Russia, 1861–1917." Ph.D. diss., University of California, Berkeley, 1992.

Thompson, E. P. "Time, Work-Discipline, and Industrial Capitalism." *Past and Present* 38 (December 1967): 56–97.

Tikhomirova, V. A. *Na bor'bu s p'ianstvom, khrestomatiia po voprosam alkogolizma i bor'bu s nim v shkole i cherez shkolu*. Leningrad, 1931.

Tlusty, Beverly Ann. "The Devil's Altar: The Tavern and Society in Early Modern Augsburg." Ph.D. diss., University of Maryland, 1994.

———. "Gender and Alcohol Use in Early Modern Augsburg." *Social History* 27 (November 1994): 241–59.

Tosh, John. "What Should Historians Do with Masculinity?" *History Workshop Journal* 38 (autumn 1994): 179–202.

Transchel, Kathy S. "Under the Influence: Drinking, Temperance, and Cultural Revolution in Russia, 1900–1932." Ph.D. diss., University of North Carolina, Chapel Hill, 1996.

Treml, Vladimir G. *Alcohol in the USSR: A Statistical Study*. Durham, N.C., 1982.

Trice, Thomas Reed. "The 'Body Politic': Russian Funerals and the Politics of Representation, 1841–1921." Ph.D. diss., University of Illinois, Urbana, 1998.

Turk, E. L. "The Great Berlin Beer Boycott of 1894." *Central European History* 15 (1982): 377–97.

Vakser, A. Z., and V. S. Izmozik. "Izmenenie obshchestvennogo oblika Sovetskogo rabochego 20–30-kh godov." *Voprosy istorii* 11 (November 1984): 93–109.

Viola, Lynne. "*Bab'i bunty* and Peasant Women's Protest during Collectivization." *Russian Review* 45 (January 1986): 23–42.

von Geldern, James. *Bolshevik Festivals, 1917–1930*. Berkeley, Calif., 1993.

Von Laue, Theodore H. *Why Lenin? Why Stalin? Why Gorbachev? The Rise and Fall of the Soviet System*. New York, 1993.

Weissman, Neil. "Prohibition and Alcohol Control in the USSR: The 1920s Campaign against Illegal Spirits." *Soviet Studies* 38 (July 1986): 349–68.

White, Stephen. *Russia Goes Dry: Alcohol, State, and Society*. Cambridge, England, 1996.

Worobec, Christine D. *Peasant Russia: Family and Community in the Post-Emancipation Period.* Princeton, N.J., 1991.

Wynn, Charters. *Workers, Strikes and Pogroms: The Donbass-Dneper Bend in Late Imperial Russia, 1870–1905.* Princeton, N.J., 1992.

Zhiromskaia, V. B. *Sovetskii gorod v 1921–1925 gg.: Problemy sotsial'noi struktury.* Moscow, 1988.

Znamia truda: Kratkii ocherk istorii Leningradskogo armaturnogo zavoda "Znamia truda." Leningrad, 1960.

INDEX

Abrams, Lynn, 6, 76
abstinence: and consciousness, 135;
    during demonstrations, 82–84,
    136–38; and femininity, 31–35, 48;
    and "intellectuals," 34–35, 48,
    131–32; and men, 34–37, 48, 121;
    oaths of, 66, 107; and *prival'naia,*
    53; and women, 64, 96, 98–99,
    102–6, 134; and youth, 32–33, 35,
    48, 66, 96, 102–6, 134
adult identity, 29, 32–33, 48, 141
advanced workers. *See* conscious
    workers; worker activists
aggression, 79–80. *See also* fistfights
Aivaz mill, 63, 114–15
alcohol boycotts. *See* demonstrations
alcohol consumption: collective,
    36–39, 60–61, 75, 85–87, 100–1; "cul-
    tured," 130; and gender, 97–99; and
    "intellectuals," 131–32; and men,
    33, 99; quotas of, 94; solitary, 36, 75;
    trends of, 11, 13, 15–21, 41–42, 140;
    Western, 5; and women, 99–105,
    119; in workplaces, 6, 38, 49–71,
    129–30, 142–43; and youth, 97–99,
    129–32, 134
alcohol monopoly. *See* liquor monop-
    oly
alcohol raids, 19, 126–27
alcoholics: and compulsory treat-
    ment, 23; "socially dangerous,"

156n56
alcoholism. *See* problem drinking
anniversaries, 54–55
Anti-alcohol Congress of 1909. *See*
    Congress against Drunkenness
Anti-alcohol Congress of 1912, 17
Anti-alcohol Congresses of 1929, 20,
    24–25, 108
apprentices, 68

baba, defined, 158n12. *See also* epithets
"backward" workers. *See* rank-and-
    file workers
bakers, 47, 64–65
bar rooms, 73–74
bartenders. *See* tavern owners
beer: consumption trends of, 20–21,
    87–88, 93; as "liquid bread," 62;
    and women, 101; in workplaces, 68
beer halls. *See* drinking establishments
Biely, Andrey, 8
billiards, 136; in dining halls, 87; sup-
    pression of, 91, 95; in taverns, 73,
    76; in workers' clubs, 88
Black Hundreds. *See* Union of the
    Russian People
Borodin, Dmitrii N., 13, 15, 17
Bouduén-de-Kurtené, R. R., 107
bowling alleys, 76
Brennan, Thomas, 76, 80
Bukharev, A. I., 107